THE MAKING OF AN ENGINEER

....

An Illustrated History of Engineering Education in the United States and Canada

THE MAKING OF AN ENGINEER

··········

An Illustrated History of

Engineering Education in the

United States and Canada

LAWRENCE P. GRAYSON

John Wiley & Sons, Inc.

NEW YORK   /   CHICHESTER   /   BRISBANE   /   TORONTO   /   SINGAPORE

Acquisitions Editor	Charity Robey
Marketing Managers	Susan Elbe, Debra Riegert
Production Manager	Lucille Buonocore
Senior Production Editor	Nancy Prinz
Text Designer	Karin Gerdes Kincheloe
Manufacturing Manager	Susan Stetzer
Cover Designer	Nancy Field
Cover Design Direction	Karin Gerdes Kincheloe

This book was set in Baskerville by Progressive Typographers and printed and bound by Quinn-Woodbine, Inc. The cover was printed by Quinn-Woodbine, Inc.

Library of Congress Cataloging-in-Publication Data

Grayson, Lawrence P.
    The making of an engineer / Lawrence P. Grayson.
      p. cm.
    Includes index.
    ISBN 0-471-59799-6 (cloth)
    1. Engineering — Study and teaching — United States — History.
2. Engineering Study and teaching Canada — History.
3. Engineering — Study and teaching — United States — History-
Pictorial works. 4. Engineering — Study and teaching — Canada-
History Pictorial works. I. Title.
T73.G75   1993
620'.0071'17 — dc20   93-10927
                                          CIP

Printed in the United States of America
10 9 8 7 6 5 4 3 2 1

To Susan
and our children
Mary Louise, Catherine, Lawrence,
Elizabeth, Maureen, and Thérèse

. . . .*The Making of an Engineer* is a fine contribution to the historiography of the profession in the United States and Canada and of the educational system that has evolved over two centuries to support it. As a trained historian, I am particularly gratified to see the story told by Lawrence Grayson unfolding in the framework of the economic and cultural institutions of our two countries.

Engineering is one of the key crafts and professions that has for millennia been part of the driving intellectual energy of economic development and social change, at least as far back as civilizations in the Indian peninsula and Tigris/Euphrates watersheds. Without engineering, the Roman Empire would not likely have achieved what it did. Fillip Brunelleschi was not only an artisan to private benefactors in fifteenth century Florence, he was also architect of the structurally innovative dome of the cathedral as well as engineer to the city state itself including its siege of neighboring Lucia in the 1440s. The whole preindustrial history of technology, roads, waterworks, shipyards, mines, temples, and so on is also the history of engineering.

A pervasive theme of Lawrence Grayson's book is the interplay between broad and rapid social change and the stresses change puts on engineers and particularly engineering educators. The consolidation of a national corporate economy in the 1890s, the two world wars, and the New Deal with its interest in economic and "social" engineering, he points out, were major crisis times that forced engineers and engineering educators to appraise critically and rigorously their social objectives and educational curricula.

In 1992, John Wiley celebrated its 100th year of publishing in engineering, just one year before the Society's own centennial. Throughout these years of industrialization and urbanization, the histories of the American Society for Engineering Education and John Wiley & Sons Publishers have been intertwined. Wiley's relationship with educational publishing and the ASEE over the past century affirms Dr. Grayson's sense that engineering and engineering education in the United States and Canada are entering another period of dramatic societal change that is causing the profession to once again critically evaluate its role in the workplace and the university.

Clearly the disappearance of the "Cold War" from the stage of history is raising major organizational performance and resource allocation questions throughout our countries and, in fact, throughout the emerging globalized economy and postindustrial culture the world over. Perhaps more challenging technical and ethical questions than have been previously askable are now going to be asked, and engineering educators will be challenged to train professionals with the increasingly diverse skills required to answer them.

My congratulations to Lawrence Grayson, on the occasion of the 100th Anniversary of the ASEE, for using his history of the organization to bring to our attention the need for the profession to respond to these issues. Education is a powerful force for good in any society and we must do all we can in ours to make the institution the best we are capable of providing.

BRADFORD WILEY II

. . . . . . .The history of the American Society for Engineering Education (ASEE) is closely linked to the history of engineering education in the United States and Canada. When the Society was founded in 1893, engineering schools already had taken root in these countries and formal education was well on its way to being universally accepted as the means for entry into engineering practice. The number of engineering schools had increased very rapidly in the previous thirty years, with individual institutions responding to the demands for engineering skills required by the industries and regions they served. As a result, there was great diversity among the engineering colleges with regard to their entrance standards, curricula, content of courses, and requirements for graduation. If engineering schools were to contribute effectively to the technological and economic development of the two nations, a mechanism was needed to identify and address common problems. The Society for the Promotion of Engineering Education, as the ASEE was then called, served that role.

The organization provided a forum for the leading engineering educators of the time to meet, discuss mutual concerns, conduct studies, and initiate unified action. As engineering education has developed, the Society has continued to provide these functions, although it has broadened its scope to undertake projects, encompass education in the various disciplines of engineering, focus on graduate study and research in addition to undergraduate teaching, and include the faculty and schools in engineering technology as an integral part of the spectrum of engineering education.

The Society has served as a means for developing resolutions to the conflicting demands to which engineering education has been subjected by the broader technical, social, and economic settings that exist in the two countries. The resolution of these tensions has led to a vibrant and effective approach to engineering education. There is continuing adaption and diversity among schools at the local level, but with an underlying commonality that assures quality programs that meet national needs.

The history of engineering education in the United States and Canada has been characterized by progressive tensions. During its early development, engineering educators were struggling for acceptability. The then traditional universities viewed engineering as too pragmatic and utilitarian for higher learning. The technical needs of the two nations required engineers with skills that often could be learned better through experience than through formal study. At that time, one could become an engineer without ever having gone to school. As the complexity of the technology increased, and the body of engineering knowledge became more codified, engineering education was more readily accepted as the basis for engineering practice and as an integral part of the university mission. Engineering became a full-fledged member of the education community with the passage of the Morrill Land Grant Act in 1862, which provided public lands to the states and territories to establish and support colleges of "agriculture and the mechanics arts."

With acceptability, new tensions arose. There has been an ongoing debate over the appropriate balance between preparing graduates for immediate usefulness in the workplace and providing them with a more fundamental knowledge that would allow them to continue their education and be more useful in the long run. This debate surfaced in the late 1800s as a struggle between the more established shop culture, in which students learned the then present-day engineering with practice on industrial-grade equipment, and a newly developing laboratory approach, in which students studied more fundamental principles. Eventually, the laboratory became dominant.

After World War I, the demands of industry for graduates with immediate utility forced more and more specialization, and the number of engineering disciplines expanded rapidly. Although there were occasional calls for a more generalized education, the laboratory became the place for teaching current industrial techniques. World War II helped swing the balance in the other direction. The war highlighted the shortcomings of engineering education, as people trained in physics were better suited to perform many of the tasks of new weapons development. Engineering education rapidly moved toward a much more fundamental approach, and in many cases the curricula became the study of engineering science. The movement toward science continued until recent problems in the competitive position of many American companies in global markets has shown the disadvantage of neglecting industrial applications. There once again is movement in the schools to reemphasize engineering practice, including manufacturing techniques, and concepts such as quality and reliability of the product.

World War II also showed the advantage of research in engineering. The federal governments in the United States and Canada began to increase by substantial amounts the funding of university-based engineering research. The more success that research brought, the greater the funding and time devoted to it, with faculty members less able to continue their traditional emphasis on the teaching of undergraduate students. A tension has developed between the need to develop new knowledge in engineering and the requirement to prepare the next generation of engineers. While many people believed the emphasis has been too much on research, there is evidence that the balance is now being righted.

These tensions have been advantageous in the long run, though not always optimal in the short run. They have assured that engineering schools could adapt their curricula to the demands of their respective countries as reflected by the needs of the industries in their locales. The result has been of great benefit to the United States and Canada, as the economies of these nations have continued to grow and their people enjoy standards of living that are among the highest in the world.

One cannot fully appreciate the changes in engineering education without an understanding of the developments in engineering and of the economic and social trends in a country. These aspects of national life are linked. Advances in engineering create a demand for changes in engineering education and provide the basis of a stronger economy. Economic growth generates the resources for education and the capitalization for engineering. Education produces men and women with the intellectual skills needed to improve engineering and to contribute to a strengthened economy. Although this is not a social history, I have tried to provide a sense of the advances in technology and of the economic and social changes in the two countries so that the changes in engineering education can be more fully appreciated.

At the start of this project, I set several objectives for the book. Since it is to celebrate the centennial of the American Society for Engineering Education, the book is presented in an attractive, appealing format. The size and style are suitable as a memento, for display and reference. The contents are centered around the photographs, since seeing people in action is an effective way to learn about and appreciate the past. Visual images portray people and events in vivid ways and convey a sense of the past that I could not capture in words. The narrative provides the background within which to view the photographs. The two are related, but not tightly linked. The reader should be able to follow the history from either the narrative or the photographs, with each presenting a complementary view. The narrative is detailed enough to get a sense of the times and events, but not an exhaustive history of engineering education. The later would be a much more voluminous work than the present one, and would be of more interest to historians of technology than to a general audience. Finally, I want the work to be accurate, with enough references to lead the interested scholar into a deeper study of the subject. How well I succeeded, I leave to the reader.

Collecting the photographs was a delight. Eleanor Baum, dean of engineering at Cooper Union and chair of the Engineering Deans Council, wrote a memorandum to the deans of the engineering colleges to encourage their cooperation with my efforts. Stephen Cheshire, president of Southern College of Technology and chairman of the Engineering Technology Deans Council, did the same with the deans of the engineering technology schools. As a result, some 100 schools provided over 1,500 photographs. They all were superb, and the vast majority met the criteria I set for publication in this book. My major problem, and disappointment, was to limit the number. In doing so, I tried to effect a balance among the various periods, disciplines of engineering, types of instructional activities, schools, prominent engineering educators, and student social activities, as well as be concerned with the quality of the photos and their ability to generate reader interest. After many iterations, I chose about 350 photographs, which was 100 more than my original estimate to the publisher. Even with that number, there are many, many additional photographs that I would like to have included, and I apologize to the people who submitted excellent shots that were not used.

The book came about because of the encouragement and assistance of numerous people. William K. LeBold of Purdue University, an old friend and a member of the ASEE Centennial Committee, first suggested that I undertake the project, reassured me when I hesitated, and even made the initial contact with the folks at John Wiley & Sons. George Burnet of Iowa State University, another long-standing colleague and fellow "Purple Badger" who served as the chair of the Centennial Committee, was enthusiastic about the project from the start and has supported it wholeheartedly and continuously with the ASEE Board of Directors and staff. Without these two individuals, I would never have undertaken nor completed this work.

O. Allan Gianniny, of the University of Virginia, read a preliminary version of the material dealing with the period prior to the Civil War. Raymond D. Findlay, of McMaster University, did the same for the material on Canada. Both are excellent historians of engineering education, and their comments were insightful. Lee Harrisberger, of the "imagineering" mind, helped me brainstorm about the title of the book.

The team at John Wiley & Sons has been a joy to work with. They agreed to the project from the very beginning and gave me their full and professional support. Executive Editor Charity Robey quarterbacked the team and was my internal link to the company. Senior Designer Karin Kincheloe asked to be assigned to the project because of her interest in it, provided several alternate designs to meet my view of the book, and was responsive to my suggestions. Senior Production Supervisor Nancy Prinz led me through the deadlines associated with the creation of a book. Marketing Managers Debra Riegert and Susan Elbe did the planning to promote the market the final product.

There was little reason for me to be surprised with the cooperation of the Wiley people. After all, the publisher has been closely allied with the ASEE for 100 years. John Wiley & Sons was the first and only exhibitor at the first meeting of the then newly created Society for the Promotion of Engineering Education at Brooklyn Polytechnic Institute in 1893. And they have been exhibiting ever since. Further, William O. Wiley, who served as chairman of the Board of Directors of Wiley in the 1930s, was treasurer of the SPEE from 1907 to 1942. He was elected to his position 35 times and served on the SPEE

Council longer than anyone else in the history of the Society. So it was natural that the company would want to be part of this centennial event.

In obtaining photographs, there were many individuals who made special efforts to help. They researched their own archives, selected photographs, developed captions (often after consultation with emeritus faculty members), and responded to further requests that I made in trying to locate photographs of and information about specific individuals or events. I hesitate to name them, only because in doing so I am bound to omit others who deserve mention. I hope they will be satisfied to realize that I know who they are and appreciate their contributions to this book.

Finally, I want to pay special tribute to the members—past, present, and to come—of the *Order of the Tattered Purple Badges*. These past presidents of the SPEE and ASEE, known by the color of the badges they wear at the Society's annual conference, have provided a century of leadership to the Society and to engineering education, and they will continue to do so. I am proud to be a part of this distinguished assembly.

LAWRENCE P. GRAYSON

CONTENTS

CHAPTER O N E

CHAPTER 1
THE SETTING

. . . . . . .1893 was a time of contrasts and change. The census of 1890 officially marked the end of America's frontier, although significant westward movement continued for many years. Before the 1890s, America was overwhelmingly rural and agricultural. The energies of the people were expended on conquering the great expanse of land, and the nation was relatively isolated from the rest of the world. Most Americans could trace their ancestry to the British Isles, Germany, or Scandinavia.

Although sectionalism still existed, memories of the Civil War were fading, while veterans in blue and gray uniforms held joint reunions.

After the 1890s, the country quickly became urban and largely industrial. It would become involved in world politics and wars. By 1896, the migration from Russia, Poland, Italy, and Austria-Hungary was consistently greater than from northwestern Europe. The new arrivals were settling mainly in cities, creating overcrowding, slums, poverty, and crime. Industry flourished, but by the ruthless exploitation of the workers. Children labored in factories and in mines, women worked 12-hour days in textile mills,

1. *The Basin and the Court of Honor at the World's Columbian Exposition. The view is looking east from the Grand Plaza. In the foreground is the Columbian Fountain.*

and absentee corporations foreclosed mortgages on distant farms. The country was experiencing convulsive changes in population, social relations, economics, and technology.

In 1893, the country was in a severe economic depression. Thousands of business firms had failed, farms were foreclosed, 600 banks shut their doors, and 74 railroads went into receivership. In late June, the stock market collapsed. There were labor protests and widespread unemployment. Yet, in spite of this economic and social turmoil, 1893 was a time of optimism and hope for the future.

Technology was advancing by leaps and bounds and was significantly changing life in the United States. In the preceding two decades, the internal combustion engine and steam turbine were developed, as was the electric generator, electric motor, incandescent lamp, phonograph, and telephone. After Thomas A. Edison established a commercially successful electric-generating plant in New York City in 1882, there was rapid application of electric power for domestic and industrial use, street lighting, and railway transportation. As a result of the work of Bessemer,

2. *The Tower of Light inside the Electricity Building at the World's Columbian Exposition.*

steel became available in quantity, with U.S. production rising from 30,500 tons in 1870 to 1,250,000,000 tons in 1884. In 1883, Washington A. Roebling completed the construction of the Brooklyn Bridge, which his father, John A., began 14 years earlier. The bridge had a record-breaking span of 1,595½ feet. In 1885, William L.B. Jenney completed the first skyscraper, which he designed for the Home Insurance Company of Chicago.

In celebration of the four hundredth anniversary of Columbus's discovery of America, the World's Columbian Exposition was held in Chicago in the summer of 1893. This was an opportunity to provide tangible evidence of America's progress as an enterprising and enlightened nation by showcasing the nation's many accomplishments in technology, science, manufacturing, art, history, and social concerns. A heady, self-congratulatory atmosphere prevailed at this world's fair, which provided one of the most remarkable exhibits of human achievements ever assembled. The exposition combined both inspiring displays of technical advances and demonstrations of American social and cultural sophistication, housed in architecturally grandiose buildings. The buildings, done in Beaux Arts classical styles, were constructed with a great array of arches, colonnades, balconies, domes, and columns. They were interspersed with sculptures, greenery, fountains, and long, winding waterways spanned by graceful arched bridges. In the middle of the fair was a lagoon 2,500 feet long and 250 feet wide. At one end was a marble boat containing several allegorical figures, while a 65-foot-high Statue of the Republic stood at the opposite end. Gondolas glided along the waterways, while full-scale replicas of the Nina, Pinta, Santa Maria, and a Viking ship were moored on the adjoining Lake Michigan.

All of the buildings in the main section were finished in simulated white marble or granite, providing a dazzling, almost ethereal effect at night when thousands of lights splayed over the area. As a result, the fair was referred to as the *White City*. The Manufacturing and Liberal Arts building, covering 44 acres, was the largest structure in the world under a single roof. The Palace of Arts had a glass transept and a spectacular dome on top of which was a statue of a mythical lady spreading her wings. The 1000-foot-long Horticultural building was topped by a 113-foot-high crystal dome. In the Palace of Mechanic Arts, there were exhibits representing almost every mechanical device fashioned by human ingenuity. Electricity Hall was decorated with Corinthian columns 42 feet high, while displays of uses of electricity, both as a source of light and a source of power, dominated the fair. Featured in the Hall were electric marvels, including electric stoves, washing machines, carpet sweepers, doorbells, fire alarms, and the Westinghouse Company's mammoth dynamos that provided for historian Henry Adams an almost spiritual experience. Displays relating to agriculture, mining, transportation, women, children, and other concerns of Americans of that day were housed in equally grand buildings.

A mile-long Midway Plaisance, which was a sharp counterpoint to the technological and cultural exhibits in the fair proper, featured Turkish bazaars, Hawaiian volcanoes, an ice railway, a simulated mountain storm in the Bernese Alps, camel rides, and circus animals. Here a young magician, who would later change his name to Harry Houdini, performed while Little Egypt danced the "hootchy-cootchy," and Scott Joplin played ragtime jazz on a piano. Visitors could ride several types of railroads, make a 1,500 foot ascent in a tethered balloon, or, in a nearby area, take in Buffalo Bill's Wild West Show. George Washington Ferris, a civil engineer, designed a giant wheel, 250 feet in diameter, on which 2,160 people, who were carried in 36 glass-enclosed cars, could ride simultaneously to view the fair and the city beyond. Along with the acts, rides, restaurants, ice cream parlors, beer gardens, and side shows, the midway contained ethnic villages showing stereotypical lifestyles of people from Europe, Asia, and Africa, as well as Native Americans.

In the summer that the fair opened, it drew 27,000,000 visitors. It is estimated that more than one of every six people in the United States visited the fair at least once. Among the foreign dignitaries who visited the fair were Archduke Ferdinand, heir to the Austro-Hungarian Empire, the Princess Eulalia of Spain, and the Duke of Veragua, a direct descendent of Christopher Columbus. The exposition was an expression of grand exuberance and great optimism, which stimulated urban planners, architects, artists, manufacturers, and consumers, all of whom had significant effects on the country in the decades ahead.

The fair was the occasion for many firsts. Thomas Edison opened the New York–Chicago telephone circuit, providing the first thousand-mile conversation. The first commemorative postage stamps and coins were issued. Sears, Roebuck issued its first catalog, and *McClure's* magazine began at 15 cents a copy. Pabst Blue Ribbon became the fair's award-winning beer, and Americans were introduced to Cream of Wheat, Aunt Jemima pancakes, Postum, Shredded Wheat, and Juicy Fruit gum. As a prelude to the fair, a new national holiday, Columbus Day, was celebrated on October 12, 1892. Francis Bellamy, editor of *Youth's Companion,* drafted a ceremony for school children, which the U.S. Bureau of Education circulated to teachers throughout the country. When the fair was officially dedicated that day, with John Philip Souza conducting "America the Beautiful," millions of children in their classrooms nationwide recited for the first time the Pledge of Allegiance to the flag of the United States. When the fair was officially opened on May 1, 1893, 100,000 people witnessed President Grover Cleveland press a button to send electricity surging through the fair site, while the enormous Statue of the Republic was unveiled.

In conjunction with the exposition, a series of 139 World Congresses were held, attracting more than 700,000 participants. These were forums for the discussion of achievements in science, literature, education, government, labor, women's issues, morals, religion, and other areas of human activity. Among the many speak-

3. *The Manufacturing and Liberal Arts Building from the west side of the Basin. In the distance is the dome of the Fine Arts Building.*

ers were educational philosopher John Dewey, suffragette Julia Ward Howe, abolitionist Frederick Douglass, historian Frederick Jackson Turner, labor leader Samuel Gompers, and lawyer Clarence Darrow. One forum was the International Congress of Engineering, which was divided into seven divisions. Division E dealt with Engineering Education.

At 11:30 AM on Monday, July 31, 1893, 70 men gathered in Hall 33 of the Palace of Fine Arts. Ira Osborn Baker, professor of civil engineering at the University of Illinois, was in the chair for Division E. For the next five days, these men would listen and respond to papers on engineering education and discuss what could be done to improve the education of engineers. By the end of the week, they created a

4. *A general interior view of the Manufacturing and Liberal Arts Building.*

new organization, the Society for the Promotion of Engineering Education, which today is known as the American Society for Engineering Education.

This was a turning point in the history of engineering education. For the previous century, engineering education developed in an unplanned, uncoordinated manner, as it responded to the changing needs for technically trained manpower of a growing, rapidly developing nation. For the century following its creation, the Society would play a significant role in improving academic quality, shaping curricula, improving teacher development, and affecting national policy on engineering education. For the coming century, I have no doubt that the Society will play an even greater role in shaping the future of engineering education in America and throughout the world.

5. *The Colonnade from the Grand Basin. The Palace of Mechanic Arts, also called Machinery Hall, is on the right.*

6. *An interior view of Machinery Hall, showing wood-working machines.*

7. *A nighttime fireworks display at the World's Columbian Exposition.*

8. *Bridge over the east lagoon. The Women's Building is in the left rear.*

9. *The Ferris Wheel on the mile-long Midway Plaisance. The domed building on the right is the Moorish Palace. The striped minarets are part of A Street in Cairo, which featured camel and donkey rides, bazaars, and Little Egypt dancing the "hootchy-cootchy."*

10. *The Palace of Fine Arts on the North Pond. This is where Division E, Engineering Education, of the World Congress met.*

CHAPTER **T W O**

. . . . . . .Engineering education in modern times may be said to have begun in France as an outgrowth of the Corps du Génie, which was created in 1676. Although the corps did not operate a school until 1749, military engineering was taught at several artillery schools, at least one of which was begun as early as 1689. Many of the engineers who fought for the Americans during the Revolutionary War studied at these artillery schools.[1]

While the primary concern in France was for military engineering, the state did not overlook civilian needs. The development and operation of roads, waterways, and harbors in France were almost entirely the prerogative of the state. When Louis XV appointed Jean Rodolphe Perronet chief engineer of bridges and highways, the king gave him the authority to establish a school within the Corps des Ponts et Chaussées, which he did in 1747. In 1775, the curriculum was structured into a three-year course of study,

and the school was renamed the École des Ponts et Chaussées. This is generally considered to be the first formal school of engineering in the world, although a number of schools had taught technical

15

subjects before then. As a result, Perronet has been referred to as the "father of engineering education." [2]

In 1794, to compensate for the poor technical training resulting from the disorganization that followed the French Revolution,[3] Napoleon created the École des Travaux Publics to train engineers for public and private service. This school, which later became the École Polytechnique, served as the model for some of the early engineering schools in the United States. Several additional schools, with curricula based heavily on mathematics, were established in France in the late eighteenth and early nineteenth centuries. These schools largely determined entry into engineering practice.

In Britain, distinct social, economic, and political conditions caused engineering education to develop along different lines. Although the Royal Military Academy in England was established in Woolwich in 1741 to instruct officers for the artillery and engineers,[4] the Industrial Revolution assured that the major concern for engineering applications was in the civilian sphere, where engineering was the responsibility of enterprising individuals. In sharp contrast to the situation in France, education for the trades and professions in England from the time of Elizabeth to 1814 was by law conducted through a system of apprenticeship. British industry in the eighteenth century and before was due largely to the inventiveness of practical and enterprising men. Many of the works that today are considered to be the result of engineering during the Industrial Revolution were done by millwrights, clock makers, and stone masons, for whom apprenticeship training, not formal education, was a prerequisite.

Before the time of America's declared independence, there was no need for a school of engineering in North America. The Europeans who came to the continent were concerned with exploration, settlement, and the development of local industries, such as fishing, fur trapping, and limited agricultural trading with the mother countries. None of these required formal education, especially in engineering. The early explorers came from many European countries, including Italy, Scandinavia, Holland, Portugal, Spain, France, and England. Settlements were under the rule and protection of the home countries. As these ties reflected the fortunes of the mother countries as powers within Europe, many did not last.

By the beginning of the eighteenth century, three European nations were vying for parts of the New World. Spain concentrated on the Caribbean and Gulf of Mexico regions and moved west and south into Central America. France settled the area north and west of the St. Lawrence River, centered around Quebec, and then moved south from Lake Erie into the area where Pittsburgh presently stands, into the Ohio Valley, and then followed the Mississippi to Louisiana. England established a series of 13 separate colonies along a crescent stretching from the Carolinas to New England, and claimed the area to the west of the French settlements in present day Canada.

11. *Jean Rodolphe Perronet (1708–1794), operating in the service of King Louis XV of France, established the first formal engineering school in the world in 1747. It was later named the École Nationale des Ponts et Chaussées.*

The engineering works that were constructed at this time were minimal. The 13 English colonies, which were the more settled, were connected by dirt roads that often were no more than paths through the wilderness. There were few bridges; shallow streams were crossed by fording, deeper ones by boats, barges, and ferries. Before their independence, the colonies' military engineering requirements were met by engineers educated in England who served in the British army or by colonists serving under them. The alliance with France during their uprising assured that many of the engineering works constructed during the Revolutionary War, and the larger public works begun in the early years following the War, were largely directed by French-educated engineers.

The situation in Canada was similar. French military engineers were the first to construct fortifications to defend their settlements against the incursions of the Indians and the British colonists to the south. Later, the French were succeeded by British military engineers, who not only created fortifications but undertook the construction of public works. The first road of any significance in Canada was opened from Quebec to Montreal in 1734, and the St. Lawrence canal system was begun in 1779. Experience rather than formal education was adequate, and often considered superior for meeting the needs of the early settlers for safety, shelter, and food necessary to sustain life and for the small commercial enterprises encouraged by England and France.

As a result, when engineering education began in America its initial development was a blending of the approaches in France and England. The early schools of engineering in the United States were established after French models, and many of the first textbooks used were either French or translations of French works. American colonists, however, were largely of English descent and shared with their English brethren a strong desire for practical and entrepreneurial activities. In this pioneering age, versatility and practical resourcefulness were prized above specialized training and the refinements of science. The interests that American colonists expressed in engineering were similar to those of their English counterparts, with initiative, imagination, and accomplishment based on individual ability, rather than formal schooling, being regarded highly. Inventions multiplied and industries developed in the hands of ingenious individuals, while the practice of any occupation at that time, including law and medicine, was the prerogative of anyone who wanted to try.

The Beginning

With the beginning of the War of Independence, America's requirement for engineers became acute. There were few experienced or educated colonists to meet the growing military need. When colonial leaders called for the establishment of engineering schools in America, they thought of engineers primarily in terms of the military. Although a few people had begun to recognize the usefulness of engineers for a wider scope of civilian activities, they did not advocate schooling for civilian engineers. The origins of engineering education in the United States thus became linked with the early history of the Army, especially of the Corps of Engineers.

At the outbreak of hostilities, one of the more experienced colonials in military matters, surveying, and construction was George Washington. His appreciation for the skills required in engineering and the benefits engineering could bring to the military were reflected in his actions, both during and after the Revolutionary War, in persistently advocating formal education for engineers.

Shortly after taking charge of the Continental Army in 1775, Washington wrote Congress about the numerous disadvantages under which the Army labored, including "a Want of Engineers to construct proper Works and direct the Men . . . I can hardly express the Disappointment I have experienced on this subject; the Skill of those we have being very imperfect." [5] Several times, he called for the training of engineers.

Washington was not alone in recognizing the need for trained officers, particularly in engineering. In February 1776, John Adams, then a member of the Board of War, wrote, "Engineers are very scarce, rare, and dear . . . we want many and seem to have none. I think it is high time we should have an Academy of this Education." [6]

Congress acceded to Washington's pleas, while the troops were encamped at Valley Forge. On May 27, 1778, Congress passed a resolution establishing an engineering department, with which Washington readily complied. In the General Orders of June 9, he issued a formal call for a school of engineering, stating:

> "3 Capt & 9 Lieut are wanted to Officer the Companys of Sappers, as this Corps will be a School of Engineering it opens a prospect to such Gentlemen as enter and will pursue the necessary Studies with Diligence, of becoming Engineers & rising to the important employments attached to that profession, such as the Direction of Fortified places &c. The Qualifications required to the Candidates are, that they be natives & have a knowledge of the Mathematics & drawing, or at least be disposed to apply themselves to those studies; They will give in their Names at Head Quarters." [7]

No school was created as a result of these orders, as apparently no one volunteered immediately, and readying for the next campaign took precedence. The mood and the tenor of the times, however, were clear. The continental army had a shortage of engineers, and almost all of those who were serving were of foreign birth and education. It was recognized that most of these men would leave the country when the war ended. America required engineers, not only for the mili-

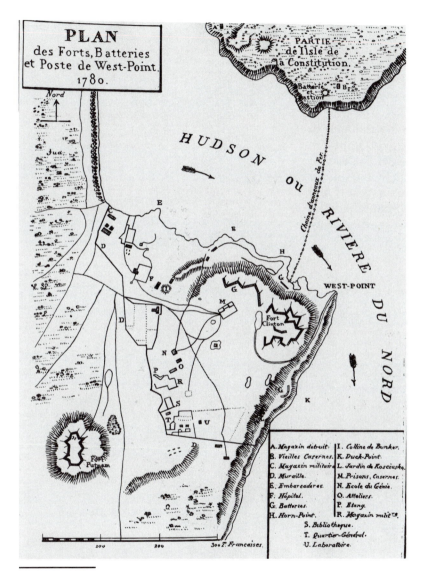

12. *A map of West Point as it appeared in 1780, showing a school of engineering (N), library (S), and a laboratory (U). This appeared in* Complot d'Arnold et de Sir Henry Clinton, *published in 1816 in Paris. A few discrepancies in the drawing lead some historians to believe the 1780 date may be too early.*

13. *General George Washington's General Order of June 9, 1778 calling for the establishment of a school of engineering, while his troops were stationed at Valley Forge.*

tary, but to meet the peacetime needs of a civilian population when the nation would be independent and developing.

On March 11, 1779, Congress formally established the engineers as a corps[8] and directed the commandant of the Corps of Engineers to "have the Sappers and Miners instructed in their duty" and "form a plan of instruction for these officers." Progress toward their instruction, however, was slow, and nothing took place during the remainder of the war.

After the Revolutionary War, the need for military education, particularly in engineering and artillery, was not forgotten. On October 23, 1783, the Committee of the Congress on the Peace Establishment, chaired by Alexander Hamilton, reported, "There must be a Corps of Artillery and Engineers kept on foot in time of peace, as the officers of this corps require science and long preliminary study and cannot be formed on an emergency."[9] The committee further recommended that the corps include among its officers four professors, one each of mathematics,

14. *West Point as it appeared in 1795. There was a school of engineering operating there at the time, but the United States Military Academy was not yet authorized.*

CONTENTS of PART I.
VOL. I.

A COURSE

15. *The table of contents of a book,* A Course of Mathematics, *which was written by Charles Hutton, a professor of mathematics at the Royal Military Academy at Woolwich, England. Published in London in 1800, it was used at West Point in the early 1800s.*

chemistry, natural philosophy, and civil architecture, and a drawing master, each of whom would be paid at the rate of $75 per month, which was equivalent to the pay of a major and considerably higher than the $40 per month recommended for surgeons. The committee, however, also stated that because of the expense of academies, their establishment "can only be an object of future consideration." [10]

Although the military did not require the inclusion of engineers in the period immediately following the close of the war, work did begin in the public sector on improving roads and building canals. Most of these activities were done and supervised either by ingenious people who had some engineering experience or by foreign-educated engineers. No further attempts were made to educate engineers in North America until after 1789, when George Washington was elected President.

At the recommendation of Washington, a military school was begun at West Point in 1794 in the old provost prison. It was suspended in 1796 when the building was destroyed by a fire, which Alexander Hamilton said, "was by some deemed a design of such officers as had been sent to the Point for instruction in the arts and sciences." [11]

James McHenry, the Secretary of War, argued that engineers required training broader than that required just for the military, stating in 1800:

> *We must not conclude that service of the engineer is limited to constructing fortifications. This is but a single branch of the profession; their utility extends to almost every branch of war; besides embracing whatever respects public buildings, roads, bridges, canals and all such works of a civil nature.* [12]

These arguments had their effect. Engineering education took root on March 16, 1802, when Congress established the United States Military Academy at West Point, with the provision that the engineers and cadets of the Academy were to be available for such duty and on such service as the President of the United States should direct. [13] This made the Army engineers available for performing tasks of a public as well as a military nature.

Loosely organized and operating on meager resources, the Academy initially had no definite or consistent system of instruction or examination. [14] This changed when Colonel Sylvanus Thayer was appointed superintendent in 1817. With the help of Claudius Crozet, an 1809 graduate of the École Polytechnic, and following a trip to France to study its educational system, he developed a sound organizational structure for the Academy. Thayer arranged the cadets into four annual classes, divided the classes into sections requiring weekly reports, developed a scale for marking, attached weights to the subjects in the curriculum necessary for graduation, instituted a system of discipline and set a standard of high achievement. These characteristics have remained with the Academy until the present and formed the pattern for technical education in America. The program Thayer

■ **BIOGRAPHICAL SKETCH**

SYLVANUS THAYER

Sylvanus Thayer is often referred to as the "Father of the Military Academy." Born in 1785 in Braintree, Massachusetts, where his ancestors had settled in the second quarter of the 1600s, he enrolled in a classical course at Dartmouth College in 1803. In 1807, he left Dartmouth for the U.S. Military Academy, where he graduated in 1808 and was commissioned a second lieutenant. After assignments in the design and construction of fortifications on the coast of New England and New York, Major Thayer was sent to Europe for two years to study military schools, fortifications, and armies. Upon his return in 1817, he became superintendent of the United States Military Academy at West Point, a position he retained until he was relieved at his own request in 1833.

developed was influenced largely by the Ecole Polytechnique, even to adopting many of the texts used at the French institution. It was based on a civil engineering curriculum, with work in the design and construction of bridges, roads, and canals, as well as fortifications.[15]

• • • • • • •

Although no degrees were granted until 1933,[16] West Point was the first engineering school in America. Its graduates played a significant role in civilian, as well as military, construction and surveying. Imbued with the spirit of Manifest Destiny, early graduates served as escorts and managers of numerous expeditions to explore and map the growing United States. Of the engineering graduates engaged in public works before 1840, a sizable fraction were West Point graduates, and at least 30 percent of them served as chief engineers of important projects on railways, canals, docks, wharves, roads, and other nonmilitary activities.[17]

Obstacles to Development in Canada

Canada, which had a much smaller population than the United States, was controlled by two nations, England and France, which were regularly at war with one another. The robust life associated with the primary industries of trapping, fishing, and agriculture drew people who were courageous and adventurous, but had little education. In contrast to the 13 colonies, there was little intellectual stimulation in early Canada. As late as 1760, no books were printed in the region, and there were few printing presses. In 1785, only one in five Canadians could read.[18]

After frequent fighting during the first half of the eighteenth century, England gained control over the French possessions in 1763 under the terms of the Peace of Paris. England faced a difficult situation. The major part of the population, who resided in the eastern portion of the country, referred to as Lower Canada, was of French culture and language and practiced the Catholic religion. As a result of a ban that existed on Huguenot emigration, Protestants were rare in this area. In contrast, the western portion, or Upper Canada, was populated by a smaller number of people, who were of English heritage. Here, they followed the English tradition that no Catholic could hold public office or be an officer in the army or navy.

As an act of expediency to maintain control of their Canadian possessions, especially with a rebellion brewing to the south, the English passed the Quebec Act in 1774. This allowed the French to maintain their customs, language, religion, and many of their laws, causing two separate cultures to remain and develop. As both Canadas remained under British control during the American Revolution, they did not experience the same need for engineers as did the 13 colonies to the south.

When he arrived, the academy was in a chaotic academic condition. He arranged the cadets into four annual classes, divided the classes into sections, developed a scale of marking, attached weights to the subjects in the curriculum, instituted a system of discipline, and set a standard of high achievement. These changes greatly improved the education at the academy, as well as formed the pattern of technical education in the United States. He also instituted a system of summer encampments, hired a number of distinguished faculty members, and offered college-level instruction in several fields.

After he left the academy and until his retirement as a brigadier general in 1863, he was engineer in charge of the construction of fortifications at Boston harbor and of the improvement of harbors on the New England coast.

Late in his life, he conceived, convinced the college authorities, endowed, and was the guiding influence in the creation of the Thayer School of Engineering at Dartmouth College. Thayer was instrumental in establishing the entrance requirements, planning the curriculum, and appointing the first director, a graduate of West Point. He also provided a fund for a public library in Braintree, and in his will provided for another scientific academy to be located in Braintree or Quincy. However, because of some poor investments, the latter could not be carried out.

Thayer died in 1872.

After the war, many colonists in the United States who had remained loyal to Britain moved north into Canada. Those who settled in the French portion caused the French people to become concerned about the survival of their culture and institutions. They sought refuge in the Quebec Act. What had been proposed as a temporary measure became a means to develop a legal sanctuary.

Canada remained relatively undeveloped. The availability of only the most primitive transportation facilities did not encourage the growth of towns and local markets. Distances between villages were long, and roads were nonexistent or exceedingly rough and treacherous. Primary routes of transportation were the rivers, which could be travelled by flat-bottomed boat in warm seasons and in winter by sleigh. With most residents living near the border, there was more incentive for north–south trade and communications between Canadian villages and those in the United States, than there was for east–west communications. The small, scattered population — in 1812, there were about one-half million people in Canada, in contrast to over six million in the United States—the friction that existed between the governors appointed by Britain and the local people in western Canada, and the tensions between the French and English people in the east, did not provide a climate for the development of engineering education.

Early Technical Schools

With the growth of the United States, there were increasing demands for technical education. In response, a variety of public and private educational institutions emerged in the eighteenth century: voluntary self-improvement groups, of which Franklin's Junto was the most famous; evening schools that taught applied science and other practical subjects to urban working people; and at an even more popular level, applied science lectures by learned men. The desire for self-improvement was so strong, that even while public elementary and secondary schools were just being established, mechanics' institutes were growing rapidly. It is estimated that by 1850, the country had about 6,000 such institutes.[19] One of the most noteworthy of these was the Franklin Institute, established in Philadelphia in 1825, which received the first government contract to conduct research on safety regulations for steam boilers.[20] By the early nineteenth century, it was becoming clear that a more systematic form of engineering education was needed to meet the nation's requirements. Neither apprenticeship systems nor the miscellany of technical instruction that had developed was satisfactory to provide the skilled manpower for the large-scale public works projects and the industrial development that was evolving. Craft traditions failed to encourage the intellectual flexibility upon which technical progress depended.

16. *West Point as it appeared in 1828. Note the substantial growth from the earlier illustration.*

17. *The Prospectus from the first catalog published in 1821 by the American Literary, Scientific, and Military Academy. Note that the courses offered include surveying, mechanics, hydrostatics, hydraulics, chemistry, electricity, field engineering, and civil engineering, including the construction of roads, canals, locks, and bridges.*

PROSPECTUS

OF THE

AMERICAN LITERARY, SCIENTIFIC, AND MILITARY ACADEMY.

CAPT. PARTRIDGE begs leave respectfully to inform the American public, that the above-mentioned Institution was opened, under his immediate direction and superintendance, at Norwich, in the State of Vermont, on the first Monday of September last. The course of education at this seminary will embrace the following branches of literature, science, and practical instruction, viz. the Latin, Greek, Hebrew, French, and English languages, Arithmetic, the construction and use of Logarithms, Algebra, Geometry, Plane and Spherical Trigonometry, Planometry, Stereometry, Mensuration of heights and distances by Trigonometry, and also Geometrically, practical Geometry generally, including particularly Surveying and Levelling, Conic Sections, the use of the Barometer, with its application to measuring the altitudes of mountains and other eminences, Mechanics, Hydrostatics, Hydraulics, the elements of Chymistry and Electricity, Optics, Astronomy, Navigation, Geography, including the use of Maps and the Globes ; Composition, Logic, History Ethics, the elements of Natural and Political Law, the Law of Nations, Military Law, the Constitution of the United States, and of the States severally, Metaphysics ; Agriculture, Permanent and Field Fortification, Field Engineering generally, the construction of Marine Batteries, Artillery duty, the principles of Gunnery, a complete course of Military Tactics, the attack and defense of fortified places, Castrametation, ancient Fortification, the ancient modes of attacking and defending fortified places, the ancient Tactics, particularly those of the Greeks and Romans, with a description of the organization and discipline of the phalanx and legion ; Book-Keeping, Music, Fencing, Military Drawing, Topography, Civil Engineering, including the construction of Roads, Canals, Locks, and Bridges ; Architecture. In addition to the foregoing, the students will be regularly and correctly instructed in the elementary school of the soldier, and also in those of the company and battalion ; they will likewise be taught the regular formation of military parades, the turning off, mounting, and relieving guards and sentinels ; the duties of officers of the guard, officers of the day, and adjutants ; the making out correctly the different descriptions of military reports ; in fine, all the duties incident to the field or garrison. The military exercises and duties will be so arranged as not to occupy any of the time that would otherwise be

Almost from its beginnings, engineering education in the United States took the form of collegiate education, instituted and directed by educators, rather than practitioners. It was firmly established before the profession organized itself, with curricula in various engineering specialties being developed and taught and degrees offered, before the corresponding professional societies were formed. As a result, engineering education did not evolve from apprenticeship training and only slowly replaced it, gaining the support of practitioners with considerable struggle. Even after the professional societies were formed, they initially did not assume responsibility for creating policy or providing guidance or control of preparatory professional education. As late as 1917, the societies granted only limited credit for academic training in their requirements for membership. Until that time, the American Institute of Electrical Engineers accepted graduation as the equivalent of only one year's experience.[21]

These beginnings were directly opposite to the manner in which education for the legal, medical, and dental professions developed in the United States, as they evolved out of apprenticeship on a purely practical and technical plane, with none of the general qualities of collegiate education. The early professional schools were usually founded as institutions independent of colleges and universities, with their corresponding professional societies assuming from their beginnings a strong concern for the educational process.[22] Many of them were profit-making ventures—a form never assumed by engineering schools—and were not endowed by private funds or supported by the state. They were organized by members of their respective professions, with the curricula determined by each profession to meet its specific needs.[23] These differences in the ways in which education for the various professions began are still evident. Today, law, medical, and dental schools operate as professional schools at the graduate level, under the aegis of a university, but with great autonomy. Engineering schools, in contrast, function at both the undergraduate and graduate levels, as integral parts of the academic and administrative structures of the university.

Most colleges founded in North America in the eighteenth century had as their primary aim an effort to promote some version of the Christian religion, both by providing leaders for the sponsoring religious denominations and by instructing all undergraduates in the conventional moral and religious beliefs. Most faculty members at these early liberal arts colleges were ministers also. They built their curricula around the classical subjects of Latin and Greek, history, philosophy, and religion, as practiced by the founding denominations. Although many liberal arts colleges began to include science as a component part of the curriculum during the second quarter of the eighteenth century, the classical curriculum remained dominant during most of that century. Shortly after the War of 1812, and especially in the 1820s, colleges began to hire permanent science professors. This change occurred first in the old colonial colleges and at several institutions in New England. By the end of the 1830s, it was common for colleges to have separate professors of mathematics, chemistry, natural philosophy, and, occasionally, geology.

■ BIOGRAPHICAL SKETCH

ALDEN PARTRIDGE

Alden Partridge was the first person to hold the title of Professor of Engineering in the United States. He was born in 1785 in Norwich, Vermont, the son of a well-to-do farmer, who had served in the Revolutionary War. As a boy, Partridge attended the local district schools in the winter and worked on the farm in the other seasons. He enrolled at Dartmouth College in 1802 but left at the beginning of his senior year to accept an appointment as a cadet in the artillerists of the United States Army.

Partridge reported to the Military Academy at West Point in December 1805 and was graduated with a commission as first lieutenant the following October. That same day, he was appointed assistant professor of mathematics at the Military Academy. He was made captain in 1810 and transferred to the civil engi-

Engineering, however, was regarded as utilitarian and was not considered a respectable collegiate pursuit. Leaders of the established colleges had little respect for and no interest in teaching applied science or the practical arts, even if the country needed such skills. Admission standards in engineering and science were lower, and the curriculum was less demanding — only three years were required to graduate in these areas, compared with four years for a bachelor of arts degree. The existing institutions had strong traditions and promoted a sense of elitism. Students majoring in engineering or science at Harvard or Yale, for instance, did not have equal status with the more elite students in the arts. Even the dining facilities were segregated.[24] Since the classical colleges did not provide fertile ground for change, many of the first schools of engineering were begun as new institutions.

Alden Partridge, an early West Point graduate, received a commission as first lieutenant of engineers in 1806. He was assigned to West Point as an instructor, was promoted to captain in 1810, and then appointed professor of engineering on September 1, 1813,[25] becoming the first person to hold this title in the United States. After serving as acting superintendent of the Academy from 1815 until Thayer's appointment in 1817, he resigned from the Army, and in 1819 established the American Literary, Scientific, and Military Academy at Norwich, Vermont. The institution was patterned after West Point, with the exception that unlike the changes instituted at the latter Academy by Sylvanus Thayer, Partridge did not require a uniform course of study for all students or a uniform length of time to complete the studies.[26] The school's first catalogue, in 1821, states that in addition to a large number of military subjects, instruction was offered in "Civil Engineering, including the construction of Roads, Canals, Locks, and Bridges," making this the first civilian school of engineering in the country. In 1834 the institution became Norwich University, awarding its first engineering degrees in 1837, when two students received the master of civil engineering after completing a three-year course of study.[27]

· · · · · · ·

The pragmatism of American society was reflected in the early schools of technical education in this country, which linked practical and theoretical instruction and connected it with a democratic ideology. In 1822, Robert H. Gardiner established the Gardiner Lyceum in Maine as a school of practical science. One of its purposes was to provide a curriculum preparatory to the higher study of agriculture, mechanics, arts, and engineering for young men of the laboring class. Its two-year course of study, later expanded to three years, included among other courses instruction in mathematics, surveying, navigation, natural philosophy, and astronomy, with civil engineering offered as an elective. In many ways its features anticipated the important aspects of the Morrill Land Grant Act of 1862, including state financial support, short courses for those not enrolled full-time, and an experimen-

neering department on September 1, 1813 with the title of Professor of Engineering. He served as superintendent of the Military Academy until the appointment of Sylvanus Thayer, then resigned from the military in 1818. The following year, he helped explore the northeastern boundary of the United States under the treaty of Ghent.

Alden Partridge had a strong commitment to the citizen soldier and believed that the best education for a youth was a combination of physical training, military discipline, and the practical application of the principles of science. In 1819, he established the American Literary, Scientific and Military Academy, which later was renamed Norwich University. This was the first civilian school of engineering in the United States, and as early as 1821 it taught courses on civil engineering, including the construction of roads, locks, canals, and bridges. He continued to lead the college until his death in 1854.

In 1822, he was appointed surveyor general of Vermont and later served several terms as a representative to the Vermont legislature. He married Ann Elizabeth Swazey in 1837 and they had two sons.

He helped establish the Virginia Literary, Scientific and Military Institute in Portsmouth, Virginia in 1839, and a similar institute at Brandywine Springs, Delaware in 1853. He was making arrangements for still another institute at Bristol, Pennsylvania when he died. ∎

tal farm operated by the students, as well as a curriculum with a uniform freshman year.[28] Due to financial difficulties, the school was closed in 1832.

Stephen Van Rensselaer, a leading public figure of his day, established the Rensselaer School in 1824 at Troy, New York "to qualify teachers for instructing the sons and daughters of farmers and mechanics, by lectures or otherwise, in the application of experimental chemistry, philosophy, and natural history, to agriculture, domestic economy, the arts and manufactures." [29] The school's first director was Amos Eaton, a lawyer, geologist, botanist, and educational pioneer. Eaton was the dominant influence on the school from its founding until his death in 1842.

While Partridge's academy clearly was an engineering school from its beginning, Rensselaer offered only a one-year general technical course during its first decade.[30] Instruction in engineering was introduced into the curriculum in gradual stages. In 1825, subjects included, "land surveying, mensuration, measurements of the flow of water in rivers and aqueducts," while the term *civil engineer* first appeared in the catalogue of 1828.[31] The New York State Legislature in May 1835 authorized Rensselaer Institute, as it was then known, to establish a department of mathematical arts for instruction in "Engineering and Technology," which led to a newly authorized degree of civil engineer being granted for the first time in 1835 to a class of four. No similar degree was granted in America or Britain at this time.[32] By 1835, the school had acquired an engineering orientation, which dominated and obscured its original purpose,[33] and, in 1849, evolved into a full-fledged polytechnic institute.

Engineering education also was developing in the south, although its evolution would be much slower than in the north. When Thomas Jefferson established the University of Virginia in 1814, he saw it teaching natural philosophy, military and naval architecture, civil architecture, and technical philosophy.[34] Charles Bonnycastle, one of the original faculty members and professor of natural philosophy and mathematics, included engineering topics in his teaching and offered his first course in civil engineering in 1833.[35] In 1835, the university appointed William Barton Rogers as professor of natural philosophy, and with Bonnycastle he shared the teaching duties in a newly established School of Civil Engineering. Rogers would leave in 1865 to become the first president of the Massachusetts Institute of Technology.

The South Carolina Railway, the first modern railroad in the United States, began passenger service in 1831, the same year the University of Alabama was founded. Southern planters quickly recognized that railroads could lower the cost of shipping their cotton to market and increase their trade. Railroad mania struck Alabama, and by 1836, 29 rail lines were chartered. The development could be stunted, however, since there were only three known civil engineers in the entire state. The University of Alabama's Board of Trustees, who were tightly linked to the railroads, instructed the faculty to begin teaching civil engineering in 1837.

18. *Charles Bonnycastle, professor of natural philosophy and mathematics at the University of Virginia, offered a course in civil engineering in 1833.*

19. *William Barton Rogers joined the faculty in the new School of Civil Engineering at the University of Virginia in 1835. In 1838, he published a textbook titled,* An Elementary Treatise on the Strength of Materials. *Rogers resigned in 1865, unsuccessfully sought a position on the faculty of Harvard University's Lawrence School of Science, and then helped found the Massachusetts Institute of Technology, of which he became the first president.*

Frederick Augustus Porter Barnard was appointed to a new professorship of mathematics and natural history, which included the teaching of surveying, construction techniques, and electromagnetism. In 1854, Barnard moved to the University of Mississippi, and then at the outbreak of the Civil War moved to the Union, eventually becoming president of Columbia University. Today, Barnard is remembered more for his promotion of women's access to college education than for his engineering teaching.[36]

In Virginia, the College of William and Mary began a School of Civil Engineering in 1836, with the professor in charge being John Millington, an engineer who had been a colleague of Michael Farrington in England in the 1820s. Virginia Military Institute opened in 1839, under the superintendency of Claudius Crozet. He used the École Polytechnique as his model. In South Carolina, The Citadel opened in 1842. Like VMI, it stressed military and civil engineering.

Public elementary education in the United States began to develop in the 1840s and 1850s, although public responsibility for secondary education did not gain momentum until after the Civil War. With limited opportunities for general education, many colleges, in order to increase enrollments and income for the school, accepted students who were not prepared for college work. They typically were enrolled in a special "preparatory" section of the college and did not count as college students. Not infrequently, the preparatory divisions had larger enrollments than the college proper, and many students never progressed beyond this preliminary stage. As public high schools became more prevalent in the 1860s and 1870s, the distinctions were eliminated and the preparatory divisions often became the first year of college study.

Engineering education suffered a setback in the late 1830s. Rampant land speculation, with payments made by paper currency issued by state and local banks, had led to inflationary prosperity. President Andrew Jackson in 1836 ordered that future payments for land purchased from the federal government would be made in gold and silver. The economy quickly deflated, loans were called, debtors defaulted, and banks closed. The United States went into the worst depression of its short history. Universities, which had operated with meager resources, were hard pressed to maintain their programs. With the development of transportation systems at a standstill, the rationale for many of the engineering programs no longer existed. The College of William and Mary closed its engineering program in 1839. Enrollments at the University of Virginia declined significantly, and the University of Alabama discontinued its engineering program in 1846. Even Rensselaer, which had perhaps the strongest engineering program outside of West Point, saw its engineering enrollment decline to six students in 1845.[37] While engineering education was deemed a necessary ingredient for future economic growth, a strong present economy was needed to maintain engineering programs.

The First Engineering Courses in Canada

Canada was struggling to develop a nation. In 1840, the British passed the Act of Union, which, on paper, blended the two Canadas into a single nation. With about 600,000 people of French extraction and 450,000 of British, there was extensive hostility, which could not be surmounted easily. Then considerable British immigration over the next 20 years balanced the two populations, causing the French to be very concerned about their cultural survival.

Railway construction in Canada began about 1830, and the first line, from Laprairie to St. Johns, Quebec, was opened in 1836. As railway construction increased, there was an influx of civil engineers, primarily from Britain and the

20. *The South Barracks at Norwich University, circa 1850.*

United States. The railway from Montreal to Toronto was completed in 1856, and when the Victoria Bridge in Montreal was built in 1860, there was an 800-mile railway link stretching from Portland, Maine to Sarnia, Ontario. Although an obvious need existed for well-trained engineers to work on the construction of canals, harbors, roads, railways, and bridges, in 1850 there were fewer than 100 engineers in the entire country.

On February 15, 1854, McMahon Cregan, an English engineer employed to conduct a railway survey, began the first formal instruction in professional engineering given in an academic institution in Canada, when he offered a two-month course in civil engineering at King's College, which, in 1859, was renamed the University of New Brunswick. Twenty-six students were enrolled.[38]

In 1855, John William Dawson was appointed principal of McGill University in Montreal. He set out to emphasize the technological needs of a sparsely populated country endowed with vast natural resources. Although Dawson was from Great Britain, he did not follow the British model. Rather, he favored the model of the land-grant universities in the United States, which provided for scientific and cultural studies, as well as the practical arts and technology. A course of engineering was established at McGill University in 1857, and continued for several years, but was discontinued in 1864 for a deficiency of funds.[39]

Although the initial step to provide formal education at the University of Toronto was taken in 1851, it was not until 1859 that the first four students were admitted. During the next two decades, there were only seven graduates, the last in 1878. The first of these, C.F.G. Robertson, received the two-year diploma in 1861, thus becoming the first graduate of an engineering program in Canada. The following year, the University of New Brunswick awarded its first engineering diploma to George Ketchum, who during his professional career made the first study of the Chignecto Canal.

Expansion of Engineering Education

In 1853, the territorial growth of the continental United States was completed when James Gadsden purchased a strip of land that occupies the present southwestern part of the country. The previous 50 years had been marked by the acquisition of a vast amount of land and expansion of the borders of the United States. Now the time was right to settle and develop that land. The movement of people and resources to the western part of the country depended upon the development of transportation and communications and required engineering skills of a far greater degree than existed before.

Benjamin Franklin Greene succeeded Eaton as director of the Rensselaer Institute in 1846 and proceeded to subject the problems of engineering education to

thorough investigation and analysis. He conceived of a polytechnic institute providing "the most complete realization of true educational culture," [40] an idea that received major emphasis after World War II. In 1849, the school was reorganized along the lines of the leading French technical schools, being particularly influenced by the programs at the École Polytechnique and the École Centrale des Arts et Manufactures. Greene began referring to the school as the Rensselaer Polytechnic Institute, a name that did not become official until 1861. Its purpose became

the education of the Architect, the Civil Engineer, Constructing and Superintending Engineers of Mechanics, Hydraulics Works, Gas Works, Iron Works, etc., and Superintendents of those higher manufacturing operations, requiring for this successful prosecution strict consideration of the scientific principles involved in their respective processes.[41]

• • • • • • •

A curriculum was developed to carry out the new aims, with the distinguishing feature of a parallel sequence of humanistic studies, mathematics, physical sciences, and technical subjects. This form of curriculum, which was new to the country at the time, but has marked American engineering curricula to this day, was intended to "contribute to the education of the man of science and the man of action, whatever be his prospective professional pursuits." This was the beginning of a shift in engineering education, from preparing a specialist with specific skills to meet the occupational requirements of the day to the education of a generalist who could more easily adapt to meet changing needs, but had less immediate utility. Although the struggle between educating an engineer as a specialist or a generalist would take several forms in the years ahead, and shift first one way then the other, the trend has been to provide a broader, more fundamental education, tempered by the needs of industrial practice.

The time requirement for the new program increased from one to three years. Experience soon showed, however, that the new curriculum was in advance of prevailing preparatory education. To remedy this, a "preparatory division" of one year was provided, but the distinction disappeared in 1862, leaving the integrated four-year curriculum, which became the accepted norm.

By 1866, only about 300 engineers had graduated from schools other than West Point during the past 31 years.[42] Most practitioners at this time still learned engineering through on-the-job experience, with the graduates seeking, but frequently not finding, employment in railroad and bridge construction. The growth of engineering education to this point had been gradual, but the lines of its development were clear. It would take only a series of events in the United States in 1862 to spur a tremendous expansion of engineering education.

His wife accompanied him to Rensselaer in 1847 and three years later she died in childbirth, as did his twin daughters. Greene never remarried, but turned his attention to building the school.

In 1851, he extended the curriculum from one to three years, and later added a preparatory division of one year which eventually led to an integrated four-year curriculum. By 1856, he had enlarged the faculty and increased the student body from less than 30 when he arrived, to 123. He subjected the problems of technical education to thorough investigation and analysis, and in 1857 presented his thoughts in a visionary report, *The True Idea of a Polytechnic.* To implement his ideas he created a curriculum that had parallel sequences of humanistic studies, mathematics, physical sciences and technical subjects. An apparent conflict between Greene and the president of the Institute's Board of Trustees led to Greene's resignation in 1859.

He decided to start another school in Troy, but abandoned the idea two years later and in 1863 accepted a position as an administrative and scientific officer in the U.S. Navy. He had a very successful career in government, conducting scientific studies on the use of the compass in iron ships, publishing papers and manuals, and touring Europe to learn about French and English scientific practices. When he retired in 1879, he returned to West Lebanon, where he died in 1895. ■

ELEMENTS

OF

CIVIL ENGINEERING:

BEING AN ATTEMPT TO CONSOLIDATE THE PRINCIPLES OF THE VARIOUS OPERATIONS

OF THE

CIVIL ENGINEER INTO ONE POINT OF VIEW,

FOR THE

Use of Students,

AND THOSE WHO MAY BE ABOUT TO EMBARK IN THE PROFESSION.

ILLUSTRATED BY NINE COPPERPLATES,

CONTAINING 273 FIGURES,

AND INTERSPERSED WITH VARIOUS USEFUL TABLES.

BY JOHN MILLINGTON,

CIVIL ENGINEER;

Formerly Professor of Mechanics in the Royal Institution of Great Britain; and of Civil Engineering and the Applications of Science to the Arts and Manufactures in the London University; and now Professor of Chemistry, Natural Philosophy and Civil Engineering in William and Mary College, Va.

PHILADELPHIA:

J. DOBSON, CHESTNUT STREET;

RICHMOND, VA.

SMITH & PALMER.

1839.

(a)

CONTENTS.

A

(b)

iv CONTENTS.

DIRECTIONS FOR FIXING THE PLATES.

PLATE 1, to face page 66.
„ 2, „ 134.
„ 3, „ 186.
„ 4, „ 360.
„ 5, „ 490.
„ 6, „ 536.
„ 7, „ 570.
„ 8, at end of book.
„ 9, facing the title page.

NOTICE.

As the plates are very long, the numbers of the figures upon them are so disposed, that the whole plate need not be unfolded from the book when first beginning to refer to it.

(c)

21. *(a) The title page from* Elements of Civil Engineering, *by John Millington, a professor at William and Mary College, in 1839, and (b) and (c) the table of contents showing the breadth of coverage in the text.*

22. *William Brydone Jack gave a series of lectures on engineering at King's College (which later became the University of New Brunswick) in the fall of 1853. The following year, Thomas McMahon Cregan offered an engineering course at the school. Jack, who became the college's president in the 1870s, was instrumental in developing the engineering program.*

23. *Student life at West Point could be joyful, as shown in this illustration of a cadet dance which appeared in* Harper's Weekly, *September 3, 1859.*

24. *West Point cadets being examined by a Board of Visitors, circa 1868.*

25. *The Polytechnic College of the State of Pennsylvania was established in 1853, and offered the first degrees in mining engineering and in mechanical engineering in the United States. The institution closed in the late 1880s.*

26. *The University of Michigan as it appeared in 1855. The university established a four-year engineering curriculum in 1850, within the School of Literature, Science, and the Arts, and offered the bachelor of science in engineering degree. The first course in metallurgical engineering in the United States was begun in 1854.*

27. *A surveying class in civil engineering at the Rensselaer School in 1862.*

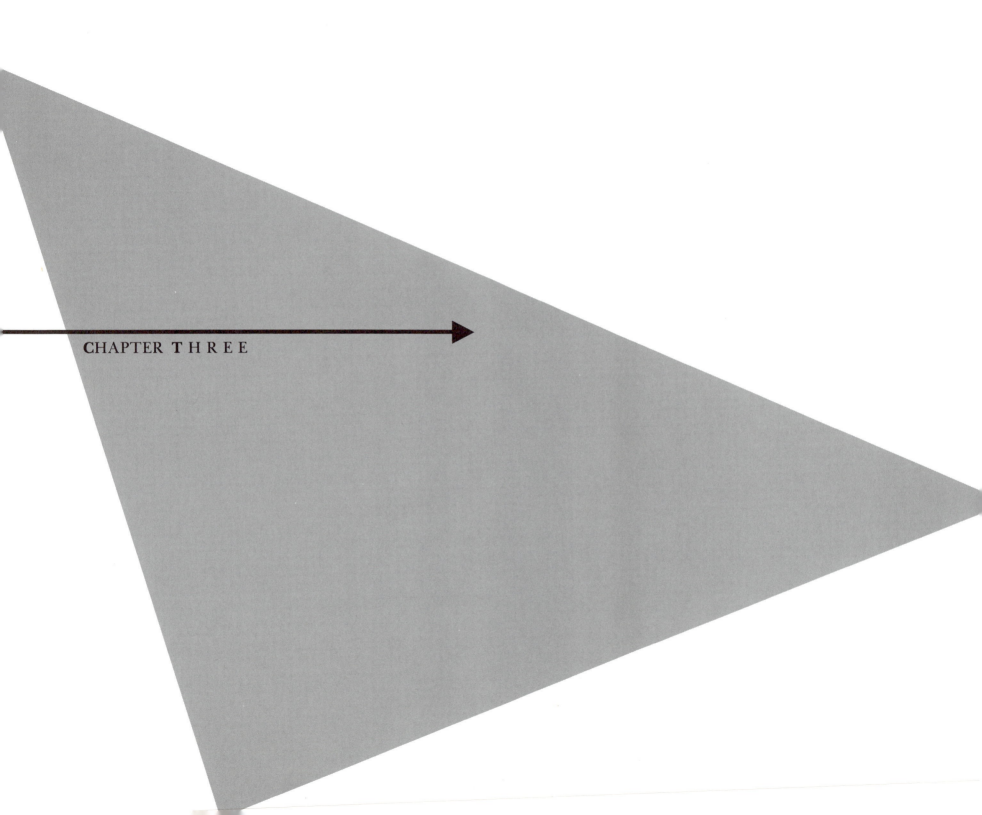

CHAPTER **T** H R E E

CHAPTER 3

THE PERIOD OF GROWTH: 1862–1893

. . . . .The early 1860s were a time of crises and setback, as well as stimulation and growth for engineering education. The Civil War, which lasted from 1861 to 1865, took a heavy toll on many colleges in the South. During the war, entire graduating classes, and in several instances, most of the student body and faculty, enlisted in the Confederate Army. Student enrollment was limited to women, the physically handicapped, disabled veterans, and young teenagers. Half of Alabama's colleges closed permanently, as did four-fifths of those in Texas.[1] The University of Alabama, which became a military school in 1860 to train soldiers for the Confederacy, was burned by northern troops in 1865 and did not reopen until 1871. The University of Virginia operated at a minimal level during the war, with many of its buildings used as hospitals for the wounded veterans of the Army of Northern Virginia.

Northern colleges fared much better. Although the demand for personnel severely affected the faculty, student enrollments, and finances, they were spared the physical destruction of the war. Many faculty members enlisted in the Union Army, and able-bodied students were drafted into service. Scientific research suffered from the shortage of college-trained technical assistants and the general disruption throughout society. However, ostensibly, as a means for academic researchers to contribute to the Union's war effort, President Lincoln authorized the National Academy of Sciences in 1865. Many professional journals and organizations perished due to economic failure in a time of rapid inflation. The opening of the Massachusetts Institute of Technology, which was incorporated in 1861, was delayed four years due to the war. Rensselaer Polytechnic Institute continued despite a complete loss of campus buildings in a nonwar-related fire.

At the end of the Civil War in 1865, there were less than two dozen engineering schools in the United States. These included: the United States Military Academy; Norwich University; Rensselaer; the dormant schools of the University of Virginia and the University of Alabama; Virginia Military Institute; The Citadel; Union College (which established a school of civil engineering in 1845); the U.S. Naval Academy (which offered courses in steam engineering from its founding in 1845 and created a separate department of engineering in 1866, when it returned to quarters at Annapolis at the end of the Civil War); the Chandler Scientific School at Dartmouth (1851); the Sheffield Scientific School at Yale (which was founded in

28. *The cadet corps at Norwich University in 1888. The school combined engineering studies with military training.*

Rules and Directions.

ADMISSION TO THE INSTITUTE.

All applications for admission to the institute, or for special information concerning it, should be addressed to the DIRECTOR OF THE INSTITUTE. Copies of the ANNUAL REGISTER may be obtained on application, either to the Director, or to W. H. YOUNG, Treasurer of the Institute, 8 First Street, Troy, N. Y.

The proper time—that is the *best* time—for entering the Classes of the Institute, is at the beginning of the scholastic year in September. Students are admitted, however, at the opening of the summer session, or at any other time in the year; but if not fully prepared on the previous work of the class, they are then obliged to make up their deficiencies by *extra efforts* during the session.

It is earnestly recommended to those who contemplate entering upon either of the courses of the Institute, to commence with the studies of Division D, rather than attempt those of Division C by means of an incomplete or superficial preparation. The requirements for entering Division D may be readily met; after which, with due attention to the studies of the class, a degree of disciplinary culture may be reached, not only sufficient for fully meeting the prescribed requirements for entering Division C, but peculiarly well adapted for *introducing* the student to the studies of this class.

EXPENSES.

Institute Fees.—In the general courses, the fees for instruction, use of astronomical and field instruments, use of consumable materials, chemicals, etc., are $75 for each semi-annual session; and in the partial courses, they are in the same proportion for the time of study. These Fees must be paid to the Treasurer in advance for each session. The Graduation Fee, including the Diploma, is $18, and must be paid to the Treasurer at least two weeks before the time of graduation. There are no extra charges.

Living Expenses.—Members of the Institute find board and lodgings with respectable private families in the city. The prices asked for board and furnished lodgings vary, at the present time, from $4.00 to $7.00 per week. The total living expenses, which include board, furnished lodgings, laundry, fires, lights, and attendance, vary from about $250 to $350 for the scholastic year.

For those parents or guardians desiring it, funds may be placed in the keeping of the Treasurer of the Institute, who will disburse and render an account of the same, (charging a commission of two and a half per cent. on the amount of his disbursements,) either to the order of the student directly, or to that of the President, Director, or other officer of the Institute. It is always liable to be injurious, unless the student be accustomed to habits of self-control, to allow him too free command of pocket money. There is little necessity for spending much money during the student's life at the Institute; and the supply of any more money than what is sufficient for his proper wants is very apt to be *worse than useless.*

STUDENT'S FURNISHINGS.

Drawing Instruments.—The instruments used at the Institute are the Swiss,—which are preferred both for their general excellence and moderate cost. These instruments, with the materials for geometrical and topographical drawing, cost from $15 to $35. The student is advised to defer his purchases of drawing instruments and materials until he comes to the Institute, when he will have the advantage of procuring them under the direction of the professors of drawing.

Chemical Instruments.—A blowpipe, platinum wire, certain re-agents, bottles, test tubes, etc., are required by each student for the courses in practical chemistry, and can be obtained at the cost of about $8.

Text-Books and Stationery.—The text-books, etc., used at the Institute, may be purchased at the city bookstores. The student is advised, however, to bring such scientific books as he may possess.

Field Service and Excursions.—All who come here are advised to bring or provide themselves with a suit of heavy and substantial clothing, boots, etc., for field service, and for the botanical and geological excursions.

SESSIONS AND VACATIONS.

The scholastic year is divided into two sessions. The first or winter session consists of twenty-one weeks, and is followed by a vacation of one week. The second or summer session consists of twenty weeks, and is followed by a vacation of ten weeks.

Students are particularly requested to be punctual in their attendance at the opening of the sessions, as indicated in the Calendar.

29. *Pages from the 1864–1865 academic year catalog of Rensselaer Polytechnic Institute. Note that there were two sessions. The winter session consisted of 21 weeks, followed by a one week vacation; the summer session consisted of 20 weeks, followed by a vacation of ten weeks.*

1847, but did not begin offering engineering until 1852); University of Michigan (founded in 1817, classes began in 1841); the Polytechnic College of the State of Pennsylvania (which was founded in 1853 and closed in the late 1800s);[2] New York University and the Polytechnic Institute of Brooklyn (both of which began offering courses in 1854 and were to merge their engineering programs in 1973 to become today's Polytechnic University); and Cooper Union (founded in 1857 as a polytechnic school "for the advancement of science and art"). In 1850, William Norton began teaching civil engineering at Brown University, and in 1865 Harvard began the School of Mining and Practical Geology. By 1874, however, there were no students at the Harvard school and it closed the following year.

Even as the war raged, three significant events occurred in 1862, which stimulated a major change in engineering education and of the United States as a nation. In that year the U.S. Congress passed the Homestead Act, which gave 160 acres of land free to any head of a family who worked for five years to improve the land. This prompted a large westward migration.

In the same year, Congress granted a charter to the Union Pacific to construct a transcontinental railroad from Nebraska to California. The largely self-taught engineers of earlier times, who surveyed the land, built roads, canals, and bridges, or were practical constructors of machinery, were not adequate for overcoming the difficulties of building a transportation system that spanned the continent. Engineers with a greater mastery of scientific and engineering skills were required to prepare and grade the terrain; lay thousands of miles of track across mountains, valleys, prairies, and desert plains; build bridges across rivers and chasms that could sustain the stress caused by tons of weight rolling forward; and continually develop larger and more powerful locomotives. Engineering schools arose out of simple necessity.

The growth of the railroads was phenomenal. The Union Pacific, completed in 1869, was quickly followed by the Southern Pacific and Northern Pacific in 1884. Between 1866 and 1876, 40,000 miles of track were laid, bringing the total to 76,808 miles of track in operation. The figure rose to 167,703 miles by 1890. In the 1880s, 520 million passengers boarded trains.

The railroad created a tremendous demand for iron, steel, and coal, which led to the growth of those industries. It opened up new regions for settlement, spawned new towns along its route by transporting food and fuel to them, made single-crop agriculture feasible by carrying the products over long distances to satisfy diverse markets, and brought cattle as well as crops to cities to feed the growing populations. It was a major factor in the development of the United States.

With the railroad came the telegraph. Supported by a Congressional appropriation of $30,000, Samuel Morse completed the first test line between Washington, DC and Baltimore in 1844.[3] Essential for the safe and efficient operation of the railroads, the telegraph paralleled the tracks and quickly provided a means of communications that spanned the country from coast to coast. At the outbreak of the Civil War, there were 12,000 telegraph offices, 9,000 of which were in railway stations. The telegraph then rapidly spread in other directions, with the Western Union Telegraph Company putting 108,000 miles of new wire into service in the decade beginning in 1866. By 1876, the total number of miles of telegraph wire in service was 184,000, which by 1890 had increased to 679,000.[4] With a growing transportation and communication infrastructure, the country was ready for further development.

Land Grant Act

The third major event of 1862 was the passage of the Morrill Land Grant Act, which laid the foundation for a comprehensive system of public higher education. This Act, introduced by Representative Justin Morrill of Vermont, was defeated in Congress in 1857 and then vetoed by President Buchanan in 1859. It finally was enacted when the Southern delegation was absent during the Civil War.[5] The Act provided for the allocation of public lands by the federal government to each state and territory for the foundation and support of colleges, "particularly such branches of learning as are related to agriculture and the mechanic arts" for the purpose of promoting "the liberal and practical education of the industrial classes in the several pursuits and professions of life." This was a typically American development, coupling the principles of science with practical purposes to satisfy democratic aspirations. The promotion of practical education had been extremely important for the utilization of the country's resources and the creation of industrial activities.

The effect of this legislation can be seen by the fact that the number of engineering schools increased from less than two dozen in 1862 to 70 in 1872, a rate of expansion without equal in American education.[6] In some states, the existing state college became the land grant institution. In other states, political considerations (and there was severe lobbying in many instances) led to new or private institutions being selected. In Texas, the legislature chose the isolated community of Bryan for the agricultural and mechanical college. In Virginia, a small college in Blacksburg won over the University of Virginia. In Alabama, which until that time never had more than 200 college students and was having difficulty supporting the University of Alabama, a small Methodist college in Auburn was chosen.[7]

Engineering schools rapidly diversified in approach and increased in number. The School of Mines at Columbia University was established in 1864, providing the prototype for most of the schools of mines and metallurgy that developed during the next 15 years. Worcester Free Institute was founded in 1868, with a distinctive form of shop training in which students served as journeymen in a pattern shop and foundry and produced commercial products, which were marketed, but for which the students received no compensation. The Thayer School of Civil Engineering at Dartmouth College was established in 1867 as a "professional" school in which the curriculum evolved into three years of study at Dartmouth for general subjects, followed by two years at the Thayer School for professional subjects, which was similar to that followed in the medical and legal professions. Cornell University, a land grant institution, was established in 1868 with the concept that education in the mechanics arts was to be "in every way equal to the learned professions." Robert H. Thurston created probably the first laboratory for engineering instruction when Stevens Institute of Technology was opened in 1871, while the University of Michigan established the first summer camp for instruction in surveying in 1874. And in the midwest, a series of institutions were founded that were to become large state universities: Iowa State University (chartered in 1858 and classes began in 1869); University of Nebraska (chartered in 1869 and classes began in 1871); Ohio State University (chartered in 1870 and classes began in 1873); Michigan State University (chartered 1855, classes began 1857); University of Illinois (chartered 1867, classes began 1868); Purdue University (chartered 1869, classes began 1874).

· · · · · · ·

On the West Coast, the University of California was established at Berkeley in 1869. When it opened, three of its six colleges were devoted to engineering — civil, mechanics arts, and mining — attesting to the field's importance to the young state of California. Its first graduating class of 12 students in 1873 included two engineers, men who in the future would become a governor, mayor, math professor, minister, and three Regents of the University.

By the end of the century, 59 separate land grant colleges had been established in 44 states under the Morrill Act. Most state universities that did not become land grant institutions expanded their curriculum extensively into the growing fields of applied science and engineering. In addition, several dozen other institutions, devoted solely or dominantly to science and engineering, were established in the latter half of the nineteenth century.

Post Civil War Industrialization

An economic boom followed the war. In the five years from 1865 to 1870 the capital invested annually in the purchase of structures and equipment for the manufacturing industries quadrupled; raw cotton used in textiles increased from 344,000 to 797,000 bales; raw sugar production went from 15,000 to 77,000 short

Thurston, who was born into a well-to-do family who manufactured steam engines, had a natural inclination to study engineering. After graduating from public high school in Providence, Rhode Island, Thurston enrolled in Brown University where he graduated three years later with degrees in both arts and civil engineering. After serving as an engineering officer on steam-powered ships for the U.S. Navy during the Civil War, he taught natural philosophy (physics) and marine engineering at the Naval Academy. While there, he published several articles on steam engines and the iron industry in the *Journal of the Franklin Institute*. When the journal's editor, Henry Morton, became the first president of Stevens Institute, he recruited Thurston as professor of mechanical engineering. Thurston remained at Stevens from 1871 until 1885, implementing his educational ideas.

Since there were few textbooks to express his ideas, he began composing his own. Eventually, he wrote 21 books, as well as 574 articles on various aspects of engineering. His three-volume text *Materials of Engineering* and his classic *A Manual of the Steam Engine for Engineers and Technical Schools* were widely used in other engineering schools in their mechanical engineering courses.

Thurston's most notable contribution to engineering education was the establishment of laboratories for both instruction and research. He equipped his laboratories with the same type of machines and devices used in the field, so that the training gained in the laboratory and shop would suitably augment the theory received in the study of higher mathematics, science, and engineering science. In 1875, Thurston received a major grant from the U.S. government to test metal alloys used in boilers, which was in addition to the contract research he already was conducting for railroad and manufacturing companies. His laboratory was probably the first in America to conduct sponsored research.

In 1885, he accepted the position of director of Sibley College of Engineering at Cornell, where he remained until his death in 1903. ∎

tons, and then to 1,397,000 short tons by 1880. There was a surge in inventions. From 1790, when the U.S. Patent Office was founded, to 1865, 60,000 patents were issued, while over 416,000 were issued from 1865 to 1890, an almost seven-fold increase in a third of the time.[8] Large numbers of European immigrants—as many as 800,000 entering the United States in a single year—helped to provide the needed labor, as well as increase the need for housing, transportation, and manufactured goods. This boom resulted in new services, new machinery, more goods, and new types of business organizations. Markets and demands increased, bringing a great amount of new capital into the economy.

By 1870, the rate of growth in the United States was considerable, and the stage was set for major advances in engineering education. The northern and western states were in the full swing of a vast process of industrial expansion, railroad building, city development, and land settlement. This industrial expansion and economic development greatly stimulated the demand for engineering services. In the older eastern states, the transition from an agricultural to an industrial society gave impetus to the subdivision and specialization of the engineering profession.

30. *Students and faculty at Cornell University prepare to take soundings for a survey of Cayuga Lake in May 1877. A French theodolite and a sounding rig are in the boat. Bricks were released to make soundings on the first survey of 1874–1878.*

In the North, wealth derived from business was supporting technology education. Ezra Cornell, who made his fortune from the telegraph, was the benefactor for Cornell University. Lafayette College was transformed from a small classical college into a flourishing institution in which engineering and the liberal arts were treated equally through Ario Pardee's coal-mining money. Lehigh College, where engineering was given the primary emphasis, was founded and supported by Asa Packer's railroad fortune.

The South, however, was destitute. The financial collapse of the Confederacy wiped out college endowments and bankrupted current and future benefactors. Faculty salaries dropped to token levels or vanished altogether. Many faculty members found different employment or emigrated to Union state universities. In contrast to the North, which was building an industrial economy and needed engineers, the South was largely agricultural and depended on the indigenous work force of former slaves and poor whites. It took half a century, until the beginnings of the twentieth century, before the economy of the South could recover, making the progress of engineering education in that region very slow and difficult.

Virginia Military Institute survived the Civil War surprisingly well. In 1867, its engineering program consisted of four years in an Academic School studying mathematics, mechanics, optics, astronomy, acoustics, chemistry, physics, mineralogy, geology, physical geography, descriptive geography, English, Latin, French, drawing (industrial, topographic, and human figure), rhetoric, logic, and moral science. This education provided a diploma, not a degree. To obtain an engineering degree, after completing the Academic School, a person had to enroll and complete a two-year course in a Special School of Applied Science, specializing in civil engineering, mechanical engineering, or mining engineering. Washington College, whose president in 1870 was Robert E. Lee, also offered three-year courses in civil and in mining engineering.[9]

To celebrate the 100th anniversary of the United States, the Centennial Exposition was held in Philadelphia in 1876. The fair was marked by a display of mechanical marvels so wondrous to behold that the *Atlantic Monthly* wrote, "Here is Prometheus unbound."[10] It was at the exposition that the Corliss engine, the electric generator and motor, and the arc lamp were first displayed, and this was where Alexander Graham Bell introduced the telephone, which within a few years would revolutionize the business routine in large cities and become a familiar convenience in thousands of American homes. The exposition provided a clear display of the rate at which America's economy was expanding, of the inventiveness of its people, and of the capacity of industry to exploit ideas, inventions, and processes through technological and financial means. It also did much to popularize technical education, particularly in the manual arts, with Russia exhibiting its methods of manual training, which influenced many of the subsequent developments in the United

States in shop training. Technology so dominated the fair that a German exhibitor remarked

The machine is the essential element in the life of North Americans. . . . Certainly it is unlimited mastery of material which speaks for the endless machinery here; certainly it is the picture of a wild chase in which all the energies are concentrated; a chase after material gain. But who can deny there is herein greatness and power?[11]

A Growing Interest in Engineering Education

Alexander Lyman Holley was instrumental in establishing a joint committee of the American Institute of Mining Engineers and the American Society of Civil Engineers, the only two engineering professional societies that existed in the United States at that time, to consider engineering education. Holley served as its secretary. This committee set up a joint meeting between the Societies to take place in June 1876, at the Centennial Exposition.[12]

Those present at the meeting expressed a wide spectrum of views about what should constitute an engineering education, ranging from the teaching almost exclusively of pure science to a heavy emphasis on practical training. Frederick J. Slade, a mining engineer, argued against teaching actual engineering practice in the colleges, and supported limiting curricula to theory with degrees to be granted only after a period of actual practice in industry. Freeman Rogers criticized the schools for teaching too many subjects and recommended the use of vacation time for workshop and laboratory practice. Robert Hallowell Richards, professor of mining engineering at MIT, called for the "synchronous arrangement of practical and theoretical work." Charles O. Thompson of the Worcester Free Institute argued for combining productive shop work and school. Robert M. Thurston of Stevens recommended "a mixed course of study and practice, extending throughout the early life of the man up to his final and complete immersion in the practice of his profession." And A.P. Baker, a practicing engineering and graduate of Rensselaer, criticized the engineering schools for having been abandoned to those who have either no experience in engineering or experience in a very limited degree.[13]

The conflicting views among the discussants was a reflection of what was occurring in the schools, as the struggle between the education of generalists or specialists continued. Two distinct approaches[14] to the education of mechanical engineers had developed. One, which was instilled at Stevens Institute of Technology, Massachusetts Institute of Technology, and Sibley College of Engineering at Cornell (after 1885), emphasized more of the theoretical concepts in higher mathematics, research, and general science, while the second, which was practiced at the Worcester Free Institute, Rose Polytechnic Institute, Sibley College (before 1865), and the Georgia School of Technology (now Georgia Institute of Technology) as founded in 1888, stressed practical shop work to produce capable machinists and shop foremen.[15] The conflict between the two approaches reached its maximum intensity in the 1880s and waned only after 1900.[16]

Professional societies maintained their interest in and desire to shape engineering education. The American Society of Civil Engineers, American Institute of Mining Engineers, and the American Society of Mechanical Engineers, which was formed in 1880, on November 1, 1882, created a joint committee to take up the subject of engineering education.[17]

In the two decades following 1862, engineering education in the United States turned away from European models and sources to seek its direction and materials in its own country. Prior to that date, engineering education was characterized by schools with very limited resources. Engineering laboratories were unknown, textbooks were few and mainly derived from abroad, and instruction was largely blackboard demonstrations prepared from texts, followed by recitation and interrogation. The primary purpose was to train civil engineers to meet the needs of geographic expansion and urban growth.[18]

31. *At Michigan State University in 1884, men and women studied engineering as part of the agriculture course. They took courses in mechanics, civil engineering, machinery, mechanical drawing, and, as these students, surveying and leveling. In 1896, women were successful in having a women's course started, and all women enrolled in it. It wasn't until 1929 that a woman, after receiving special permission, again studied engineering.*

After 1862, there was an expansion in the number of schools, aided mainly by the Land Grant Act. The collegiate type of curriculum with its extended base of science, mathematics, languages, and social studies, although modified by the pressure of expanding technical knowledge, proved its stability and became firmly established as the basic structure for engineering education in the United States. Curricula began to diversify to meet the specialized need for engineering talent. The lecture system became widespread. By 1885, shop work had obtained its maximum position in engineering curricula, as measured by the time allotted for it, and considerably overshadowed the developing instruction on laboratory instruction.

Of all the elements of progress at that time, possibly the most important was the beginning of a period of notable teaching and authorship. Engineers, rather than scientists, took increasing leadership in education, and an American literature was developed through the writing by faculty members of textbooks and articles in the journals of the newly forming technical societies. Engineering education in the United States was moving into a period of consistent development.

Distinct Curricula Arise

Engineering began to diversify into its major branches during this period. The first distinctive curriculum in civil, as distinguished from military, engineering was offered at Partridge's Academy in 1821, which was followed in 1828 by Rensselaer, with the latter institution granting the first degree in civil engineering in 1835. Mechanical engineering was first offered at the Polytechnic College of the State of Pennsylvania which awarded the first degrees in the subject in 1854. Yale taught mechanical engineering as dynamical engineering in 1863, Massachusetts Institute of Technology offered it in 1865, and Worcester Free Institute in 1868. In 1871, Stevens Institute of Technology was founded specifically for the professional education of mechanical engineers. A significant asset in the development of mechanical engineering curricula resulted when the U.S. Navy went into a period of reduction in the 1870s. To utilize the educated and experienced naval engineering officers, the government legislated the assignment of those officers to teaching positions mainly in civilian colleges and universities to promote "knowledge of steam engineering and iron shipbuilding." The authorizing bill was passed in February 1879, and 49 appointments to 39 institutions were made in the following 17 years.[19]

The diversification continued with the first degrees in mining engineering awarded in 1857 by the Polytechnic College of the State of Pennsylvania and the creation of the School of Mines at Columbia University in 1864. Electrical engineering followed as an outgrowth first of mechanical engineering and then of

32. *Students not only mixed chemicals, but also had to make their own cupels at the University of Missouri in 1885.*

physics departments, evolving from the scientific to the technical, rather than in the reverse direction, as did the earlier branches of engineering education. Topics in electricity were taught at an early stage. Frederick Barnard, for example, included electromagnetism, along with hydraulics and surveying in his engineering course at the University of Alabama about 1840.[20] Electrical engineering, however, was first introduced as a formal course of study at MIT in 1882, then at Cornell and several other schools in 1883, with perhaps the first department of electrical engineering organized at the University of Missouri in 1886.[21] The growing electrical industry, which began to flourish in the preceding decade, and the popularity of the subject led Senator George Hoar of Massachusetts to remark in 1886 that "every technical school in the country has established, or is seeking to establish, a department of electrical engineering."[22]

A need for engineers knowledgeable about chemical processes was fostered by the high rate of production and consumption of oil in the United States in the late nineteenth century, first for ship transport, and then for the automobile. A further stimulus was the enormous demand for explosives and chemicals during the First World War. Chemical engineering was similar to electrical in that it evolved from a scientific rather than a technical base. Chemistry applications were taught as early as 1866, when John William Mallet was appointed professor of analytical, industrial, and agricultural chemistry at the University of Virginia.[23] It was introduced as a curriculum at the University of Illinois in 1885.

National engineering societies were established shortly after their respective curricula, showing that the profession had not yet assumed leadership and responsibility for professional education. The founding of the American Society of Civil Engineers in 1852 was followed by the creation of the American Institute of Mining and Metallurgical Engineers (1871), the American Society of Mechanical Engineers (1880), the American Institute of Electrical Engineers (1884), and the American Institute of Chemical Engineers (1908).

Engineering Education Takes Root in Canada

By the end of the U.S. Civil War, with an expansionist mood stirring the United States, Britain was very concerned for the survival of Canada. To strengthen the country, the British North America Act was passed on March 28, 1867, which created a federation of the provinces of Ontario, Quebec, Nova Scotia, and New Brunswick. British Columbia, which was made a province in 1858, was soon added to the Dominion.

To tie the country together and protect the 250,000 square miles of Hudson Bay Territory in the west, plans were developed for a transcontinental railroad that would span the country from the Atlantic to Pacific Oceans. Although the line was started in the 1860s, progress was slow, and it remained in the east. It was not until

1880, when the Canadian Pacific Railway Company was reorganized, that rapid development occurred. Contending with immense financial problems, an armed rebellion and bitter political controversy, the builders laid 2,000 miles of steel track across plateaus, swamps, prairies, and the formidable Selkirk and Rocky Mountain ranges in five years—exactly half the time stipulated in the contract. The construction of this railway, which began in 1881, is perhaps the most spectacular engineering enterprise ever undertaken in Canada, and had a most significant effect. When the final spike was laid on November 7, 1885, Canada was linked by transportation, if not culture and language, into one nation.

Engineering classes at the University of Toronto began in the fall of 1878. The program was of three years' duration, leading to a diploma entitling the graduate to the standing as an "Associate of the School." In 1884, the University Senate replaced the diploma with the degree of Civil Engineer. Following two common years, the student entered in one of three departments: engineering (civil, mechanical, and mining), assaying and mining geology, or analytical and applied chemistry. Seven full-time students, three in mechanical engineering and four in civil engineering, enrolled for the 1878–1879 session. By 1892–1893, entrance requirements for the engineering program had been strengthened and a fourth "postgraduate" year had been added. In 1893, George Downing, an electrical engineering graduate of the Massachusetts Institute of Technology, was appointed as professor of physics and electrical engineering.

33. *The University of New Brunswick (formerly known as King's College) in 1867, the year of Canada's confederation.*

With Confederation in 1867, funding of education became a provincial responsibility. Although McGill University was the only engineering school in Quebec, it was apparent that as an English, Protestant institution, McGill would receive very meager support from the French provincial government. Rather, the Quebec Ministry of Public Instruction quickly entered negotiations to establish classes in applied science and the issuing of engineering diplomas by the newly established École des Sciences Appliquées aux Arts et à l'Industrie in Montreal. This provided the first formal French-language engineering instruction in Canada. In 1877, the government passed a bill renaming the school École Polytechnique. That year, the first five students received diplomas from that institution. By the end of the nineteenth century, nearly 400 students had graduated from the departments of civil, mechanical, mining, electrical, metallurgical, and chemical engineering at the École Polytechnique.

In 1874, the Canadian Parliament created the Military College of Canada "for the purpose of imparting a complete education in all branches of military tactics, fortification, engineering, and general scientific knowledge in subjects connected with and necessary to a thorough knowledge of the military profession." On June 1, 1876, the college opened its doors to 18 cadets. Two years later, Queen Victoria granted the institution the right to add the prefix "Royal" to its name. Beginning with the first graduating class of 1880, a diploma of graduation was granted. Engineering education had taken root in Canada.

Urbanization and Invention

During this era, North America was still predominantly agricultural, but changes were occurring rapidly, particularly in the United States. The U.S. Bureau of the Census declared 1890 the official end of the American frontier, as the census of that year showed for the first time that the increase in urban population for the preceding decade was greater than the increase in rural population. Although it was not until 1920 that urban residents exceeded rural dwellers, the trend was clearly evident.

In the preceding two decades the internal combustion engine and the spark-ignition engine were developed, as were the steam turbine, electric generator, electric motor, storage battery, voltage transformer, incandescent lamp, phonograph, and telephone. Major engineering works were proliferating. J.B. Eads completed a 500-foot center span bridge across the Mississippi in 1874, after 17 of the leading civil engineers of the day differed over how it should be designed.[24] By the middle of the 1880s, the Brooklyn Bridge was complete, Jenney built the first skyscraper, and Edison's electric-generating plant was operating at Pearl Street in New York City. Further, technological developments and a growing emphasis on standard-

34. *Although women were rare in engineering, a few did attend and graduate from engineering schools in the 1800s. Elizabeth Bragg was the first woman to graduate from engineering at the University of California in 1876.*

ization and production techniques set the stage for the establishment of mass production techniques.

American higher education also underwent a major step in its evolution. Colleges grew in number and in the number of students who attended. The purpose of college education had begun to change. There was a definite movement to give education a greater utilitarian emphasis, which appealed to a large segment of the American population. Practical subjects were introduced into the curricula, and graduation from college was connected more closely with skilled vocations and professions. Engineering was widely accepted as worthy of being taught in college, solidifying engineering into a collegiate rather than professional school model of education.

Graduate study also was beginning in earnest. Yale granted the first PhD degree in 1861, and The Johns Hopkins University, which is considered a prototype for graduate education in the United States, was founded in 1876. The German approach of connecting original research and graduate study, along with its methods of science, was the model that was adopted.

By 1892, there were about 100 engineering schools in the United States, graduating some 1,200 students annually.[25] Most elements of the structure of the American system of higher education were now in place. The numbering of courses, the credit system, major fields of study and departmental organization, the lecture, recitation, and seminar mode of learning, the elective system, and the administrative hierarchy involving presidents, deans, and department chairmen had all emerged and were accepted with little variation among institutions. The conceptual design of the collegiate structure and of the baccalaureate curriculum have not changed since that time.

In spite of similar structures, the schools exhibited significant differences in standards, course content, the balance between liberal arts and technical subjects, the mix of theory and practice, and even the length of study for a degree. Some institutions required six years and others three, while people still could enter the profession by the simple expedient of hanging up a shingle.[26]

· · · · · · ·

With the great diversity of approaches, it was evident that a consensus had to be developed on what constituted an engineering education. In 1890, Stillman W. Robinson, a professor of mechanical engineering at The Ohio State University, organized a "Mechanical Engineering Teachers Association."[27] The group held its first meeting the following year at Columbus, Ohio and met again in Buffalo in 1892, at which time its members voted to change its name to "Engineering Teachers Association," presumably to broaden its appeal to engineering educators other than just teachers of mechanical engineering.[28] Although this society did not last more than another year or two, it did indicate that the time was right for creating a society to focus on engineering education.

BIOGRAPHICAL SKETCH

STILLMAN WILLIAMS ROBINSON

Stillman Robinson was a practicing engineer, inventor, author, consultant, and dedicated teacher. He organized the Association of Teachers of Mechanical Engineering in 1890 and served as its president and, in 1893, was an active participant in the formation of the Society for the Promotion of Engineering Education and a member of its first governing council.

Born on a farm near South Reading, Vermont on March 6, 1838, Robinson became an apprentice in a machine shop at the age of 17, where he served for four years. In 1860, he decided to study engineering, and journeyed from Vermont to

Michigan, making the 625 mile trip mainly on foot and working at odd jobs along the way. He entered the University of Michigan in January 1861 and graduated from the three-year course in June 1863. He then accepted a position with the United States Survey of the Northern and Northwestern Lakes as an assistant engineer, where he remained for three years.

In 1866, he returned to the University of Michigan as an assistant in civil engineering and the following year was appointed assistant professor of mining engineering and geodesy. He was awarded 39 patents for a wide range of inventions, including a thermometer graduating machine, timepieces, a steam rock drill, photograph cutter, telephone, air compressors, automatic car brakes, shoe-making machinery, substructures for elevated railways, hypodermic syringes, and a lens grinding machine. He also published 70 articles in professional journals.

In 1870, Robinson accepted a position as professor of mechanical engineering and physics at the Illinois Industrial University, which at the time offered little engineering instruction. Anxious to carry out some of his ideas regarding the use of shop practice and experimental work in teaching, he appeared before the Board of Trustees ten days after arriving at the university, presented a case for uniting theoretical and practical instruction, and was granted $2,000 to purchase tools and partly finished apparatus. With the help of his students, he proceeded to construct a steam engine, adapting it with special features for experimental purposes. His was the first distinctly educational shop in America. It was run on a commercial basis, taking contracts to make articles

for dealers and to repair machinery. In recitation classes, Robinson often worked with students to design machines that were then built in the shop.

In 1878, Robinson moved to Ohio State University as professor of mechanical engineering and physics. Again, he began by creating a mechanical laboratory, constructing much of the equipment himself. While at the university, he was appointed by the Railroad Commission of Ohio to inspect the track, bridges, and equipment of all the railroads in the state, which led him to develop new methods based on mathematical analysis for constructing easement curves to produce smooth transitions from straight to curved tracks. Robinson participated in the organizational meeting of the American Society of Mechanical Engineers in April 1880, and was active in the society's first meeting in November of that year. Robinson resigned from the university in 1895, but maintained his outside activities until his death on October 31, 1910. ■

35. Columbia University's School of Mines in 1865, one year after it was founded, was housed in a former broom factory. Passing trains were so loud that lectures had to be suspended until they passed.

36. Students working in the wood room of the Washburn Shops, the commercial branch of the Worcester Free School (now known as the Worcester Polytechnic Institute), in the 1870s.

37. *The University of Michigan established a surveying camp on Crystal Lake near Frankfort, Michigan, in 1874. It later was named Camp Davis in honor of civil engineering professor Joseph Baker Davis.*

38. *The students in 1879 stand in front of one of the tents in which they lived during their stay at Camp Davis.*

39. *Students at the University of California, Berkeley, wore formal clothes in the field. From the late 1870s until 1911 students' class years could be distinguished by the hats they wore; seniors sported black top hats, while juniors wore battered gray ones.*

40. *At the U.S. Military Academy, students constructed field fortifications as part of their military engineering training, circa 1880.*

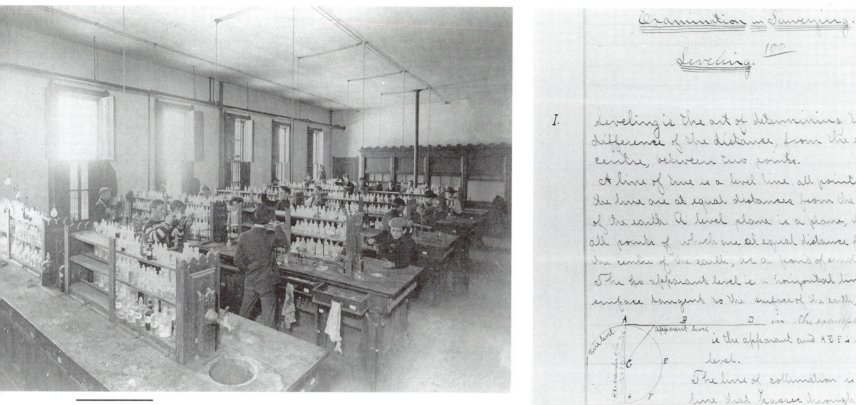

41. *Chemistry students at the University of Missouri experimented in a quantitative analysis laboratory in 1885.*

42. *An examination in surveying taken by student W.W. Averiett at the University of Alabama in 1887.*

43. Students at the University of Missouri learned to conduct an assay in 1885.

44. Bertha Lamme received a degree in mechanical engineering with a speciality in electricity from The Ohio State University in 1892, when this picture was taken. She worked at Westinghouse Electric Company until 1905, when she married Russel S. Feicht, the firm's director of engineering. Her brother, Benjamin Lamme, designed the first Niagra Falls generators, and in his will endowed the Lamme Medals, still awarded by the American Society for Engineering Education and by the Institute of Electrical and Electronics Engineers.

45. *An electrical engineering class at Notre Dame University, circa 1892.*

46. *Blackboard techniques were important in this descriptive geometry class at the Rensselaer Polytechnic Institute in 1890.*

47. *Founded as a military college in 1889, the cadets in the 1890s formed "CAC" for Clemson Agricultural College. The Cadet Corps existed for over 65 years.*

48. *In 1892 three professors from New Mexico College of Agriculture and Mechanic Arts engaged in a bit of high jinks at Shedd Ranch.*

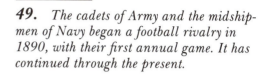

49. *The cadets of Army and the midshipmen of Navy began a football rivalry in 1890, with their first annual game. It has continued through the present.*

50. *Athletics were an important part of student life. In the 1880s, baseball was played near the Old Chem Lab at Cornell University.*

51. *Students at Rensselaer Polytechnic Institute competed in Tug of War in 1892. The school had both a "light" squad, shown here, and a "heavy" squad.*

52. *Engineers also showed their musical talents. The RPI Banjo and Guitar Club in 1892 included mandolins, guitars, banjos, and a piccolo banjo.*

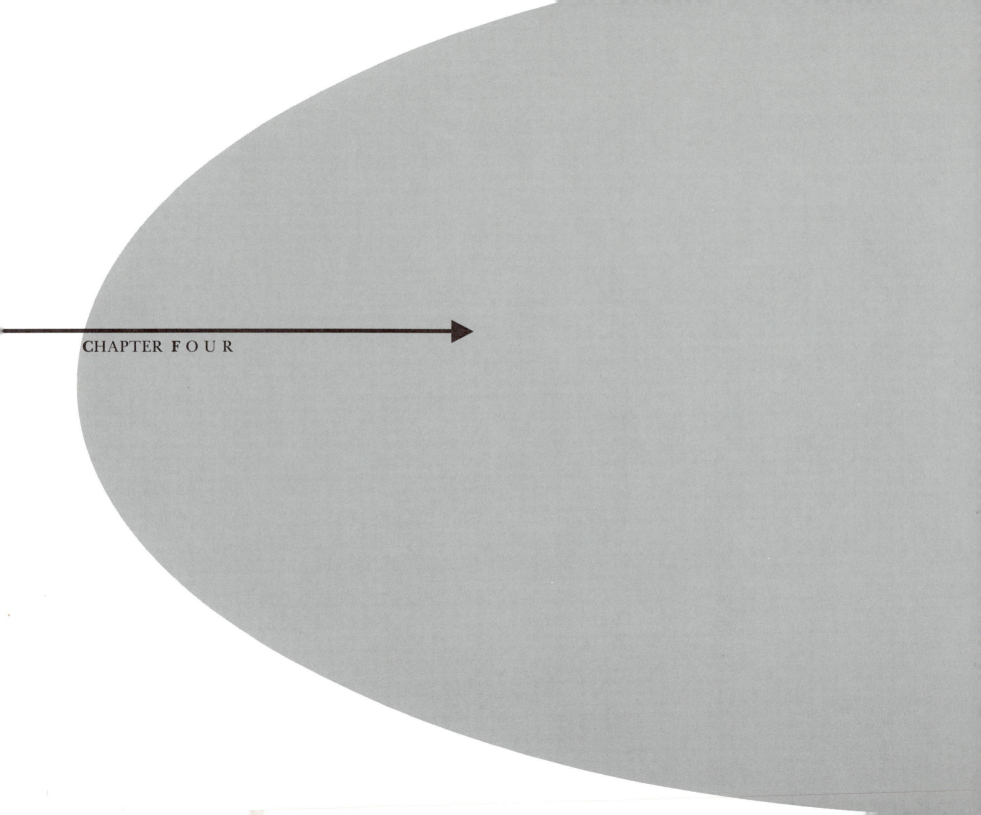

CHAPTER FOUR

CHAPTER 4

THE PERIOD OF
DEVELOPMENT: 1893–1914

. . . .**B**y 1893, American technology had come of age and the profession of engineering was taking form. Civil, mining and metallurgical, mechanical, and electrical engineers had established separate disciplinary societies to advance their respective technical interests. With the growth of industry and its demands for engineering graduates, educational problems were increasing rapidly. Engineering education, however, did not yet hold a high place as preparation for the profession or as essential to its practice. A "self-made" practical man was still considered more useful to industry than a college-educated engineer. Even at the beginning of the twentieth century, the American Institute of Electrical Engineers counted a college education as only one year of experience in qualifying for membership.

Engineering teachers also were striving for recognition and were not regarded as highly as practicing engineers. It was only after 1893 that engineering education began to be viewed as desirable preparation for practice.

Founding of **ASEE**

The World's Columbian Exposition, held in Chicago in 1893, was a natural opportunity to bring together a group of engineering faculty members to discuss the problems facing engineering education and suggest possible actions. A number of congresses on important branches of knowledge and industry were being established in connection with the exposition. Ira Osborn Baker, a 39-year-old professor of civil engineering at the University of Illinois, convinced the organizers that the International Congress of Engineering should consider engineering education as a topic separate from the disciplinary discussions. His suggestion was accepted and resulted in Division E, Engineering Education, whose sessions were organized and chaired by Baker. This was the first major meeting on engineering in which engineering education was recognized as an important subject and indeed was given equal status with the branches of engineering.

• • • • • • •

When Baker opened the meetings of Division E on July 13, 1893, 70 individuals were present, an attendance considered to be very large. While most of the attendees were young (in their 20s or 30s) a significant number were highly experienced educators.[1] The group represented a large cross section of schools from every region of the country. In the formal sessions, the participants listened to papers on various aspects of engineering education and discussed their implications. Quickly, there was a general feeling that a permanent organization devoted to the advancement of engineering education was necessary.

Stillman W. Robinson, president of the Mechanical Engineering Teachers Association,[2] was at the session. Robinson, then 55 years of age, began his teaching career in 1866, when he accepted a position as assistant in civil engineering at the University of Michigan under Professor De Volson Wood. Wood, 61, was perhaps the most senior engineering teacher in the country, having taught continuously since 1849, first in a local public school, then while he was a student at the Rensselaer School in its preparatory division, and then from 1857 in engineering. The two men worked closely together and in 1867, jointly developed a steam rock drill.[3] Although Robinson moved to the Illinois Industrial University, which became the University of Illinois, in 1870, and although Wood moved to the newly founded Stevens Institute of Technology in 1872, the two men remained close. When Wood was writing his book, *A Treatise on the Resistance of Materials,* Robinson working from a prepublication copy, solved many of the tutorial problems.[4]

A year after Robinson moved to the Illinois Industrial University, Ira O. Baker enrolled there as a student. For two years, Baker took classes from Robinson and for four years served as an assistant to him in physics laboratory practice. Although 20 years later, Society records would state that the organizers of the congress were apparently unaware of the existence of Robinson's organization until just a few days before the meetings began,[5] there clearly was a long-standing relationship

■ BIOGRAPHICAL SKETCH

IRA OSBORN BAKER

Ira Osborn Baker is proclaimed as the person primarily responsible for the founding of the Society for the Promotion of Engineering Education. Born on September 23, 1853 in Litton, Indiana, he attended high school in Illinois, then returned to Indiana to teach in a country school for six months. In March 1871, he enrolled at the Illinois Industrial University (later renamed the University of Illinois) in civil engineering. He was one of five civil engineers among the university's 19 graduates in June 1874. He then assumed a position teaching civil engineering and physics, beginning a 48-year faculty career at the University of Illinois. For 39 of those years, he was head of the civil engineering department. When the university was authorized to offer degrees, rather than certificates, he was among the first to be awarded the degrees of bachelor of civil engineering and of civil engineer in 1878 and an honorary doctor of engineering degree in 1903.

As no satisfactory textbooks existed for the subjects he was teaching, Baker developed his own by writing the text on tracing paper and blueprinting the necessary copies. Several of these evolved into standard textbooks. His *Treatise on Masonry Construction,* first published in 1889, was the first comprehensive textbook published in English dealing with foundation methods and principles involved in the use of cement. The book was reprinted in several editions and was used widely in schools in the United States, as well as in Japan, China, Mexico, and other countries. His book *A Treatise on Roads and Pavements* was published in 1903 and also went through several editions.

Baker pioneered in laboratory development at the university, creating a cement-testing laboratory in 1889 and later a road-materials laboratory. These were used for teaching and research. Baker himself conducted investigations of brick, stone, cement, and concrete, making many valuable contributions to the knowledge of these materials.

In addition to his efforts in founding the Society for the Promotion of Engineering Education, which he served as president from 1899 to 1900, he organized the Illinois Society of Engineers in 1886 and was active in the American Society of Civil Engineers and the Western Society of Engineers. Baker often served as an advisor to public officials in the State of Illinois on matters dealing with drainage, highway bridges, and building codes.

After his retirement from the University of Illinois in 1922, he retained the title Professor Emeritus of Civil Engineering until his death on November 8, 1925.

between Robinson and Wood and between Robinson and Baker at the time of the Columbian Exposition.

During the session of Division E on Tuesday, August 1, Robinson described the objectives and organization of his society and invited those interested in engineering education to meet the following morning to consider methods of organizing the engineering teachers from all engineering disciplines.[6]

Before the week was out, Baker appointed C. Frank Allen of the Massachusetts Institute of Technology, John B. Johnson of Washington University, and Mansfield Merriman of Lehigh University as a committee to draft a constitution for a new organization. This they did, with Merriman suggesting that the name be the "Society for the Promotion of Engineering Education."[7] The committee went beyond its charge and nominated a slate of officers:

DeVolson Wood, Professor of Mechanical Engineering, Stevens Institute of Technology — President

Samuel B. Christy, Professor of Mining and Metallurgy, University of California at Berkeley — Vice President

George F. Swain, Professor of Civil Engineering, Massachusetts Institute of Technology — Vice President

John B. Johnson, Professor of Civil Engineering, Washington University — Secretary

Storm Bull, Professor of Steam Engineering, University of Wisconsin — Treasurer

When asked if this did not exceed the committee's charge, Allen responded that it did, but if the organization was to become a reality, it was necessary to move rapidly. The attendees elected those nominated as officers, as well as a 21-member council to oversee the organization. The council included two members from Canada: John Galbraith, professor of engineering and principal at the School of Practical Science in Toronto, who later served as vice president of the Society, and H.T. Bovey, professor of civil engineering and applied mechanics at McGill University. Galbraith, one of the most prominent engineering educators in Canada,[8] would host the fifth annual meeting of the Society at the School of Practical Science in 1897. The attendees also decided that those in attendance at the meetings of Division E should become the first members of the Society.

When the closing session of the International Congress of Engineering was called to order on Saturday, August 5, 1893, C. Frank Allen, the secretary of Division E, reported that a permanent association of engineering teachers had been organized by the members of that division. Engineering thus became the first profession with a society devoted exclusively to education for the profession. The papers presented at the congress became volume one of the *Proceedings* of the SPEE.

• • • • • • •

■ BIOGRAPHICAL SKETCH

De VOLSON WOOD

De Volson Wood was the first president of the Society for the Promotion of Engineering Education. A dedicated, exemplary teacher, he spent 48 years in the classroom, 40 of which were in engineering. He was reported to have rarely missed a day of class in his many years of teaching. At the time of his election to the SPEE presidency, Society records referred to him as "the senior teacher of engineering in the country, if not in the world."

Wood was born in 1832 near Smyrna, New York. At the age of 17, after completing his secondary education, he began teaching in his native town, an occupation in which he engaged continuously for the rest of his life. A year later he enrolled in the Albany State Normal School, while continuing to teach, and graduated in 1853. After a year spent as principal in a public school, he returned to the Albany normal school as assistant professor of mathematics.

The following year he enrolled as a junior at the Rensselaer Polytechnic Institute. A Preparatory Division was just being organized, and he was asked to take charge of the mathematical studies of the preparatory students, which paid for his Rensselaer education. Upon graduating as a civil engineer in 1857, he decided to move to Chicago. On the way he visited the University of Michigan's campus, where he was asked by President Tappan

to fill in for a few days for a recently appointed professor of civil engineering who had not appeared. Wood remained on the faculty for fifteen years, organizing its department of civil engineering. While there he received honorary degrees of A.M. from Hamilton College and M.Sc. from the University of Michigan.

In 1872, he accepted an offer from President Morton and the Trustees of the newly established Stevens Institute of Technology to become professor of mathematics and mechanics. He remained at Stevens until his death in 1897. His influence as a teacher was renowned. The *American Mathematical Monthly* wrote,

"The civil, mechanical, and electrical engineers, architects, railroad managers and presidents, college professors and presidents, etc., who formerly were Prof. Wood's students, and who now are scattered over the whole world, would, if simultaneously rounded up, form the most intelligent army that ever moved on the face of this mundane sphere."

The inventor with Stillman W. Robinson of a steam rock drill in 1866, Wood published textbooks on trussed bridges and roofs, elementary mechanics, resistance of materials, analytical mechanics, coordinate geometry, mechanics of fluids, trigonometry, thermodynamics, and turbines. He also authored some 69 papers and chapters for several encyclopedias. ∎

its dean from 1896 until his death in November 1914. Christy also served as vice president of the American Society of Mining Engineers. He believed strongly that engineers should be cultivated and advocated that they study Greek, Latin, mathematics, and philosophy. An accomplished musician, he was a strong supporter of the arts at the university, after his death a chair in Greek theater was named in his honor.

53. Samuel Benedict Christy, professor of mining and metallurgy, University of California at Berkeley—vice president of the Society for the Promotion of Engineering Education. Born in San Francisco in 1853, he graduated from the University of California, Berkeley in 1874. His senior thesis was titled "Faraday's Theory of Electrostatic Induction." He joined the faculty upon graduation as an instructor of chemistry, became an instructor in mining in 1879, and a full professor in 1885. He created the College of Mining and served as

54. George Fillmore Swain, professor of civil engineering, Massachusetts Institute of Technology—vice president of SPEE. He was born in San Francisco in 1857, into a family that first settled in America in 1635. His father was one of the most successful merchants in the city. He entered the Massachusetts Institute of Technology to study civil engineering at the age of 15. After graduation, he worked as a civil engineer for three years, then pursued studies in structural, hydraulic, and railroad engineering at the Royal Polytechnicum in Berlin. In 1881 he accepted a position in civil engineering at the Massachusetts Institute of Technology, where he remained until he

accepted the Gordon McKay Professorship of Civil Engineering at the Graduate School of Applied Science, Harvard University, in 1909. He served in many professional organizations, including as president of the SPEE from 1894 to 1895, and of the American Society of Civil Engineers. The first recipient of the SPEE's Lamme Medal, he died in 1931.

55. *John Butler Johnson, professor of civil engineering, Washington University—secretary of SPEE. Johnson was born on June 11, 1850 and attended school in Marlboro, Ohio. His high school principal was T.C. Mendenhall, who served as SPEE president from 1898 to 1899. After attending a teachers college, he taught school for several years in Indiana and Arkansas. In 1874, he entered the University of Michigan, where he graduated as a civil engineer in 1878. After working as an engineer on the Great Lakes survey and then for the Mississippi River Commission, he became the William Palm Professor of civil engineering at Washington University. While there he wrote five textbooks and began the "Descriptive Index of Engineering Literature." In 1901 he became dean of the Col-*

lege of Mechanics and Engineering at the University of Wisconsin. Johnson served as president of the SPEE from 1897 to 1898, before he died of an accident at his summer home on the shore of Lake Michigan, June 23, 1902.

56. *Storm Bull, professor of steam engineering, University of Wisconsin—treasurer of SPEE. Bull was born in Bergen, Norway, October 20, 1856. At the age of 18 he entered the Technical School in Zurich, where he graduated in 1877. For the next two years, he practiced engineering in Europe, and in 1879 moved to the University of Wisconsin, where he became an instructor in engineering. In 1886 he was made professor of mechanical engineering, and in 1891 professor of steam engineering. In 1890 he served as vice president of the Jury of Award in the machinery department of the Paris Exposition, and in 1902 served a similar role at the St. Louis Exposition. Bull was proficient with the cello, served as*

a trustee of his local Unitarian church, and was elected mayor of Madison, Wisconsin in 1900. He died after a prolonged illness in 1908.

Shortly after the congress ended, the 70 attendees were sent information forms and requested to submit an admission fee of $3 and annual dues of $2.[9] Of the original members, 58 were engineering faculty members in 32 United States schools and three were practicing engineers in this country, while three were from England, two were from Canada, and the remaining four were from France, Germany, Russia, and Switzerland.

The organization rapidly drew to itself the leading figures in engineering education, with its officers and members coming from institutions that had sound academic standards and progressive policies. When the Society held its first meeting as an official organization the following year at the Brooklyn Polytechnic Institute, it had an international membership of 156 people. President DeVolson Wood noted, "This is the first meeting of a society for the promotion of engineering education in a broad sense in this country, if not in the world."[10] The men who founded the Society had a strong belief in the significance of their efforts and stated in the preamble to the 1894 proceedings: "There is now little question that this society will have a great and lasting influence in shaping the development of our Engineering schools."[11]

57. *From 1904 to 1913, Iowa State College was designated as the state Highway Commission, and dean of engineering Anson Marston was appointed highway commissioner. In 1907, the college was using mule teams for operating road construction machinery.*

In his inaugural address as president, Wood noted that the requirements for membership in the SPEE were not limited to men, but were open to women. He pointed out that the Society's constitution did not include the word "male," stating:

"in these days of the great enlargement of the educational field for women, it looks like a stroke of wisdom to so form the organic law that the admission of women to this Society might be possible without calling a constitutional convention and entering into political strife over such a minor point. Who would not feel that this Society would be honored by enrolling among its members that woman who . . . became the head, hands and feet of him who was the official engineer of the East River bridge, Roebling? Or of that woman who designed for the Columbian Exposition, at Chicago, a building to commemorate the work of women of the nineteenth century?" [12]

In addition to the paper presentations, "John Wiley & Sons sent sample copies of all their engineering publications, and had placed them on exhibition in a room in the building where an assistant would be in constant attendance." [13] Thus, John Wiley & Sons, which began publishing engineering textbooks only a few years earlier, became the first exhibitor at the first annual conference organized by the Society for the Promotion for Engineering Education. This combination of formal sessions and exhibits has been the pattern of the Society's annual conferences ever since.

Industrial Engineering

Sparked by activities at the World's Columbian Exposition, as well as the first automobile exhibition held at Madison Square Garden in 1900 and the Wright brothers' first flight in 1903, great industrial expansion took place as America turned more to the exploitation of ideas and the production of goods. Engineers became deeply engaged in the industrialization of the nation and focused their efforts on the improvement, operation, and maintenance of a growing complex of devices and processes.

The electrical industry grew rapidly in this period. The Westinghouse Electric Company was formed in 1886, and the General Electric Company in 1892 as an outgrowth of a company formed in 1882 by Thomas Edison to exploit his work in electric lighting. In 1895, a power plant was opened at Niagara Falls, with part of the power transmitted to Buffalo rather than being used locally. A decade later, some 175 textile mills used electricity to drive their machinery. Markets for electric power were being extended from the source of generation, allowing industries to develop rapidly throughout the continent. By 1917, the country produced almost 43.4 billion kilowatt-hours of electrical energy, compared to 6 billion kilowatt-hours in 1902. [14]

Herman Hollerith, then working for the U.S. Patent Office, invented in 1890 an electromechanical machine to tabulate information using cards with punched holes. These machines were first used to tabulate mortality statistics in New Jersey, Baltimore, and New York City, and then were selected for compiling the Census of 1890. In 1906 Hollerith formed the Tabulating Machine Company, which through mergers and growth, later became the IBM Corporation.

As corporations grew, new industrial organizational forms were created, with white-collar managers overseeing clerical workers and blue-collar laborers, under the ownership of anonymous stockholders. American producers were communicating with their suppliers and customers by telephone and distributing their goods over greater distances by truck and railroad.

The railroads posed special problems. They had to coordinate the daily activities of hundreds of operators, conductors, brakemen, station agents, clerks, and work crews scattered across thousands of miles of track. They also had to know the whereabouts of their rolling stock, where to route their trains, and how to bill, collect, and maintain an accounting of fees from shippers and passengers throughout the system. To meet their needs, the railroads created a structure that resembled more a military organization than a family-owned enterprise. They developed specialized departments, such as finance, scheduling, production, purchasing, sales, and marketing, with hierarchical chains of command and authority concentrated upward. By the end of the century, this type of organization, which became the prototype of the modern corporation, was duplicated in steel making, farm-implement manufacturing, oil, chemicals, and rubber. Centralized hiring and firing was added in 1902 when the National Cash Register Company established the first personnel department.

With the growth of the corporation, the introduction of mass production, and the desire to improve productivity, came an interest in scientific management and the beginnings of industrial engineering. H.R. Towne in the 1870s and 1880s pioneered in methods to increase production after he joined Yale's company to produce pin tumbler locks. His ideas developed and spread rapidly during the two decades following 1890. Frederick W. Taylor introduced concepts of efficiency engineering, the piece rate system and job analysis, as he analyzed tasks into their component parts and timed their performance with a stopwatch. With wage payments based on the amount of finished product, manufacturers introduced quality-control inspectors to review the finished work, a procedure that remained until recently. Hugo Muensterberg coupled psychology with industrial development, and Frank and Lillian Gilbreth developed time and motion studies. Frank Gilbreth later became a vice president of the SPEE, and Lillian, who was the first woman granted membership in the National Academy of Engineering, a professor of industrial engineering at Purdue University.

Collegiate education closely followed industrial developments. The first course in management in an engineering college appears to have been offered by Hugo

Diemer at the University of Kansas in 1902, while a similar course was created at Cornell in 1904. Diemer subsequently moved to Pennsylvania State College, where he began the first curriculum in industrial engineering in 1908.[15] Several societies for the science of management were formed about 1912, but with the trade unions resisting in the belief that efficiency meant speeding the production process and exploiting labor, the movement slowed considerably.

Engineering Schools Increase

With the rising industrial demands for greater and greater numbers of engineers with increased technical specialization, the number of engineering colleges grew rapidly. In 1892, the United States Bureau of Education published a list of 101 schools called *engineering schools* by the Bureau, and an additional 141, "which gave degrees in science and which could conceivably also become engineering schools." [16] Much of this expansion, however, had taken place at a fairly low level of academic quality and was viewed as a demoralizing influence by the better engineering schools.[17] A classification[18] done in 1896 of 110 engineering colleges, according to their entrance requirements, gave the following groupings:

Class A: Requiring for entrance at least algebra through quadratics, plane geometry or plane trigonometry, one year of foreign language, and moderately high requirements in English — 31 colleges.

Class B: Requiring algebra through quadratics and plane geometry — 33 colleges.

Class C: Requiring less than algebra through quadratics and plane geometry — 25 colleges.

Class D: Not offering complete courses in engineering, but giving analogous work generally under the heading of mechanic arts; many in the process of developing into true engineering schools — 18 colleges.

Class E: Having no entrance requirements as such, but doing engineering work of good grade — 3 colleges.

The first decade of the twentieth century saw engineering education in America continue to rise in popularity. The number of engineering students in the United States increased from 10,000 to 30,300 in the period 1890 to 1910.[19] In 1900, there were three engineering schools with enrollments of over 500 students; in 1909, there were 30.[20]

It was at this time that engineering education began to develop on the West Coast. The University of California at Berkeley was founded in 1868 and Stanford University in 1891, with instruction in engineering begun from the start in each case. Throop Polytechnic Institute began offering degrees in electrical, mechanical, and civil engineering in 1908, before becoming the California Institute of Technology in 1921. The foundations for major developments in engineering education on the West Coast, which were to be stimulated particularly by World War II, were now in place.

While the United States grew by leaps and bounds, Canada remained stable. Between 1870 and 1900, the Canadian population of some 3.5 million grew by less than 60,000 people a year. After 1900, with the opening of virgin lands and free homesteads, settlers from eastern Canada, the United States, and Europe swarmed into Canada at the rate of 200,000 to 300,000 a year. The Canadian Pacific Railway allowed them to move west. As a result, two new provinces, Alberta and Saskatchewan, were created in 1905. By 1911, there were about 1.3 million people in the Canadian west.

The growth of engineering education in Canada paralleled the population growth. As people settled the west and new opportunities for economic development arose, new engineering schools were established. Just prior to the turn of the century, only five universities and one military college offerred engineering instruction, and then in only six disciplines.[21] They were McGill University, University of Toronto, University of New Brunswick, École Polytechnique, University of Kingston, and the Royal Military College of Canada. Because none of these institutions was west of Toronto, they served primarily the developing needs of the eastern portion of the country.

Initially, the University of New Brunswick (which until 1859 was known as King's College) offered only diplomas in engineering. Then in 1899, after the engineering students petitioned, the university senate sought and received the approval of the provincial legislature to confer degrees in engineering. That same year, the first school of engineering in Nova Scotia was established at St. Francis Xavier University. In 1907, Nova Scotia's legislature established the Nova Scotia Technical College, which, in 1980, was renamed the Technical University of Nova Scotia. It was created as an upper-division institution, with only the final two years of the engineering programs offered. The preparatory years were left to "feeder colleges."

As the western provinces of Canada were established in the first decade of the twentieth century, engineering schools were created in Saskatchewan, Alberta, Manitoba, and British Columbia. In 1906, the newly formed province of Alberta established the University of Alberta on 250 acres of scrubby wilderness. Classes began in 1908, and a department of civil and municipal engineering was created the following year. In 1913, the first graduating class in engineering numbered five people.

The University of Manitoba was established in 1907, with the first class of students in civil and electrical engineering enrolled that September. Two years after Saskatchewan achieved provincial status, the provincial legislature in April 1907 created the University of Saskatchewan. The campus was an expanse of

58. *John Galbraith, first professor of engineering and principal of the School of Practical Science (which later became the Faculty of Applied Science and Engineering of the University of Toronto), was a member of the first Council of the SPEE. He hosted the Society's annual meeting in 1897 in Toronto. This photo of him lecturing was taken in 1900.*

prairie grass, broken only by a weathered settler's shack, a small barn sheltering half-broken broncos and a clump of poplar saplings. When classes commenced in 1909, the college included a department of agricultural engineering.

The University of British Columbia was established by legislation in 1908. When it began operation in 1915, it contained departments of civil, chemical, and mining engineering.

With the creation of these four institutions, Canadians now had the opportunity to undertake engineering education throughout the vast country. Except for these four engineering faculties established in the first decade of this century, no new engineering educational institutions were developed until just prior to the Second World War. Educational expansion would await a new stimulus for economic growth.

Diversification of Curricula

Along with growth, there was a large diversification in the types of engineering curricula offered in the United States. Without a strong professional body to formulate or encourage more focused professional objectives, engineering colleges operated only under the general rules of their respective universities. Schools concentrated on educating specialists rather than generalists, so that their graduates would be immediately useful upon employment in different parts of the country. As a result, curricula to prepare engineers for textile manufacturing, for example, developed in the south at Georgia Institute of Technology, North Carolina Agricultural and Mechanic Arts College, and Clemson Agricultural College, and in the northeast at Lowell Textile School; for coal mining, at the West Virginia University; for copper mining, at the Michigan Mining School; and for agriculture, throughout the midwest.

As interests expanded, and engineering colleges adapted their offerings to meet local needs, splinter disciplines were created. Refrigeration engineering evolved from mechanical engineering, railroad engineering from civil engineering, and illumination engineering from electrical engineering. A committee of the SPEE reported that 90 different engineering degrees were offered by the colleges in 1904; 68 of the degree types were undergraduate (only 47 types were actually conferred, however) and 22 were graduate (12 were conferred). The 82 colleges reporting awarded 2,393 baccalaureate degrees and 84 graduate degrees, with the major fields being civil (641 degrees), mechanical (635), electrical (414), mining (231), and general engineering (409).[22]

The diversification of curricula was paralleled by the creation of new professional societies. In 1904, the American Institute of Chemical Engineers, the Society for Heating and Ventilation, and the American Society of Refrigeration Engineers were created. In 1905, the American Concrete Institute and the Society of Automobile Engineers were formed, and the next year the Illuminating Engineering Society was established. As more societies formed and set different requirements for membership, the possibility of developing unity within the profession decreased.

It was at this time more than any other that the laboratory method of instruction in engineering grew to its dominant position. This change was due in part to the growth in electrical engineering and the emphasis in mechanical engineering on scientific rather than shop approaches. Early curricula had been dominated largely by the pattern of civil engineering, with its emphasis on design and field work, which, in turn, had been largely influenced by models of French schools. The latter were characterized by an emphasis on didactic methods of instruction and on

59. *Certain aspects of electrical engineering depended upon chemistry, as seen in this 1912 laboratory of Charles P. Steinmetz, professor of electrical engineering at Union College. Steinmetz also was the senior researcher for the General Electric Company at the time and maintained an affiliation with both organizations.*

mathematics and analytical, rather than experimental, methods. By 1900 it was generally recognized that American laboratories and methods for the teaching of engineering were not surpassed in any other part of the world. This could not be claimed, however, for much of the theoretical and design instruction.

Although engineering schools were expanding rapidly, some prejudice against engineering as an academic discipline still existed. In 1903, a graduate of Worcester Polytechnic Institute was refused admission to the University Club of Brooklyn on the grounds that he was a graduate of a polytechnic.[23]

60. *Lectures with demonstrations were an important teaching technique at the turn of the century. Cornell was a pioneer in teaching electrical engineering, with Professor Henry J. Ryan handling all of the instruction for many years. In the safety cage behind him is a high-voltage transformer.*

First Experiment Station

As a result of the Land Grant Act and its provision to promote knowledge in agriculture and the mechanic arts, agricultural experiment stations and agricultural extension grew rapidly. Similar growth in these areas did not occur in engineering, but beginnings were made. America was still an agrarian country at the turn of the century, so that research and dissemination of information in agriculture was viewed as a benefit to large numbers of people and to have direct results in terms of productivity. This latter was an important objective since the country was on its way to becoming an urban industrialized society, and higher yields from the farms with less labor would be needed to feed the growing population. Research in engineering, however, was not considered as necessary, since great technological developments were being made by individual entrepreneurs without the benefit of government subsidies.

Eugene Hale introduced a bill into Congress in 1896 to establish engineering experiment stations at land-grant colleges, but it was defeated.[24] Although monies were not available from the federal government, individual states gradually took the initiative. The University of Illinois established the first engineering experiment station in December 1903. The following year under the newly appointed dean of engineering, Anson Marston, a second experiment station was established at Iowa State College of Agriculture and Mechanics Arts. Marston, who would become SPEE President in 1914, helped get the college designated as the State Highway Commission in 1904 and took an active role in improving the roads in Iowa.

• • • • • • •

In short order, after the first engineering experiment stations were created, similar stations were organized at Pennsylvania State College, University of Missouri, University of Kansas, Kansas State Agricultural College, University of Ohio, Texas A&M College, and the University of Wisconsin. Their purpose was to assist and promote the industrial interests of the state through the publication of bulletins, research on industrial or public works problems, and technological assistance to industry.

By 1924, 503 engineering research bulletins had been issued, research funds amounted to $663,456, and there were 110 full-time and 358 part-time staff members in the engineering experiment stations of the land-grant colleges in 29 states.[25] Eventually, all land-grant institutions having engineering programs followed this lead. In the area of extension services, the growth was much slower, with the Pennsylvania State College beginning a program of industrial extension in 1907.[26]

Railroad. Upon graduation, he became resident construction engineer for the railroad at St. Joseph, Missouri. Shortly after he joined the Missouri Pacific Railroad, rising from transitman to supervisor of construction of the Ouachita River Bridge.

On December 14, 1892, he married his childhood friend and schoolmate, Mary Alice Day. Their fathers had served together in the Civil War. The couple honeymooned in Ithaca, New York, where Marston completed a study on stresses in bridge rollers.

A few months before his marriage, he had accepted a position at Iowa State College, where he rose quickly to professor and head of civil engineering. In 1898 he was given responsibility for overseeing the construction of the campus buildings. In 1908, he was appointed dean of engineering, as well as director of the Iowa Engineering Experiment Station, which was only the second such organization to be founded in the United States. In 1908, the university was given responsibility as Iowa State Highway Commission and Marston was named the Commissioner. In the early 1900s, he consulted on the construction of water works, sewage systems, drainage systems, and bridges in Illinois, California, and Florida, as well as Iowa.

During World War I, Marston was commissioned in the U.S. Army as a major in command of the 1st Battalion, 109th Engineers. In 1918, he was promoted to lieutenant colonel commanding the newly formed 97th Engineer Regiment (Highway Engineers). On horseback, with his long "walrus-type" moustache, he bore a striking resemblance to Teddy Roosevelt, and was dubbed "Old Handlebars." After the war, he was made a reserve colonel of engineers.

Marston was one of the original members of the SPEE, and served as its treasurer from 1906 to 1907 and president from 1914 to 1915. He also served as president of the American Society of Civil Engineers, Iowa Engineering Society, American Association of Land Grant Colleges and Universities, and American Association of Land Grant Colleges and Experiment Stations, and served on the governing board of the American Society for Testing and Materials.

Marston retired in 1932, and was named dean emeritus five years later. A gregarious man known for his sense of humor, he enjoyed sports and outdoor activities. He died in an automobile accident on October 21, 1949, at the age of 85. ■

Part-Time and Co-op Programs

In order to meet the needs of older adults and those who could not financially afford the cost of full-time study, engineering schools instituted part-time education. This took several forms. In 1904, the Polytechnic Institute of Brooklyn offered undergraduate engineering courses in the evening. This was well-suited to the needs of the large, urban population in the New York City area, and the program grew rapidly. By 1990 over 41,000 or 11 percent of all undergraduate and over 45,000 or 39 percent of all graduate students in U.S. engineering schools were enrolled part-time in degree programs.

A second approach in which students alternated periods of full-time instruction with appropriate employment in industry was introduced by Herman Schneider in 1906 at the University of Cincinnati. It was an attempt to blend the strengths of the university with those of industry. Students could learn the fundamentals of science and engineering in school, while employment provided the essentials of engineering practice. Similar approaches for cooperative education were initiated at Northeastern University in 1910, the universities of Georgia and Pittsburgh in 1912, Akron in 1915, Marquette and MIT in 1919, Harvard in 1920, and Antioch and New York University in 1921.[27]

· · · · · · · ·

As the plan spread, the pattern of spending periods in college and industry varied. At Cincinnati, students pursued alternating two-week sessions. At Pittsburgh, the periods consisted of four weeks in class and four weeks in industry. The MIT plan at this time, carried out in conjunction with the General Electric plant at Lynn, Massachusetts, consisted of three months in industry followed by three months at the Institute and began during the junior year. At Harvard, students spent three periods consisting of one-half semester each off-campus. New York University proposed to alternate the work of the junior and senior years on the campus, so that only the juniors or seniors would be on campus at any one time. Antioch proposed to make shop work self-sustaining and of financial aid to the students.[28] In 1927, MIT introduced cooperative education at the graduate level, in study toward the master of science in electrical engineering.[29] Drexel University currently has one of the most extensive co-op programs, with all students in engineering, science, and management required to complete three six-month assignments in industry as part of the university's 5-year degree program.

Cooperative education programs expanded steadily. In 1925 there were 5,500 cooperative students in 16 schools; in 1930 there were 9,550 students in 19 schools;[30] and in 1970 there were 104 engineering schools that had adopted them.[31] In 1993 over 150 schools of engineering and engineering technology in the United States enrolled 35,000 cooperative students.[32] Today, cooperative

HERMAN SCHNEIDER

Herman Schneider was the originator of cooperative education, beginning it at the University of Cincinnati in 1906. He was born in 1872 in Summit Hill, Pennsylvania. As a boy, he worked in his father's general store, attended the village public school, and at the age of 14 went to work as a breaker-boy in a coal mine. An older brother decided on a career in civil engineering, and Herman followed his example. After preparatory courses at the Pennsylvania Military Academy, he enrolled at Lehigh University in 1892.

Following his graduation in 1894, Schneider was employed at a Maryland ironworks for three years and then on the engineering staff designing bridges for the Oregon Short Line Railroad Company. In 1899, he returned to Lehigh as an engineering instructor, where he conceived of the idea of having students work in shops as a regular part of their instruction and not merely as a means of earning tuition. He found little support for his idea and abandoned it to accept an appointment at the University of Wisconsin. A Lehigh graduate then teaching at the University of Cincinnati suggested that he and Schneider exchange positions. Schneider accepted and, in 1903, moved to Cincinnati, where he was named dean of the college in 1906. With the support of the president, the university's Board of Trustees approved the cooperative plan for a one-year trial, but assumed no responsibility if it failed.

Schneider quickly enlisted 27 students who alternated weekly between classroom instruction and work experience, with one group always on the job. The program was a great success. By 1908, 70 freshmen were admitted from among 400 applicants. By 1912, there were 294 students and 55 firms cooperating in the program.

In 1917, Schneider was called to report to the War Department, where for two years he headed the Industrial Service Section, handling all production and labor matters. When he returned to the university in 1919, he became dean of the newly combined College of Engineering and Commerce. He arranged for the commerce students to co-op in banks, advertising agencies, and other businesses, and soon had students working in six states. By 1920, the regular program was abandoned, and Cincinnati became the first school to conduct a solely mandatory co-op program.

In 1928, Schneider reluctantly served as acting president of the university, and the following year accepted the presidency while the trustees searched for a new president. In 1932, Schneider resumed the engineering deanship, which he retained until his death in 1939. ■

education programs take five or six years to complete, and have the same entrance requirements and use the same instructional materials as the full-time, four-year curriculum.

Cooperative education in Canada began much later than in the United States, and its subsequent growth has been slow but steady. When its Faculty of Engineering was established in 1957, the University of Waterloo became the first school in Canada to offer cooperative education in engineering. By 1988, over 6,000 engineering students were enrolled in cooperative programs at 12 universities, including Waterloo, Alberta, Sherbrooke, Ottawa, British Columbia, Guelph, Regina, Victoria, Concordia, Memorial, and Simon Fraser Universities, and the Technical University of Nova Scotia.

Industrial Training

In the late 1880s, applications of electricity were starting to develop. Street cars were a major application, and electric lighting was beginning to come into use. As the equipment for electric power was large and complex, companies found it necessary to train employees to test their equipment, and then to troubleshoot and repair it after it was installed and operating in the field. The Thompson-Houston Company in Lynn, Massachusetts, established an "Experts Course" in the late 1880s, and the Edison General Electric Company in Schenectady, New York, began a "Test Course" about the same time. When the two companies merged in 1892 to form the General Electric Company, the courses were continued under an "Experts Department."

Soon after the merger, General Electric changed its policy to have the employees pay for the training. An entrance fee of $100 was set for the one-year course, during which employees were given extensive shop programs in winding, assembling, and testing of small and large motors, dynamos, generators, and transformers, as well as in arc lamps and the use of instruments.[33] Employees also were paid while in training at the rate of 5 cents, 7 cents, 10 cents, and 12 cents per hour during successive three month periods. The policy was short-lived. The program, however, continued and expanded, at no expense to the employee.

State Licensing

In order to protect the public from unqualified and unscrupulous persons who practiced engineering, states began to license engineers for practice. Wyoming passed the first state law to register engineers in 1907 to ameliorate the chaotic conditions that developed when homesteaders "surveyed" their own water rights and signed their names as "engineers." Louisiana followed in 1908 with a law regulating the practice of civil engineers. This development had an effect on engineering curricula, particularly those branches that dealt with the health and safety of the public.

Registration was, and continues to be, based on professional competence. It required a certain amount of experience in responsible engineering positions, as well as the passing of an examination in the theory and practice of engineering before a license would be granted.[34] As concern for public safety grew, all states eventually adopted licensing laws. In 1991, there were 320,949 registered engineers in the United States.[35] Canada followed a similar procedure in requiring engineers practicing in areas affecting public safety to be certified by a professional body. Canada introduced certification of engineers in the early 1930s, and by 1990, about 157,000 engineers were certified in that country.[36]

Growth of **SPEE**

The Society experienced rapid growth after the turn of the century. In 1900, there were 249 members, which increased to 503 by 1907. In 1914, when schools were first admitted as institutional members, there were 1,339 individuals and 47 institutions enrolled in the Society. Indicative of the growing stature of the Society was the participation of prominent practicing engineers as well as of the leading engineering educators in its meetings. Charles P. Steinmetz, who was one of the most outstanding electrical engineers of the period, was active in the 1912 annual conference.[37]

Most of the annual meetings during the formative years of the Society were held in cities, at sites that would accommodate large gatherings of conferees. Many of these meetings were organized in conjunction with conferences of other societies. Beginning in 1906, when the Society was hosted by Cornell University, through the mid-1980s, almost all of the annual meetings were held on university campuses. This allowed the participants to tour other universities and provided a relaxed, congenial atmosphere. Many attendees combined the business of the annual meeting with a family vacation, bringing spouses and children. In the mid-1980s, the conference became too large for most university facilities to accommodate. Attendees often were anxious to return home to their summer research assignments. Most recent conferences have been held in large hotels and conference facilities, rather than on a university campus.

When it began, the Society had one publication, *Proceedings,* which included the papers presented at the annual meeting, as well as the minutes of the meetings of the board of directors. In order to provide improved communications about technical education with its members, the Society created a monthly magazine, *Bulletin,* in June 1910. In 1916 the name of the magazine was changed to *Engineering Education.* In 1924, this publication was merged with the *Proceedings* to become the *Journal of Engineering Education,* although the bound annual volumes were still called *Proceedings.*

The Society took seriously its responsibility to promote the improvement of engineering education. Committees were appointed to collect statistics on engineering education, to study problems of common interest to engineering schools, such as entrance requirements and degree standardization, and to develop policies for the Society. Many of the reports were circulated widely among engineering administrators and influenced the development of engineering education.

Social Changes

The United States had undergone significant changes in the 38 years that elapsed from the nation's centennial in 1876 until the country entered World War I in 1914. At the beginning of the period, America still was an agrarian country of 46,107,000 people. By 1914, the population had more than doubled to 99,111,000, with the country being largely urban and industrial. There was almost continuous immigration from abroad and high rates of natural population increase at home. In 1893, 439,730 people entered the United States. By 1914, the annual total reached 1,218,480. These immigrants were different from earlier people who migrated to the country. Before 1880, those who emigrated were mainly Protestants from northern and western Europe. After 1880, there were Catholics from Italy and Poland, Orthodox from Greece, Jews from Russia, and Buddhists from China and Japan, among others. These people spoke numerous languages, came from a variety of cultures, and were generally poorer and less well educated than those in the society they entered. They became the manual laborers needed to produce more goods and services, as well as the basis for expanded markets.

Dynamos and motors drove American industry, while electric lighting and power improved life at home. Advances in communications and transportation rapidly moved people, goods, services, and ideas. As a result, the pace of the country was determined no longer by the cycle of the seasons for farming, but by timetables and time clocks in factories and offices. The man-made environment was increasing in size, as Americans built enormous bridges, skyscrapers, apartment houses, multistory hotels, department stores, and other facilities of steel, concrete, and glass.

There was a great belief in the power of technology to transform society. Henry Adams, after touring the St. Louis Exposition in 1904, wrote:

"The new American showed his parentage proudly; he was the child of steam and the brother of the dynamo, and already, within less than thirty years, this mass of mixed humanity, brought together by steam, was squeezed and welded into shape; a product of so much mechanical power and bearing no distinctive marks but that of pressure."[38]

Department stores and franchised businesses, mail-order houses, metropolitan newspapers, and mass-circulation magazines grew to satisfy expanding consumer needs and desires. Tootsie Rolls, Cracker Jacks, flavored chewing gum, ice cream cones, Horn and Hardart's Automat, the *Saturday Evening Post,* and Sunday color comics all came into existence in this period. Editor-publishers like William Randolph Hearst, Joseph Pulitzer, and Edward Wyllis Scripps helped increase the number of daily newspapers from 971 in 1880 to 2,580 in 1914.

Vaudeville, motion pictures, amusement parks, and professional sports, none of which existed to any degree in 1876, catered to the leisure of the people in 1914. The telephone and phonograph came into existence in 1876 and 1877. By 1914, there were 10 million telephones in the United States, and 500,000 phonographs were sold that year, which reached 100 million by 1921. The availability of records and the phonograph promoted an American dance craze that began about 1910. To attract those who lived in cramped apartments, movie theaters became large, architectural extravaganzas, with statues, tapestries, and mirrors inside, and electric-light marquees outside, creating a dreamlike atmosphere.

The middle class was growing and changing. This was reflected in the increase in the number of school graduates and the changing purpose of education. In 1893, 59,000 students completed secondary school, of which 24,000 were male. Of the men, 20,550 or 85 percent graduated from college four years later, indicating that, for males, secondary school was primarily a preparation for further education. By 1910, high school graduation was becoming an end in itself. That year, the number of students completing high school swelled to 157,000, but only 50 percent of the 64,000 males graduated college four years later.[39]

The same trend, but with smaller numbers of people, was true at the collegiate level. In the mid-1800s, only a small minority, primarily Anglo-Saxon, Protestant males, attended college or practiced a profession. By 1914, more men and some women from many other backgrounds were becoming accountants, educators, engineers, librarians, psychologists, physicians, and civil servants. Their activism was reflected in increased intellectual pursuits, such as the large number of congresses and meetings held at the World's Columbian Exposition in 1893 and at various fairs. The expanding middle class led to the demand for improved health and social services, the growth of hospitals, universities, urban reforms, and compulsory school attendance. America was becoming more institutional, homogeneous, and materialistic.

61. *The Brooklyn Polytechnic Institute building at 99 Livingston Street was the site of the first annual meeting of the SPEE, held on August 20–21, 1894.*

62. *The Academic Chapel at the Brooklyn Polytechnic Institute was the room in which the SPEE met in 1894.*

63. *At the Pennsylvania State College, a mechanical engineering class learned to design a lathe.*

64. *Drawing was an integral part of design. Professor Henry H. Norris, head of the department of electrical engineering at Cornell University, used it to teach the "Design of Street R'y [railway] Motors," circa 1910.*

65. *Although few women were enrolled in engineering, there were two in this 1907 class at Ohio State University.*

66. *The student at the table is using a cylindrical slide-rule in this mechanical drawing class at the Thayer School in 1895. Patented by E. Thacher in 1881, the slide-rule could be used with a compass for computations that were accurate to four places.*

67. *Cooperative learning is not a new concept, as seen in this 1907 mechanical engineering class at Ohio State University.*

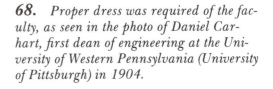

68. *Proper dress was required of the faculty, as seen in the photo of Daniel Carhart, first dean of engineering at the University of Western Pennsylvania (University of Pittsburgh) in 1904.*

69. *George Swain, one of the first two people elected as a vice president of SPEE, lectured on structures at the Massachusetts Institute of Technology in the early 1890s.*

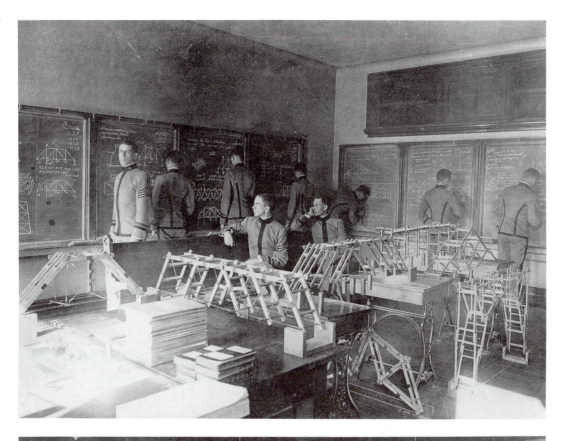

70. *Careful blackboard work was stressed in this 1914 class in bridge analysis at West Point.*

71. *The chemistry laboratory at the Case School of Applied Science was a busy place in 1893.*

72. *When not teaching, Estévan A. Fuertes, director of civil engineering at Cornell, could keep up with administrative work in the office he shared with his secretary in the late 1800s.*

73. *Mixtures were made in large quantities in the 1893 industrial chemistry class at the Massachusetts Institute of Technology.*

74. *At the University of Rochester, a woman and several men studied optics under the guidance of Professor Ernsberger in 1910.*

75. *Engineering has always been a profession in which practice is important. This 1910 foundry class at the Cornell University was taught molding, core-making, mixing of metals, in addition to learning how to operate a cupola.*

76. *Mechanical engineering students at Pennsylvania State College learned to make forms in this 1894 photo.*

77. *These students working with molten metal were among the first engineering graduates at the University of Wyoming in 1897, when it awarded bachelor's degrees in mechanical engineering and in mining engineering.*

78. *At the University of Michigan in the 1890s, students worked with the forge and anvil.*

79. Working with industrial grade equipment was an important part of the instructional process in the 1899 machine shop at Washington State University.

80. In 1910, students were learning to cut models in the department of ocean engineering at the Massachusetts Institute of Technology.

81. *At the U.S. Naval Academy, midshipmen in 1905 received instruction on the rigging of a scale-model of the man-of-war* Antietam.

82. *In 1910, students learned to test the strength of materials in Cornell's Sibley College.*

83. *In the early 1900s several students at Colorado's Agricultural College (now Colorado State University) worked on a grain binder.*

84. *At Washington State University circa 1910, students were taught to repair broken or worn-out parts of farm tractors.*

85. *Electrical engineering was concerned mainly with power generation and distribution, as illustrated in this dynamo lab at the Massachusetts Institute of Technology in 1905.*

86. *At Throop College of Technology (now California Institute of Technology), electrical engineering students measured the impedance of motors in 1914.*

87. *Engineering studies were not only conducted indoors. This 1910 agricultural engineering class at Iowa State College did field work in farm drainage.*

88. *A hydrology class at the Pennsylvania State College measured the velocity of a stream with a current meter, circa 1900.*

89. *In the summer, there was engineering camp. At the University of New Brunswick, a civil engineering surveying class gathered outside their tents, circa 1900.*

90. *The 1901 class at Colorado State University took their level rods to the top of Long's Peak after running a line of differential levels from Estes Village, Colorado.*

91. *Six weeks in a tent, food included, cost $35 in the early 1900s at this Iowa State College camp. Here mining engineering students gather before mapping the terrain.*

92. *At the University of Missouri, mining students tested a steam drill in 1895.*

94. *Professor Albert W. Smith taught his metallurgy and mining students about a cyanide process in this early 1900s laboratory at the Case School of Applied Science.*

93. *At Michigan Technology University, the mining class of 1898 visited the Lake Angeline Mine.*

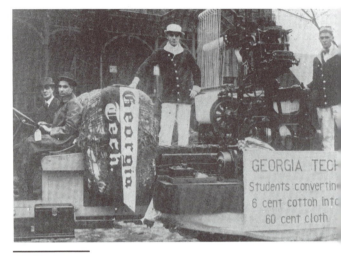

96. *The Georgia Tech students had an opportunity to publicize their contribution to the economy with this float in the 1914 "Hog and Hominy" parade.*

95. *At Georgia Tech, industrialist Aaron French endowed the A. French Textile School, which prepared students to meet the needs of the state and regional textile mills for the then-emerging industry. This is how the dye house looked in 1900, a year after the school opened.*

97. *Several engineering schools worked closely with the railroads in the early twentieth century. By 1913, the University of Illinois had a locomotive testing laboratory in which engines were run at high speed on wheels to duplicate actual operation.*

98. *In 1902, Embury A. Hitchcock, professor of mechanical engineering and future dean at Ohio State University, and his "testing crew" performed research on an operating locomotive.*

99. Students at Worcester Polytechnic Institute experimented with a trolley inside the school's electrical engineering laboratory. From 1907 to 1929, the trolley traveled throughout New England to test track and equipment.

100. Engineering schools have always served the needs of their states. The School of Engineering at the Pennsylvania State College secured the cooperation of the Pennsylvania Railroad, Pennsylvania Department of Highways, and U.S. Bureau of Roads to outfit a "Good Roads Train." The train, which consisted of seven cars equipped for presenting illustrated lectures and containing scale-model displays of highway construction machinery and methods, embarked on a statewide tour in January 1911.

101. *Pennsylvania State College began extension classes in the early 1900s, as shown in this picture of Allentown, Pennsylvania.*

102. *By 1913, students at the School of Engineering of Milwaukee were experimenting with a complete seven-pole transmission line and substation laboratory, which was donated by the Milwaukee Electric Railway & Light Company.*

103. *In 1910, Ira O. Baker published this illustration of an "elevating grader" being used to construct an earth road in his book* A Treatise on Roads and Pavements *published by John Wiley & Sons.*

104. *The same equipment that was described in Ira Baker's book was used in the early 1900s to construct roads in Illinois.*

106. *Engineering students did not spend all their time in study. There was time to parody themselves, as these engineering drawing students did in parading around campus during the Ohio State University 40th anniversary celebration in 1913. T-squares, ink bottle, and pens were in evidence.*

105. *At Michigan College of Mines (now Michigan Technological University), students at the turn of the century gathered for relaxation in the lounge of a gymnasium/clubhouse.*

107. *Students at Michigan College of Mines often dressed in night shirts for parades and fund-raising rallies, as well as for sleepwear.*

108. *At Mississippi A&M College (now Mississippi State University) students enjoyed pillow fights in the 1910s.*

109. *A lacrosse game played by the Lehigh University "Engineers" on November 24, 1903 drew a large and interested crowd.*

110. *Some students preferred to restrict their exercise to the gym, as did these students at Worcester Polytechnic Institute in 1914.*

111. *Football in 1894 was viewed by students at the University of Kentucky as a rough-and-tumble game, as shown in this illustration from their yearbook.*

113. *Engineering was growing throughout the country, in cities like New York, where Cooper Union is located, as shown, circa 1900.*

112. *When University of Michigan students completed their courses and received their degrees in 1912, Professor Charles S. Denison led the faculty commencement procession via the Denison Archway, which he designed and has since become a university tradition for blossoming romance.*

114. *Engineering was also expanding in rural areas, where chickens were fed outside of Mechanical Hall at West Virginia University in 1903.*

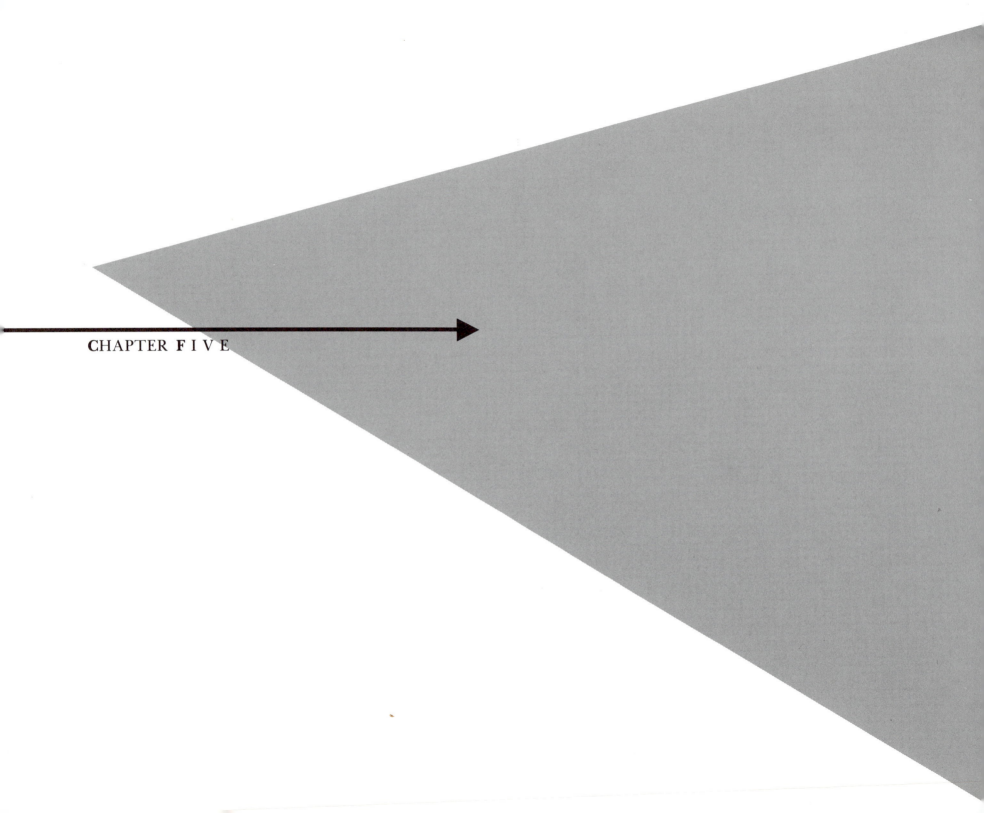

CHAPTER **F** I V E

. . . . . . .The development and demand for the automobile and airplane, the growing need for petroleum and electric power and the techniques of mass production, amplified by the requirements generated by the First World War, brought engineering and engineering education into a new phase. Nothing was more representative of the developments of this period than the automobile. In 1913, the year Henry Ford set up a moving assembly line to produce the Model T, there were 1.25 million motor vehicles registered in the United States. Ford reduced the time to assemble a chassis from 12½ hours to ½ hour, and thus greatly increased production while holding down costs.[1] As a result, by 1918 there were more than 6 million cars registered in the United States.

With the economy in a healthy state, the number of vehicles rose dramatically to 26.7 million by 1929 when the Great Depression began. After a period of stagnation, the number of vehicles registered began to rise again to 32.5 million in 1940.[2] Although the rise was great, it is more dramatic when viewed in a global perspective. In the period from 1914 to 1940, Americans bought about three-quarters of all automobiles produced in the world. This enormous output of automobiles stimulated other industrial activity by increasing the demand for steel, petroleum, rubber, and plate glass.

The airplane underwent similar rapid adoption. Its early employment by the U.S. Post Office, its use in World War I, the establishment of transcontinental service in 1921, and Lindbergh's historic flight in 1927 stimulated the growth of a new industry and aided the acceptance of the airplane by the American public. It was used for crop spraying, irrigation work, and planning for towns and railroads, as well as military applications. Between 1914 and 1940, the United States produced a total of 38,000 aircraft for the military and almost 40,000 more for civilian use.[3] This was far more than what was being produced or used in any other country.

In line with these developments, departments of aeronautical engineering were created in the colleges, with Felix W. Pawlowski beginning the first program at the University of Michigan in 1914. The airplane also had significant effects on other branches of engineering and technology. It called for precision engineering, high tensile steel, the machining of light alloys, the creation of fiberglass and plastic adhesives, new lubricants, high-quality fuels, and powder metallurgy.

The demand for oil and petroleum also rose significantly during this period. America was the major oil producer and consumer, consistently producing about two-thirds of the world's oil. Its rate of consumption per capita was ten times that of any other country.[4] While the automobile created a demand for large quantities of fuel, the airplane increased the requirements on fuel quality, with resulting improvements in the distillation process, thermal cracking, the production of petroleum (which up to the war was mainly a waste product), and the creation of tetraethyl lead. The need for chemical engineers rose, and many departments of chemical engineering came into being.

Radio was another outstanding technological development of this period. The broadcast of the news of Harding's election as President of the United States by Westinghouse Station KDKA in November 1920 caught the public's attention. Although there were very few radio sets in existence, the event was widely noted in the press. The following year, Westinghouse started three additional stations: WBZ in Springfield, Massachusetts, WJZ in New York, and KYW in Chicago. General Electric established WGY in Schenectady in 1921, and a year later AT&T set up WBNY in New York. In 1922, the number of receiving sets in use was estimated as 60,000. This figure jumped to 1.5 million the following year, and by 1927, it reached 6.5 million, or one set for every 20 inhabitants of the country.[5] Electrical engineering was expanding beyond power and lighting to communications.

The focus on producing graduates who upon employment could be immediately useful to industry — which was what business and industry wanted — had begun in earnest with the passage of the Morrill Act, and increased significantly in the first decade of the 1900s. Engineering curricula rapidly became more diverse, as engi-

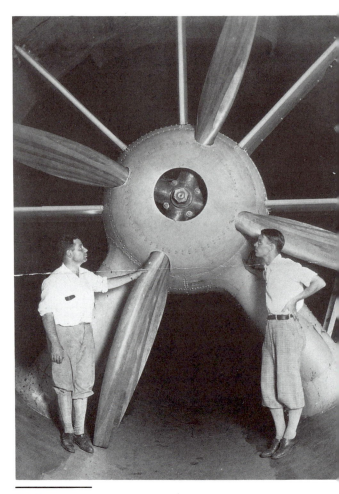

115. *World War I left its mark on engineering education. In the late 1920s, Arthur L. Kline and Clark B. Millikan (right) experimented with a 10-foot wind tunnel at the California Institute of Technology.*

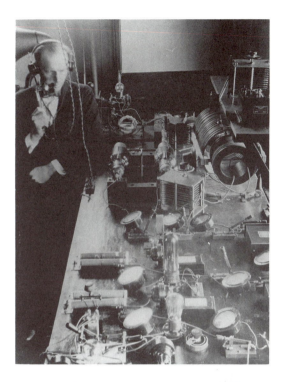

116. *Michigan College of Mines (now Michigan Technological University) operated radio station WWAO in 1924—an engineer's delight.*

117. *The Milwaukee School of Engineering established radio station WSOE in the 1920s, over which President Herbert Hoover, Vice President Charles Dawes, and Colonel Charles Lindbergh spoke to Milwaukee audiences.*

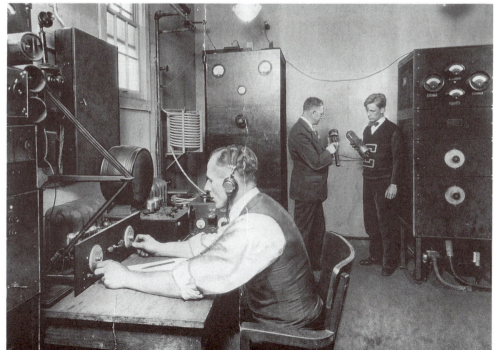

118. *Radio communications became a part of the curriculum as a result of World War I. In 1922, Ralph Willis Goddard, professor of electrical engineering at New Mexico College of Agriculture and Mechanic Arts, seen here on the dome of the engineering building, helped to erect a 120-foot radio antenna.*

neering schools initiated courses of study dealing with specific technical applications. There were programs in aeronautical, agricultural, architectural, automobile, bridge, cement, ceramic, chemical, civil, construction, electrical, heating, highway, hydraulic, illumination, industrial, marine, mechanical, metallurgical, mill, mining, railway, sanitary, steam, textile, telephone, and topographical engineering, as well as engineering administration. This extreme diversification placed severe demands on engineering colleges. It was time to examine the structure of engineering education and relate its objectives to the long-term needs of the country.

Taking Stock of Education

At the annual meeting of the SPEE in 1907, a resolution to form a Joint Committee on Engineering Education, proposed by Society President Dugald C. Jackson, professor of electrical engineering at MIT, was passed. Invited to be members of the committee were representatives of the American Society of Civil Engineers, the American Institute of Mining Engineers, the American Society of Mechanical Engineers, the American Institute of Electrical Engineers, and the American Chemical Society.[6] The committee was charged to examine all branches of engineering education, including research, graduate professional courses, undergraduate instruction, and the proper relations of engineering schools to secondary industrial schools, and to recommend the degree to which the curricula of engineering schools should be common.

· · · · · · ·

The progress of the committee was glacially slow. In 1912, with almost nothing accomplished after five years, the Carnegie Foundation for the Advancement of Teaching provided funds for the effort and Professor Charles R. Mann of the University of Chicago was appointed as an impartial observer. In 1917, ten years after the study began, Mann took charge of the committee. The committee's report, known as the Mann report, was issued the following year. It was the first comprehensive study of engineering education in the United States.[7] The report began a series of periodic evaluations by the profession, which has continued up to the present.

The report described the conditions that existed at that time; it analyzed statistics; it discussed admission problems, time schedules, course content, testing and grading, and shop work; and it dealt with suggested solutions to the problems it found. It recommended the establishment and adoption of standards or tests to evaluate the ability of students to assimilate and coordinate knowledge in terms easily understood by educators and employers. It recommended further that

DUGALD CALEB JACKSON

Dugald C. Jackson was an international authority on electricity, and head of the department of electrical engineering at the Massachusetts Institute of Technology for more than a quarter of a century. Born in Kennet Square, Pennsylvania, on February 13, 1865, he was the son of a professor of mathematics at Pennsylvania State College. He graduated from Penn State as a civil engineer at the age of 20, and for the next two years he pursued graduate studies at Cornell University. Then he helped organize the Western Engineering Company in Lincoln, Nebraska.

In 1889 Jackson became chief engineer of the Sprague Electric Railway Company, and the following year chief engineer of the Central District of the Edison General Electric Company. He accepted a position as head of electric engineering at the University of Wisconsin in 1891, where he wrote three textbooks on electricity and magnetism, and alternating current machinery.

In 1907, he became head of electrical engineering at MIT. Jackson was retained by the British Government in 1911 to make an assessment of the telephone system of England, in preparation for the government's purchase of 1,500 exchanges operated by private companies and the nationalization of the system under the post office. During World War I, he served as major and later as lieutenant colonel of engineers in France, and as chief of the Power Board with the American Expeditionary Force, where he was responsible for the planning and installation of power supply systems. For this work he was made a Chevalier of the Legion of Honor.

In 1919, he organized a consulting firm which allowed him to participate in many public utility activities, including hydroelectric projects, the electrification of railways, and the development of lighting systems for several cities. Jackson was awarded patents in electric rotating machinery, electric motors and instruments, electric motor starting devices, telephone equipment, and train lighting. A founding member of the SPEE, he served as its president from 1906 to 1907. He also served as president of the American Institute of Electrical Engineers, and the American Academy of Arts and Sciences.

Although he retired from MIT as professor emeritus in 1935, his activities continued. Jackson served as a lecturer on electrical engineering in Japan in 1935, the following year lectured at several universities in China on engineering education, and edited a series of technical books. He also was active in the Engineers' Council for Professional Development from 1932 to 1938, and chaired the Engineers Joint Committee on Ethics from 1940 to 1950, when he turned 85 years of age. Dugald Jackson died on July 1, 1951. ∎

119. *Electronics and power were developing into separate specialties in electrical engineering in the 1920s. Harold B. Smith, the founder of Worcester Polytechnic Institute's electrical engineering department, used a large demonstration panel for his lectures during that period.*

120. *At the Case School of Applied Science, classroom demonstrations were popular in the 1920s.*

121. *Mechanical engineering students at the University of Maine were taught using industrial-grade equipment, circa 1930.*

122. *William "W. O." Wiley, who was a traveling sales representative, secretary, and, in 1925, president of the publisher John Wiley & Sons, was elected treasurer of the Society for the Promotion of Engineering Education (SPEE) in 1907. He was re-elected to the SPEE position every year until he retired in 1942.*

schedules of study for engineering students should require no more than 48 hours per week, including recitation, laboratory, field work, and home preparation, and in conjunction with other engineering societies, to establish a classification of engineering work and the preparation necessary for those positions.[8]

A sense of stability took hold in the Society. The organization was established, operated, and staffed totally by volunteers. The Society records, which resided with the secretary and treasurer, were relocated every year or two as new volunteers were elected to these positions. But this was to change. In 1907, William O. Wiley, who would become chairman of the Board of Directors of the publisher John Wiley & Sons, was elected treasurer for a one-year term. He was reelected each succeeding year until he retired 35 years later in 1942. Wiley served on the SPEE Board of Directors longer than any other person in the history of the Society.

Serving almost as long was Frederic Lendall Bishop, dean of the School of Engineering at The University of Pittsburgh. He became secretary in 1914 and was annually reelected for 33 years until his retirement in 1947. In 1918, Bishop hired Nell McKenry as assistant secretary, the Society's first regular employee; she remained in that position until 1948.

· · · · · · ·

World War I

In June 1914, a Serbian shot and assassinated Archduke Ferdinand, the heir to the Austrian-Hungarian empire. A intricate web of military alliances and mutual defense pacts quickly drew all of the great European powers into conflict. In August, Austria and its ally Germany invaded Serbia. Russia went to the aid of Serbia, and France, an ally of Russia, entered the war. England, allied to both France and Russia, tried to remain out of the fighting, but came in when Germany invaded Belgium. Turkey and Bulgaria entered on the side of Germany, while Italy, Greece, Romania, and Japan joined the other side. When England declared war, Canada as part of the British empire, was automatically in the conflict. The United States, whose foreign policy was to remain neutral in European affairs, did not become involved immediately.

When war began, Canadian schools of engineering put themselves at the disposal of the government. At the time, engineering was taught in ten universities located in the four western provinces, Nova Scotia, New Brunswick, and two each in Ontario and Quebec. Almost immediately, large numbers of engineering students and professors began enlisting in the armed forces. While the scale of engineering instruction diminished, most of the programs continued to operate, but with the barest number of students and faculty. In several universities, space was turned over to the armed forces. For example, at the University of Toronto two-thirds of

FREDERIC LENDALL BISHOP

Frederic Lendall Bishop served as secretary of the Society for the Promotion of Engineering Education from 1914 until 1947, which for much of this time also meant he served as editor of the *Journal of Engineering Education*. His 33-year tenure in this volunteer, part-time position to which he was reelected each year was marked by significant growth and development in the Society. It was the time when several significant studies of engineering education were conducted, including the Mann report, the Wickenden report, and the two Hammond reports.

Bishop was born in St. Johnsonbury, Vermont in 1876. After attending a local academy, where he was a classmate of Calvin Coolidge, he enrolled at the Massachusetts Institute of Technology, from which he received a bachelor of science in electrical engineering in 1898. Upon graduation, he accepted a position as professor of physics in the newly founded Bradley Polytechnic Institute in Illinois and began to study physics at the University of Chicago under the soon-to-be Nobel Laureate Albert Michelson. In 1905, Bishop received a doctorate in physics, and in 1909, as the Western University of Pennsylvania was evolving into the University of Pittsburgh, Bishop joined that institution as professor of physics. A few months later, he was made dean of engineering, a position he held for 18 years.

In 1910, he introduced the cooperative system into engineering, making Pittsburgh the second institution in the country to adopt the approach. With America's entry into World War I, Bishop was put in charge of the university's war training program and the some 5,000 men who studied there. When the School of Mines was combined with the School of Engineering in 1920, he became the dean of both. In 1923, he was instrumental in establishing a department of industrial engineering at the university.

With the national preparedness, which preceded World War II, Bishop, as a primary representative for SPEE, became a spokesman for engineering education. From 1940 until the end of the war, he served first as a member of the National Advisory Committee on Engineering Training for National Defense to formulate national policy for the training of hundreds of thousands of men and women for war industries, and later as a member of the National Coordination Committee on Education and Defense, which was instrumental in creating the Army Specialized Training Program at U.S. colleges.

Bishop maintained an active research interest in glass, working at one time on laminated automobile windshields and wrote papers on thermal conductivity, heat of dilution, electric furnaces, viscosity, and highway engineering. Throughout his entire career at Pittsburgh, in spite of the many demands of his administrative, society, and governmental work, he continued to teach physics to sophomore engineering students.

Bishop died in 1947, a few months after he resigned as secretary of SPEE. ∎

the students and many of the staff joined the Canadian Officer's Training Corps, and a large part of the Engineering Building was put at the disposal of the Royal Flying Corps.

At the beginning of the hostilities, America maintained its policy of free trade and argued it had the right to trade with all nations during time of war. This policy was of great benefit to American business, which stood to make huge profits while the merchant fleets of the warring nations were confined to port. The belligerent nations objected. Great Britain declared a total blockade of German ports, and Germany announced that their U-boats would sink any ships headed for Allied ports. America's strong and historic ties to England skewed the trade relations. United States trade with Germany and Austria declined from $169 million in 1914 to less than a million in 1916. In the same period, trade with the allies increased from $865 million to over $3 billion. German U-boat attacks increased, public sentiment in America swung to the Allies, and on April 6, 1917, America declared war on Germany.

123. *At New Mexico College of Agriculture and Mechanic Arts, students assigned to a radio detachment were given field buzzer practice in 1918.*

124. *At Worcester Polytechnic Institute, students from the Army and Navy could find relaxation at the YMCA during World War I.*

Engineering schools in the United States, as in Canada, fully supported the war effort, even as it caused considerable disruption in their normal operations. It was evident that the military would need men trained in technical skills, and the engineering schools operating through the SPEE responded quickly. The Society rescheduled its 1917 annual meeting, which marked the organization's twenty-fifth anniversary, from Northwestern University to Washington, DC, to facilitate conferences with government leaders.

Soon after, Hollis Godfrey of the government's Advisory Commission of the Council of National Defense appointed a committee to study the relation of the engineering schools to the national government during the war. The five-member committee included Milo Ketchum, SPEE president that year; Frederic Bishop, the Society's secretary; and Charles Mann, who was heading the study of engineering schools. The committee convened in Washington from August 7 to August 10, met with the heads of various government agencies, and developed recommendations on how the engineering schools could be part of the war effort. Two weeks later, the secretary of war assigned an officer from the General Staff to secure the cooperation of the educational institutions in meeting the nation's need for technical manpower. The committee assembled for two days on August 31 and met with the officer.[9]

On April 10, 1918, the War Department drafted 10,000 young men and placed them in engineering schools for eight weeks of intensive military and technical training. The program consisted of military drill, practical technical training in areas such as machine shop and motor mechanics, and a weekly one-hour seminar on the international situation and current events. By June 15, 50,000 men were in training at 155 schools. Each month, 25,000 men were graduated and entered the army as technicians. By the time the armistice was signed on November 11, 1918, 130,000 men had been trained and the schools had contracted to train 220,000 more.[10]

But training was not to be restricted to preparing technicians. In June 1918, the 60 leading engineering schools graduated 1844 civil, mechanical, and electrical engineers. Most went into the service, leaving few for the essential industries, such as ship building. The colleges responded again. The Massachusetts Institute of Technology (MIT) instituted an intensive ten-week, seven-day-a-week program for technical college graduates to train them in naval architecture and marine engineering. Cornell, MIT, and Throop College of Technology continued their regular classes during the summer and fall of 1918 for the junior class, graduating them between September and December rather than the following June.[11]

On September 18, 1918, the War Department announced the creation of the Student Army Training Corps (SATC) to prepare officers as engineers for both the army and navy. All physically fit male students in engineering schools were to be members of the SATC. By condensing the courses and eliminating unnecessary

125. *In 1918, aviation was a new, but important field. At Ohio State University, the Curtis Wright biplane, known as the* Jenny, *served as a trainer for cadets enrolled in the School of Military Aeronautics.*

activities, educational programs were developed in civil, mechanical, and electrical engineering. Each consisted of eight terms of 12 weeks each, during which students would receive both academic and military training. Students were expected to devote 53 hours per week to lectures, recitations, laboratory work, examinations, military training, and supervised study.[12] The program was to begin on October 1, but because of a national influenza epidemic, the opening was delayed for at least three weeks in most institutions, and then operated only three weeks before the armistice was signed. The program ended with the end of hostilities.

The war had a significant effect on the colleges. In 1917 and 1918, the services took virtually all engineering graduates, with some schools accelerating their programs to graduate juniors early. Further, undergraduates left the institutions to enlist in great numbers. The upper three classes were depleted, while the freshmen in 1918 were filled by the SATC. Further, large numbers of engineering teachers enlisted in the army or navy or left the colleges for industry. In order to accomplish its aim, which it did very successfully, the government took an active role in the

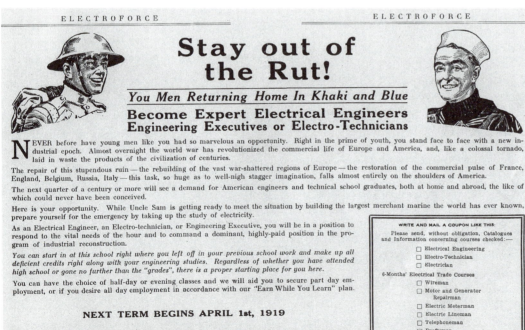

126. *After the war, the School of Engineering of Milwaukee advertised for returning veterans.*

higher educational institutions of the country, supplanting the normal academic governance and organization. The need to produce graduates rapidly and the presence of large numbers of military students were serious sources of friction between most faculties and military officers. Then, with the advent of peace, the military suddenly withdrew leaving the schools in a very disorganized state.

In spite of the difficulties of responding to wartime needs, the colleges did benefit from their involvement. The program provided a large freshman engineering class, which would otherwise have been empty. In 1918, the military draft age was lowered from 21 years to 18 years. In one day (October 18, 1918) 140,000 male students were inducted simultaneously into active duty in the Army. Without the SATC on campus, many colleges would not have enrolled essentially any able-bodied males over the age of 18. In addition to the regular SATC students, large numbers of wounded veterans were sent to the engineering schools for rehabilitation work.

The SATC also shattered standardized traditions and customs in the engineering schools, providing an opportunity for significant improvements. Division of the academic year into shortened terms or "quarters" was imposed by the SATC at all participating institutions. The quarter calendar persisted for decades at these schools, and Michigan State University did not return to the semester system until 1992. Further, ROTC, which was established under the Morrill Act, was introduced as a permanent policy to avoid causing future sudden deficiencies in trained technical personnel in the event that World War I did not bring about the predicted lasting peace.

Perhaps the major result of the relationship was the recognition that the federal government was willing to spend $200 million for a single year of education. This was the largest educational appropriation made in this country to that time. It showed that the government was willing to spend extremely large amounts on education if it was obvious to the public that the needs of the country would be served effectively.

Education for Engineering Management

The war brought out a significant shortcoming of mobilization. While people could be trained rapidly, it was not as easy to focus the aims of individual companies to a unified goal of production. A long time elapsed between the decision to produce and the production of aircraft, ships, clothing, and other supplies. In spite of the desire and patriotic response of individual owners and managers, it was a difficult process to subordinate the private interests to the public good. There was a belief that this could have been effected more quickly if engineers were trained in management and production organization.

127. *Students at the School of Engineering of Milwaukee formed a jazz quartet in 1919. The student in uniform was a member of the Student Army Training Corps.*

128. *A class in hydraulics at the North Carolina State University prepared to measure the horsepower of a stream at Lassiter's Mill in 1918. At the far left is Carroll L. Mann, class of 1899, who joined the engineering faculty in 1901 and headed the civil engineering department from 1916 to 1948.*

The need to provide engineers with management education was reinforced in peacetime. At the war's end, the United States undertook to help restore the economies of Europe. To meet the combined demands of domestic and export markets, industrial equipment and consumer goods had to be produced at previously unprecedented rates. This led to a rapid growth in mass production manufacturing methods. Ford, for example, in 1925, turned out on the average one car every ten seconds of the day, or a total of about 50,000 cars a week. Mass production greatly increased the amount of product produced per worker, but required an increase in the management and economic sides of engineering. This prompted changes in engineering education. Distinct curricula to emphasize the administrative rather than the technical aspects of engineering were introduced widely. The place given to economics in all curricula was augmented, and business electives in engineering education were more generally provided.

In line with the recommendations of the Mann report, there was a noticeable trend away from specialization for undergraduates. The effort to stretch a four-year program into both an all-around and a specialized training was abandoned, with a movement toward simplification of programs and a greater emphasis on general training. The extreme diversification of curricula which had been growing for several decades was reversed, and a period of consolidation followed. In order to prepare engineers to serve in the full scope of technical, administrative, and executive responsibilities, engineering schools developed general types of curricula that would be useful in a wide range of occupations. These were built on a foundation of science, humanities, and social relationships, rather than on the practical techniques required for specific industries or occupations. The curricula were functional, similar to those in agriculture, commerce, journalism, or education; but they emphasized the professional responsibilities of the graduate much more than did these other curricula.

State licensure and the registration of engineers continued to expand after the war. In 1920, seven states had licensure laws, which increased to 26 states by 1932, and then to 41 states by 1940. Requirements for licensure varied greatly by state. In 1934, all states allowed a person to become registered without having graduated from engineering school, with the number of years of professional experience for licensure varying from 10 years in Kansas, Pennsylvania, and West Virginia to no experience in Louisiana. The latter required, however, an examination that was almost impossible to pass without a reasonable amount of professional experience. All states reduced the amount of professional experience required if the applicant graduated from an approved engineering school.[13]

In order to promote uniformity in the administration of state registration laws and provide for reciprocity among states in recognition of engineers, the National Council of State Boards of Engineering Examiners was established in 1920. As more engineers became registered, the National Society of Professional Engineers

129. *In the electrical engineering department of the University of Illinois, Professor Joseph T. Tykociner provided the world's first demonstration of synchronized sound-on-film movies on June 9, 1922. The university showed little interest in patenting it, and he did not pursue commercial protection.*

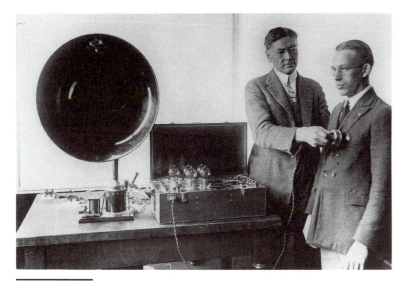

130. *At Purdue University, electrical engineering professor R. B. Abbot demonstrated a stethoscope in the early 1920s.*

132. *In 1929, at Ohio State University, K. Y. Tank studied illumination from a window, an incandescent lamp, and a mercury vapor bulb to improve factory lighting.*

131. *At the University of Michigan, motion pictures were used in 1929 to study chip formations under a microscope.*

was organized in 1934 to meet their special needs. In spite of this growth in licensed professionalism, few, if any, engineering schools made the preparation for registration and licensed practice their predominant objective, as is the norm in law and medicine.

Wickenden Report; ECPD Founded

In order to reassess the findings and recommendations of the Mann report in light of the experiences of World War I, in 1923, the Society for the Promotion of Engineering Education established the Board of Investigation and Coordination. William E. Wickenden was appointed director and Harry P. Hammond was appointed associate director. Wickenden formerly had been an assistant professor of electrical engineering at MIT and coordinator of cooperative education at AT&T, before being promoted to assistant vice president of the Bell System, the position from which he resigned to direct the study. Hammond was a professor of civil engineering at the Polytechnic Institute of Brooklyn.

• • • • • • •

This second major evaluation of engineering education was extremely comprehensive. With 95 colleges cooperating, the study was the most thorough that had ever been carried out in any country on the problems, aims, and programs of engineering education. While the Mann report was prepared under the auspices of a joint committee of the national professional societies, the new investigation originated within the colleges. As such, it was an introspective study of engineering education conducted by the colleges, rather than an assessment by practitioners in the profession.

The board completed its work in 1929, after six years of effort. Its report,[14] which ran over 1,300 pages and was published as two large volumes, examined virtually every aspect of engineering education in the United States, including its historical development and how it compared with engineering education in Europe, curricula, faculty development, relationships with industry, and opinions of past graduates. It provided data and described specific ideas for both improving the quality of engineering education and expanding it to serve more students. The second part of the report, published in 1934, was devoted to the less-than-baccalaureate programs.

The Mann and Wickenden reports outlined curricula for engineering schools, but unlike the medical and legal professions, no agency existed to assure the quality of American engineering schools. A principal recommendation of the Wickenden report, therefore, was to create an agency to set standards and inspect engineering schools for compliance with such standards. This was carried out in 1932, when the Engineers' Council for Professional Development (ECPD) was established as a joint

BIOGRAPHICAL SKETCH

WILLIAM ELGIN WICKENDEN

For six years, William Elgin Wickenden was director of a most comprehensive study of engineering education for the Society for the Promotion of Engineering Education. In 1930, the two-volume report *A Comparative Study of Engineering Education in the United States and Europe*, which became known as the Wickenden report, was released. It had a great effect on the development of engineering and technology schools.

The grandson of an English schooner captain who was lost at sea, and son of a self-educated civil engineer, William Wickenden was born in Toledo, Ohio in

1882. One of eight children, seven of whom went to college, he was valedictorian of his high school class, delivered papers and labored in the summer as a draftsman for the Toledo Bridge Company for a dollar a day. He went to Denison University, a liberal arts institution, where he graduated in 1904 as class valedictorian and a member of Phi Beta Kappa. He then received a scholarship in physics to the University of Wisconsin, where he subsequently served as instructor in electrical engineering. In 1909, he published his first book *Illumination and Photometry* and moved to MIT as assistant professor of electrical engineering. Five years later, he was promoted to associate professor. During his ten years at the Institute, he instituted cooperative courses at the Western Electric Company, where he moved in 1919 to become personnel manager. In 1921, he was appointed assistant vice president of the American Telephone and Telegraph Company in charge of technical training for the entire system. Two years later, he left to head the SPEE study.

Upon completion of the study in 1929, he became president of the Case School. A gifted orator with an expansive vision, he immediately announced his plans to merge Case with Western Reserve. The Great Depression, however, put an end to his hopes, as the college faced a declining enrollment, faculty reductions, and a budget decline. In spite of financial difficulties, he was responsible for the introduction of a comprehensive program of graduate studies and degrees, for upgrading the educational background of the faculty, and for stressing the importance of the humanities in the education of engineers. In 1931, a graduate division was opened for both men and women. When Wickenden assumed the presidency of Case, it had 650 students, all of them undergraduates. When he retired in 1947, there were 3,000 students, 200 of whom were at the graduate level.

Just before the Japanese bombed Pearl Harbor, Case contracted with the federal government to operate the Engineering, Science, and Management Defense Training Program for civilians working on defense projects in factories. Almost 10,000 people were trained in four and a half years. From 1943 to 1945, Case also trained sailors under the Navy's V-12 program, many of whom then completed their education to become ensigns at the Naval Academy. Wickenden died on September 1, 1947, the first day of his retirement. ∎

effort of the engineering schools, the professional societies, and the licensing boards. ECPD, which was given authority to accredit engineering curricula, was the vehicle for the profession to impact directly on the education of future engineers.

The first accreditation action took place in 1935. On November 21, the Committee on Engineering Schools of ECPD met in New York City to begin the inspection procedure. The Stevens Institute of Technology in nearby Hoboken was visited that day, and Columbia University was visited the following day. The team reviewed their curricula in chemical, civil, electrical, mechanical, metallurgical, mining, and industrial engineering. By December 16, 1935, 33 institutions in New England and the Middle Atlantic states had requested examination,[15] and by the end of 1936, all but three or four of the engineering colleges in the Northeast had been visited. In 1937, ECPD reviewed 626 curricula and accredited 374 for the maximum period of four years, and accredited 71 for lesser periods. The remaining 181 programs were not accredited.

The number of schools with accredited curricula continued to grow, increasing to 125 in 1940, to 159 in 1960, and to 310 in 1991. By 1991, there were over 1,432 basic-level and 30 advanced-level engineering curricula accredited by the Accreditation Board on Engineering and Technology (the new name for ECPD).[16] Accreditation continues to be voluntary and is much sought.

Technical Institutes

The second volume of the Wickenden report pointed out the need for technical institutes to provide post-high school, nondegree programs to train engineering technicians as supporting personnel required by the burgeoning industry in the United States. It concluded that technical institutes could be more readily justified in many regions of the country than additional engineering colleges could, and that they were better suited than engineering schools to produce certain types of technically trained personnel. As a result, the report made a large number of recommendations for the development of technical institutes. It stressed that the institutes were not to be extensions of engineering schools to which dropouts would be relegated, but that they should have their own distinctive character to provide positive appeal to a distinct group of individuals with genuine promise. Further, the institutes were to be staffed by people who knew industry intimately and who could blend scientific and practical instruction; and their graduates should receive nationally recognized credentials.

The subsequent development of technical institutes has, in general, followed these suggestions. Two-year technical programs became firmly established in the period between the Great Depression and World War II.

133. *Large-scale models were often built for research. At the Massachusetts Institute of Technology, this model of the Cape Cod Canal was built in 1935 to study possible improvements for the canal.*

In reviewing the operation of technical institutes, the Wickenden report also concluded that their faculties suffered from a sense of professional isolation. The SPEE moved to overcome this by offering itself as a forum for these people. In 1937, technical institutes were admitted as Institutional Members of the Society. As membership grew, the Society established in 1960 the Engineering Technology Division for individual faculty members and the Technical Institute Council to represent the institutions. The latter has become the present Engineering Technology Council. The Society accepted the responsibility and exercised leadership to help ensure the rational and organized growth of technical institutes, which evolved into the engineering technology colleges of today.

Preparation of Engineering Teachers

The improvement of engineering teaching has been a concern of the SPEE and the ASEE throughout its history. The Society was founded as an organization of persons involved in engineering teaching, and it has devoted a great deal of effort to improve instruction. As early as 1901, Society President John B. Johnson declared, "The time is ripe for men to prepare themselves expressly to teach in the engineering colleges." [17]

In 1911, Society President Arthur N. Talbot, was more explicit in discussing the role of the engineering teacher, stating:

> *Not only must he be able to impart knowledge, but he must know the principles of education, appreciate the aim of teaching, and use the methods which are necessary to obtain results . . . Courses in pedagogy or in principles of education and psychology will be found to be of great value.* [18]

The following year, William T. Magruder, in his SPEE Presidential Address, expanded on the theme:

> *faculties of some of those universities which maintain both colleges of engineering and of education should offer in their summer terms strong courses of study in psychology and education considered both as a science and as an art . . . college presidents, deans, and heads of departments should influence their younger assistants and fresh graduates who expect to go permanently into the work of education to take these proposed courses of study.* [19]

In 1911, Westinghouse Electric and Manufacturing Company decided that engineering faculty members required more knowledge of industrial practice. It invited 30 teachers with two or more years of teaching experience to spend six weeks at its Pittsburgh plant. The teachers worked in the testing department,

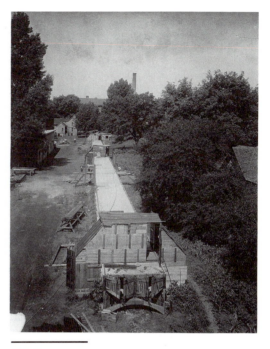

134. *At the University of Illinois, an above-ground model of the Holland Tunnel (which runs between New York and New Jersey) was constructed in the 1920s to conduct research on the tunnel's ventilation system.*

manufacturing department, or engineering department, were paid at the rate of $0.22 per hour for a 54-hour week, and spent one evening a week discussing teaching problems. The program was a success and was continued annually through the summer of 1915.[20] Although this did not go as far as Talbot and Magruder had proposed, it was a beginning in the direction of pedagogical training for engineering teachers.

The Mann and the Wickenden reports were critical of the limited pedagogical preparation of engineering teachers and advocated that they receive training in educational methods. In response, the SPEE organized Summer Schools for Teachers. With a grant of $7,500 from the Carnegie Foundation, the first programs were held in 1927, one at Cornell University under the direction of Dexter F. Kimball, Cornell's dean of engineering, and a second at the University of Wisconsin under Edward R. Maurer, professor of mechanics. The object of the three-week sessions was to bring together experienced teachers who had mastered both the content and methods of presenting their subjects and young teachers who were just beginning teaching careers.[21] Thereafter, two sessions, conducted at different institutions, were held each summer until 1933.[22] Each session focused on a specific disciplinary theme, such as engineering mechanics, electrical engineering, civil engineering, engineering drawing, and descriptive geometry, as well as economics and English, and concentrated on both the content of the subject and on methods of organizing and teaching it.[23]

The SPEE had become the leading proponent for improving engineering instruction.

Social Involvement

When Herbert Hoover, an engineer, became president of the United States in 1929, the social role of the engineer gained prominence. There was a growing awareness that technology was causing effects on society that no one had anticipated. Hoover called attention to the unplanned effects, to the waste and inefficiencies in industry, and to the plundering of natural resources that resulted from industrial developments. It was the Great Depression, which began in 1929 and lasted until the United States entered World War II, however, that brought new responsibilities to the American engineering profession. Large numbers of people, including many engineers, were out of work as industries began to produce less and less. The economic upheaval of the depression brought to the fore the need for engineers to understand better the social, political, and economic environments in which they were working. As a result, there arose a considerable demand to give engineering students significant training in the liberal arts in order to make them aware of and share in the control and consequences of expanding technology.

Franklin D. Roosevelt, Hoover's successor as president, stressed the relationship between engineering and society even further. Under his administration, the Tennessee Valley Authority was started in 1933, as the largest federally initiated effort ever attempted in America to apply engineering to the needs of society. The Authority, which has been a major contributor to the development and economy of its region, is engaged in flood control, soil conservation, fertilizer development, reforestation, public health, construction of an inland waterway, and generation of hydroelectric power. Today it is one of the largest consumers of coal and largest producers of electricity in the United States, with an installed generating capacity of 31,783 megawatts in 1990, which will increase to over 37,000 megawatts by the end of the decade.

President Roosevelt's interest in applying engineering to social issues continued. On October 7, 1936, the president wrote to the Society:

> *Events of recent years have brought into clear perspective the social responsibility of engineering. . . .*
>
> *In respect of the impact of science and engineering upon human life—social and economic dislocations as well as advance in productive power—the facts are revealed with distressing clearness in public records of unemployment, bankruptcies and relief. . . .*
>
> *The design and construction of specific civil engineering works or of instruments for production represent only one part of the responsibility of engineering. It must also consider social processes and problems, and must coöperate, in designing accommodating mechanisms to absorb the shocks of the impact of science.*
>
> *This raises the question whether the curricula of engineering schools are so balanced as to give coming generations of engineers the vision and flexible technical capacity necessary to meet the full range of engineering responsibility.*
>
> *I am calling this matter to the attention of educators of high administrative authority in the hope that it may be thoroughly explored in faculty discussions and in meetings of engineering, educational and other pertinent professional associations.*[24]

The response was immediate. On October 27, Harry P. Hammond, the current president of SPEE, wrote[25] to President Roosevelt on behalf of the Society, stating that engineering educators had "during the last dozen years . . . given extended attention to the problem of the development of the social and economic elements in the education of engineering students, and to the better coördination of engineering education with the social order in which engineers function." He pointed out that there was a clear trend toward "broadening and enrichment" of engineering curricula, with more emphasis on economics and social sciences. He also noted that in engineering subjects, greater emphasis was being placed on the fundamentals of science and technology and less on technical specialties. Such developments were, he observed, related to the basic recommendations set down by the Wickenden report as well as a result of numerous addresses and reports made at national and regional meetings of SPEE.

T. North Whitehead of the Harvard Graduate School of Business Administration continued the criticism, writing:

> *I do not believe that our Society can continue to tolerate highly trained engineers whose interest is exclusively centered in the details of their mechanisms . . . Unless we can train engineers whose interest in the vital social processes is comparable to their technical interests, I fear that we engineers may be paving the way for a companion volume to Gibbons' 'The Decline and Fall of the Roman Empire.'* [26]

Samuel Earle, in his 1938 SPEE presidential address, further pointed to the need:

> *Are not many of our curricula simply a collection of courses each of which may be good but with little thought as to the relation of one with the other? . . . The engineering teacher should also bring to his students the fact that the professional engineer . . . should be able to converse at least with some intelligence about music, art or literature, as well as economics and politics.* [27]

Andrey A. Potter, dean at Purdue University, while taking umbrage at the criticism from nonengineers, agreed that too many of the humanities courses taught to engineers were presented at the high school level. [28]

The movement to require liberal studies in the engineering curriculum reached a peak when, in 1939, the National Society of Professional Engineers joined with other groups of engineers to advocate a change in the New York State educational law. A bill was presented to the New York legislature, which would require young engineers applying for licensure to successfully complete two years of liberal arts and four years of engineering college work. [29] In June of that year, the SPEE Council appointed a committee under the chairmanship of Harry Hammond to consider the desirability of a preliminary period of study in a liberal arts school before admission to a school of engineering and to present a report in November of that year.

• • • • • • •

The report, which was called the *Report of Committee on Aims and Scope of Engineering Curricula,* [30] stated that although a four-year bachelor's degree curriculum was appropriate for a large majority of students, this would not be the case if the course of study were extended to five- or six-years. It recommended that graduate education should be expanded for "adequate time . . . to be allowed in the undergraduate period for a thorough grounding in the basic sciences, for laying the foundation of a social philosophy, for developing powers of effective expression

■ BIOGRAPHICAL SKETCH

HARRY HAMMOND

Harry Hammond was a very active member of the Society for the Promotion of Engineering Education. He served as the associate director of the Wickenden report, and later chaired two additional SPEE studies on engineering education, *Aims and Scope of Engineering Education* in 1940, and *Engineering Education After the War* in 1944. The latter studies have become known as the Hammond reports. From 1929 to 1933, he directed the SPEE program of summer schools for engineering teachers, and served as president of the Society from 1936 to 1937.

Hammond was born in Asbury Park, New Jersey on December 21, 1884. He attended the University of Pennsylvania from which he was awarded a bachelor of science in civil engineering in 1909 and later received the degree of civil engineer from the university. Upon graduation in 1909 he accepted a position at his alma mater as an instructor in civil engineering. Two years later, he accepted a similar position at Lehigh University, and in 1912 became assistant professor of civil engineering at Brooklyn Polytechnic Institute.

The following year, he married Margaret L. Raymond, the daughter of William G. Raymond, one of the founders of the SPEE and its president from 1911 to 1912.

Hammond remained at the Polytechnic until 1937, becoming professor of sanitary and hydraulic engineering and in 1927 head of the department of civil engineering. In 1931, he received an honorary doctorate in engineering from the Case School of Applied Science. In 1937, Hammond became dean of engineering at The Pennsylvania State University, where he remained until his retirement in 1951. During his tenure at Penn State, the engineering enrollment grew from 1,000 to 2,500 students, and the research facilities were greatly expanded.

While at Brooklyn Poly, Hammond was active as a consultant on bridges and water supply systems for the City of New York, and assisted in studies of several universities. During World War I, he served as chairman of a Selective Service Board in New York City, and during the Second World War, he held a number of government advisory positions, including member of the national advisory committee for the Engineering, Science and Management War Training Program. Harry Hammond died on October 21, 1953. ∎

and for cultivating reflective and critical habits of thought." The value of a four-year program would be enhanced if in addition to the other objectives an adequate introduction was provided in engineering methods of applying science to actual problems. The committee recommended that courses in the science–technology and humanities–social science stems be given concurrently, rather than sequentially as had been previously suggested. The committee also found that although engineering was taught in a wide variety of institutions, engineering curricula were very similar throughout the nation. This was a major change from two or three decades earlier, when engineering programs were highly specialized and very diverse to meet local industrial needs. They recommended that there should be more diversification and variation among curricula in order to prepare engineers for a wide range of technical, administrative, and executive responsibilities.

Discussions of the proper balance between cultural and engineering subjects provided in the engineering curriculum began before the Society was founded, reached a peak during the Depression, have persisted throughout the Society's history, and no doubt will continue to be a concern of engineering educators in the future.

135. *At the University of Cincinnati, seven women were admitted to the co-op program in 1920 to study either chemical engineering or commercial engineering (a business education program). They quickly became known as* co-eps.

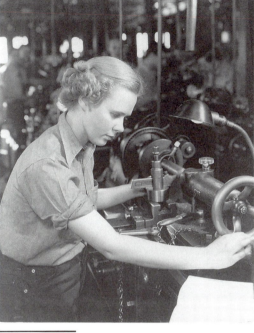

136. *At Purdue University, a female student worked at a lathe in 1937.*

137. *Women worked in the machine shop at Washington State University, which had its first female graduate in 1899.*

138. *Women were scarce, but not absent, from engineering in the early part of the century. In 1919, the University of Wisconsin conducted a women's mechanics class.*

The 1930s mark the beginning of a period of societal change in the public's concept of the need for a college education. Prior to 1930, about 5 percent to 10 percent of Americans aged 18 to 24 attended college. Between 1930 and 1950, colleges and universities provided access for between 30 percent and 50 percent of the 18- to 24-year-old population. This was a transition from elite to mass education. As an engineering degree provided a route to a well-paying future, engineering students came disproportionately from modest families with modest incomes and education and were usually the first generation in their families to enroll in college. Engineering education, thus, was able to combine the ideals of equality and merit.

Developments in Canada

After the cessation of hostilities in 1918, Canadian schools quickly surpassed their prewar size. Engineering students and staff swelled significantly, as special accelerated programs were implemented in most universities for the benefit of returning veterans. In addition, rapid industrial expansion in the 1920s, particularly in Ontario, increased the demand for engineers and thus for engineering education.

139. *Proper dress was required in the chemistry lab at École Polytechnic de Montreal in 1923.*

In 1927, Elsie Gregory MacGill became the first female engineering graduate at the University of Toronto. She later became the first female member of the Engineering Institute of Canada and the first female to receive a master's degree in aeronautical engineering at the University of Michigan. Ms. MacGill went on to have a distinguished engineering career. Having flight-tested the first Canadian metal plane, she supervised all of the engineering work for the Canadair production of the Second World War Hawker Hurricane fighter for the United Kingdom and the Curtis Wright Helldiver for the U.S. Navy. Later, she headed her own aeronautical engineering consulting firm.

With the stock market collapse of 1929, business, manufacturing, and construction activity was sharply curtailed in Canada, as well as the United States. While Canada's ten engineering faculties were maintained, student numbers declined again and only three new engineering programs were introduced in the entire country during the early and mid-1930s. Ironically, those three programs were at the University of Saskatchewan, a province that suffered grievously from the combined effect of the economic depression and the worst drought ever experienced in Canada.

140. *At Ontario's Queen's University, students had a relaxed method of preparing for final exams in about 1920. It seemed to work for John Bertram Sterling (standing). He had an outstanding career as an engineer, was elected president of the Engineering Institute of Canada, and served as chancellor of his alma mater from 1960 to 1974.*

141. *At Norwich University, a group took advantage of a tower constructed by civil engineering students to enjoy the water in 1925.*

142. *Elsie Muriel Gregory MacGill was the first woman to graduate from an engineering program in Canada, receiving a degree in electrical engineering from the University of Toronto in 1927, the year this photograph was taken. In 1929, she became the first woman to receive a master's degree in aeronautical engineering from the University of Michigan, and, in 1940, she became the first female professional engineer in Ontario. Despite crippling polio, she made significant contributions in aeronautics and other fields. For her accomplishments she received her government's highest civilian award, when she was made an Officer of the Order of Canada.*

In 1937, Université Laval in Quebec City became the eleventh Canadian university to offer engineering degrees. Prior to that time, students completed two years of engineering at Laval and then transferred, usually to the École Polytechnique, to complete the degree requirements. As the École Polytechnique then offered only civil engineering, a need was felt to have French-language instruction in other engineering fields. Consequently, mining engineering was introduced at Laval in 1939, and during the next decade, six additional engineering programs were introduced.

Growth of Graduate Study

Prior to 1890, only six institutions in the United States offered education beyond the baccalaureate. Rensselaer in its very early years encouraged the enrollment of individuals who had completed a baccalaureate degree from another college; Norwich granted master's degrees as early as 1837; and Iowa State College awarded its first post-baccalaureate degree in engineering, a C.E., in 1879. The first graduate programs that followed a four-year undergraduate education began in the 1890s. The Lawrence Scientific School at Harvard offered a graduate program in electrical engineering in 1893, while MIT offered a master's degree in civil engineering in 1894 and graduate programs in chemical, mechanical, and sanitary engineering within the next ten years.

For the most part, graduate work was limited to comparatively few students and often was no more than a fifth year of undergraduate instruction. In 1904, 114 engineering colleges reported a combined enrollment of 15,004 undergraduates and 249 graduate students.[31] In 1922, there were only 368 graduate students enrolled and 18 advanced degrees granted.

World War I brought a recognition of the important contributions that could be gained through academic research. The war effort proved conclusively the benefit of applying fundamental knowledge to practical applications. It further demonstrated to industrialists the importance of engineering research, as distinct from scientific research, thus initiating a new source of revenue for engineering schools. Others, however, lamented the tremendous cost to the nation's academic community. Frank B. Jewett, president of the Bell Telephone Laboratories, evaluated the war's impact by stating:

> By robbing the colleges, universities, and industries of trained scientists for war's sweat shop, it was inevitable that stupendous results should be obtained, but at the expense both of basic research and of training new men. While I am not in a position to know the exact situation elsewhere in the world, I do know that we in the United States had early in the summer of 1918 arrived at the state where scientific man-producing machinery no longer existed.[32]

Total expenditures for research in engineering colleges amounted to almost $1,500,000 in the academic year 1924–1925.[33] About half came from industrial sources, with certain industries recognizing the commercial value of research. The American Railway Association, for example, contributed over $500,000 to Purdue University during the preceding two years for research in its field of interest. The automobile industry, in contrast, contributed only $10,000 for cooperative engineering research during the same period.[34] Although university-based research was increasing, the amounts of money expended were still minimal. General Electric and Westinghouse, for example, each spent more than twice as much on research as all engineering colleges combined.[35]

Although the total funds expended for research in engineering colleges in 1925 was less than one-thirtieth of the amount spent by these institutions for undergraduate instruction,[36] it stimulated a rapid growth in graduate study. From 1921 to 1930, graduate enrollments in electrical engineering increased ninefold, in mechanical engineering they increased sevenfold, and in chemical engineering they increased sixfold. By 1934, there were 2756 graduate students and 1197 graduate degrees awarded, with 86 colleges offering work beyond that required for the bachelor's degree.[37] By 1938, graduate enrollment exceeded 5,000 students. Of the 75 schools offering graduate work, seven enrolled half of the students, while one-third of the institutions had less than ten students each.[38]

Although much of this growth was in part-time and evening study, particularly in the metropolitan areas, and most often terminated with the master's, education for the doctoral degree also increased at this time. Yale University awarded the first PhD in engineering in 1873 to Augustus J. Dubois, who subsequently became professor of civil engineering at that institution. The School of Mines at Columbia awarded the second shortly thereafter, but the third doctorate in engineering was not awarded until 1896 by Cornell. In 1920, 11 engineering schools awarded the doctorate, which increased to 30 institutions by 1933.[39]

As graduate programs expanded, engineering schools adopted the M.S.–PhD pattern that was common in the arts and sciences. As a result, the administration of their programs came within the scope of established graduate schools. Like undergraduate engineering education, graduate programs thus became an integral part of the university structure, instead of developing as separate professional schools, as in medicine and law.

In Canada, the focus remained almost totally on undergraduate education, with little emphasis on graduate education or research. Prior to the Second World War, only McGill University and the University of Toronto had acquired reputations for their engineering research.

Aviation Supply Officers Training at Ga. Tech — 1918

143. *Troops came in great numbers to the colleges during World War I. At Georgia Tech, the Aviation Supply Officers' Training School housed its students in tents on the campus quadrangle in 1918. There was also a School of Military Aeronautics, a radio course, and a motor transport course. ROTC was instituted and the entire student body donned uniforms and drilled every day.*

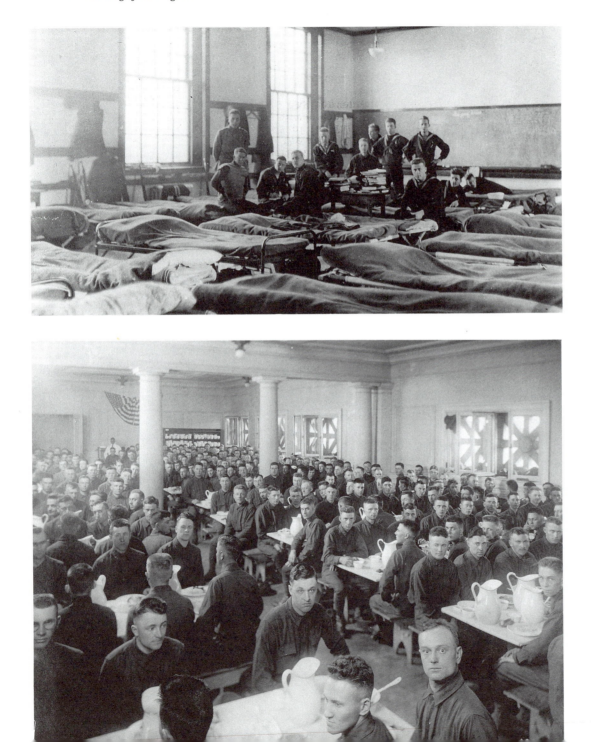

144. *At The Johns Hopkins University, laboratories, classrooms, and attics in the engineering buildings were turned into barracks for the 500 members of the Student Army Training Corps in 1917.*

145. *At the University of Pittsburgh, the enlisted men in the five-week, gas engine and automechanics program ate dinner mess-hall style.*

146. At the University of Pittsburgh in 1918, students learned how to repair the Liberty truck, known in the army as the standard class B truck. The vehicles were mass-produced according to government specifications that made them more rugged and reliable than any truck then produced for the civilian market. The government also required, under a strategy developed by the Quarter Master Corps in consultation with the Society of Automotive Engineers, that there be uniformity in the components produced by various manufacturers to allow the trucks to be made in the maximum number of factories with the minimum number of spare parts required in the field. The Liberty truck became the Army's standard heavy-duty truck, and was in use until the 1930s.

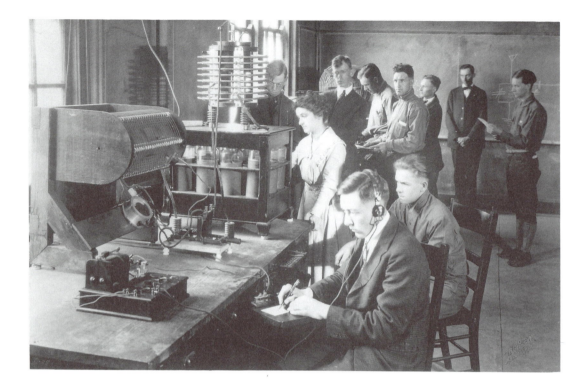

147. At Iowa State College, wireless telegraphy was taught. Military communications was a subject addressed by the school's Engineering Experiment Station.

148. In 1918, navy students learned drafting at Stevens Institute of Technology.

149. At the Pennsylvania State College, in addition to their regular classes, the military drilled with the bayonet.

150. Telephone electrician students practiced pole climbing in the 1917 linesman's course at the University of Michigan.

151. At the United States Military Academy, cadets practiced building a pontoon bridge on the Hudson River in about 1920.

152. Students at Rensselaer Polytechnic Institute ran tests with a small wind tunnel in 1937.

153. *The University of Alabama began courses in aeronautical engineering in 1929. By 1940, students were assembling a fuselage as part of an experimental civilian pilot program supported by the Civilian Aeronautics Authority.*

154. *Students at Colorado's Agricultural College (now Colorado State University) experimented with heavy-duty equipment in the alternating current laboratory in 1920.*

155. *At the Polytechnic Institute of Brooklyn, the combustion laboratory in 1928 included work on an automobile.*

156. *In 1920, University of California at Berkeley mining engineering students dressed for work in the Lawson Adit, a training mine that still is used occasionally by students in mining and mineral engineering.*

158. *Lightning was a phenomenon that was studied in electrical engineering at Purdue University in 1931.*

157. *By the late 1930s, Professor Howard Gardner, the first faculty member in chemical engineering at the University of Rochester, worked with students on a newly installed double effect evaporator.*

159. *The Milwaukee School of Engineering established a traveling lecture-demonstration titled "Wonders of Electricity," used to reach the general public at local high schools throughout the midwest in the 1930s.*

160. *At Worcester Polytechnic Institute, students in the 1930s learned the management aspects of running industrial plants, including planning, costing, personnel, and sales.*

161. *Agricultural engineering students at the University of Idaho in 1929 had lectures on tractors in a workshop.*

162. *At the University of Cincinnati, students in mechanical engineering kept refreshed as they worked on some taxing problems.*

163. *At the Pennsylvania State College, engineering students observed the mechanical harvesting of potatoes in 1934.*

165. *Dr. O. R. Sweeney, first head of chemical engineering at Iowa State College, conducted research on making insulation board from corn cobs in the 1930s.*

164. *Textile engineering was an important part of the curriculum at Clemson University during the 1930s, because of the large textile industry in South Carolina. Here, a faculty member operates a weaving machine.*

166. *Railroad engineering was a popular subject at Purdue University in 1935.*

168. *Research was becoming a more important part of a faculty member's responsibilities. In 1929, Herbert F. Moore, professor of theoretical and applied mechanics at the University of Illinois, shown here conducting a test on the load capacity of rails, concluded a ten-year investigation of fatigue of metals.*

167. *Michael Idvorsky Pupin, a Serbian immigrant, was professor of mathematical physics at Columbia University from 1901 to 1931. His patent on inductively loaded telephone lines significantly increased transmission distance without the need for a repeater. His autobiography,* From Immigrant to Inventor, *won a Pulitzer Prize.*

Engineers' Day
1928
March 16

ford race
barbecue
open house
dance

University of California Campus

169. *The University of Illinois celebrated its first Engineers' Day in 1924. The float indicates that electricity was then used for illumination, communication, and power.*

170. *Engineers' Day was already a decades'-old tradition at the University of California at Berkeley in 1929. It featured parades, car races, and other festivities.*

171. *St. Patrick has been considered the parton saint of engineers for many years. In 1939, the University of Missouri at Rolla recognized engineers with three days of festivities.*

172. At the New Mexico College of Agriculture and Mechanic Arts, radio was used for one of the first times in the nation to broadcast a football game in November 1925.

173. Students at Washington State University demonstrated in 1936 by blocking entry to the Mechanic Arts Building to protest a strict, unwritten code of ethics enforced by a domineering dean of women.

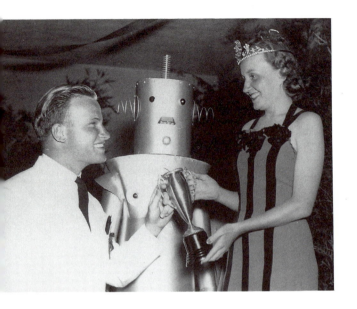

174. In 1940, the Queen of the Engineers' Ball at the University of Florida presented a mechanical engineering student with the Sigma Tau trophy.

175. Milkshakes and sandwiches were typical lunches for students at the Polytechnic Institute of Brooklyn in 1935.

176. In the 1930s, pipes were de rigeur for Duke University students, shown studying in a dorm room.

177. At the University of Kentucky, engineering students in 1939 became concerned with the way the Student Union conducted May Queen elections. The engineers ran Bill Dunlap, shown marching through an arch of T-squares, and because nearly all engineers voted for him as a block, he received the most first place votes. He and the Union's declared winner were each crowned as queen by the university president before a large crowd in the football stadium.

178. *At Michigan College of Mines and Technology (now Michigan Technological University), the school's female engineering students rode in a car in the 1934 winter carnival parade.*

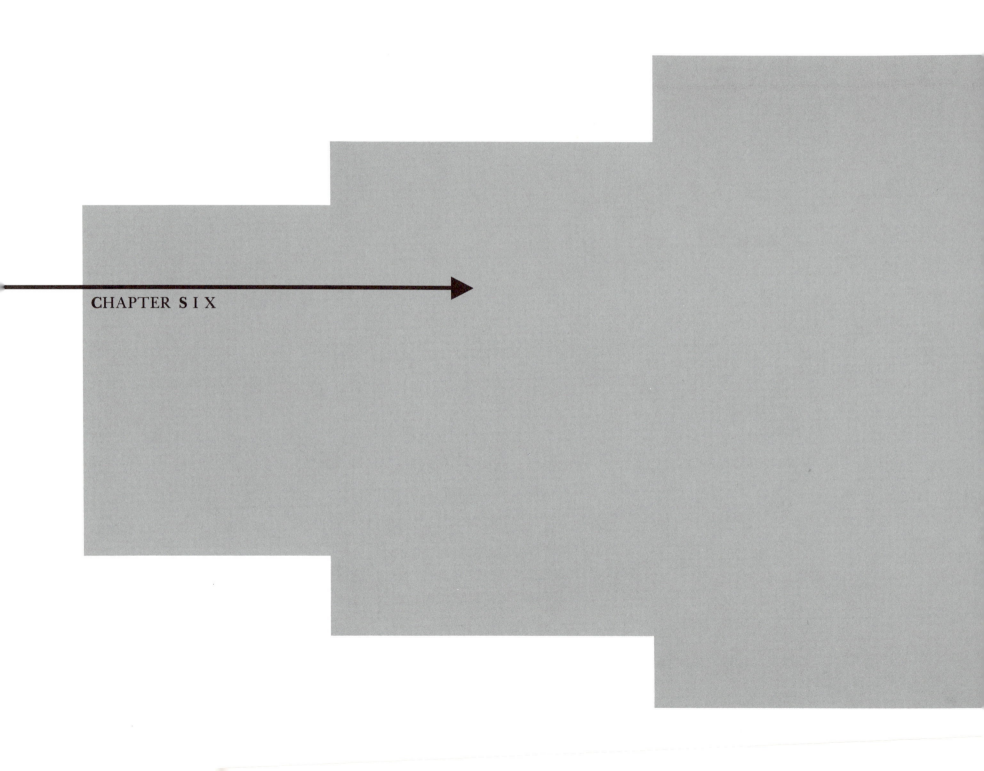

CHAPTER S I X

. . . . . . .The engineering schools in both the United States and Canada were involved heavily in the Allied effort during World War II. When hostilities began, faculties and administrations once again placed their institutions at the disposal of their governments. The schools provided technical training for an unprecedented number of people for the military and defense industries. Without that contribution, the productive capacities of the two nations to maintain their war efforts probably would have been hampered significantly.

In spite of the success, involvement in the war revealed weaknesses in engineering education, particularly in the electrical and electronics areas. The United States previously had depended almost completely on European scientific research to act as the source of ideas and principles for exploitation by American industrial capability. When the flow of European scientific information was cut short by the war, American engineers reacted as well as they could. But the wartime demand for new and advanced knowledge in almost every branch of engineering and science showed the shortcomings of engineering education.

167

While engineers made contributions to the development of ships, tanks, planes, and armament, it often was the physicist with advanced fundamental training who took the initiative in creating new devices and systems. It became obvious that in order to cope not only with the wartime needs but with the postwar problems and meet the changing technical needs of industry, new developments in engineering education were required. This stimulated a change from a strong emphasis on subjects that emphasized engineering practice to a stress on the scientific principles underlying the technology. This movement was further advanced as a result of the Soviet – United States tensions of the 1950s and 1960s, which resulted first in a cold war and then in a race to dominate outer space and land a man on the moon.

Impact of World War II

When Hitler invaded Poland on September 1, 1939, England declared war on Germany. As in 1914, Canada was immediately drawn into the conflict as a member of the British Commonwealth, while the United States tried to remain out of the war by the Neutrality Act of 1939. Canada was not prepared for war. Practically all of the nation's military hardware was obsolete, and the military had almost no research capability to help in the development of modern equipment. Canada's National Research Council had been established in 1916, but had a small budget and a minor significance. As in World War I, the nation's universities were placed

179. *With the beginning of World War II, the military relied heavily on colleges and universities. Men in uniform came* en masse, *marching to class through the city streets to the Polytechnic Institute of Brooklyn in 1942.*

on wartime footing, and large numbers of students and faculty enlisted in the armed forces. Nearly every university in the country offered to place their facilities at the disposal of the government for work on the war effort.

German conquests were swift. In April 1940, Germany overran Denmark and Norway; in May, Holland and Belgium surrendered; and in June, France fell. With Britain seriously threatened and with the possibility of the British Navy being absorbed by Germany, the enemy would soon be at America's shores. The isolation of the United States came to an end. On December 7, 1941, the Japanese bombed Pearl Harbor. The next day, the United States declared war on Japan, and three days later, Germany and Italy, honoring treaty agreements with the Japanese, declared war on the United States.

180. *At the University of Illinois, the military marched in formation to class during World War II.*

The speed of the German "blitzkrieg" convinced even the most ardent isolationists that mechanized warfare had come into its own. And mechanization meant engineering. Warfare had become a test of the scientific, engineering, and manufacturing skills and capacities of the belligerent nations. To be successful in this type of war, a nation must have available large numbers of people well prepared in science, engineering, and technology, both for the military and to staff new production facilities generated by expanding orders for war material.

It became evident as early as the spring of 1940 that the number of engineering graduates from the country's colleges would not be sufficient to meet the needs of the national defense. Many small companies would quickly expand to several times their prewar size. Others would be called upon to manufacture items that were radically different from their normal products. Still others, such as the large airplane factories to be built in Kansas, Oklahoma, and Texas, would be located in areas that were predominantly agricultural and did not have a base of men and women experienced in industrial production.

The SPEE began to explore ways to meet the needs for engineers. It looked toward evening engineering education, and a conference was called in June 1941 at the Society's annual meeting held in Berkeley, California. It also set up a Committee on Acceleration of Regular Engineering Programs, which met on December 17, 1941. The committee recommended to the United States Commissioner of Education that the engineering class of 1943 be graduated early and that the Congress appropriate funds to the colleges to partially offset the cost to the colleges for such acceleration. The Commissioner of Education was negative, and the plan was abandoned. Then came Pearl Harbor, and ten days later the committee submitted a new plan to the Commissioner of Education. However, government action was still not forthcoming. Without waiting for the Office of Education to act, the colleges themselves announced accelerated programs.[1] This was a short-term measure that could produce only limited results.

In July 1940, Andrey A. Potter, dean of engineering at Purdue University and Society president from 1924 to 1925, was appointed expert consultant to the U.S. Office of Education to prepare a proposal for the Defense Council and Congress on how engineering colleges could contribute most effectively to the defense effort, and to serve as liaison officer between the engineering schools and the appropriate federal agencies.

· · · · · · ·

Potter recommended in August 1940 that a national advisory committee be appointed to aid the Commissioner of Education in formulating policies and facilitating the cooperation of the engineering colleges. Following his suggestions, the commissioner established a committee consisting of 11 engineers and engineering educators. The educators believed that engineering colleges could make a valuable

■ BIOGRAPHICAL SKETCH

ANDREY ABRAHAM POTTER

A.A. Potter was given the title "Dean of the Deans of Engineering Universities," by MIT in 1949. He deserved the honor, serving for 40 years as a dean of engineering.

Potter was born on August 5, 1882, in Vilna, Russia, under Tsarist rule. He studied at the people's elementary school, but found the teachers to be stern and sometimes cruel taskmasters. At home, he learned French and German and discussed literature with his grandfather. When he was eight, his father gave him a china ocarina, which he learned to play so well that he taught other children and formed an ocarina band. When he was ten his father gave him a copy of *The Autobiog-*

raphy of Benjamin Franklin, which deeply impressed him. Potter wanted to emulate Franklin in every way, and to obtain the freedom to do so he emigrated to America via cattle boat from Liverpool when he was 15 years of age. He arrived in Boston in 1897 to live with an aunt and uncle.

The following year he took the entrance examinations for MIT, passed mathematics, French and German, but not the English portion. After a year of language study, he entered MIT and received a degree in 1903 in mechanical engineering, with a concentration in electrical engineering. During college, he taught at Boston YMCA College, now Northeastern University, to earn money. Upon graduation he accepted a position with the General Electric Company in Schenectady, New York, working on steam turbines. His pay was 12 cents an hour.

A year and a half later, he was loaned to Kansas State Agricultural College, where he taught mechanical engineering. He never returned to GE. In 1906, he married Eva Burtner. Potter became full professor at Kansas State in 1910 and dean of mechanical arts and director of the engineering experiment station in 1913. He was an early advocate of applying engineering to agriculture and in 1914 began an agricultural engineering department. In 1920, he accepted a position as dean of engineering at Purdue University, where he remained until he retired in 1953. He served as acting president of Purdue from 1945 to 1946, but refused an offer to accept it permanently.

In World War I, Potter served on several governmental boards for industrial preparedness and education for the Department of the Navy and the War Department. In World War II, he was very instrumental in organizing the Engineering, Science, and Management War Training program, which trained 1.3 million people for defense industries, and served as executive director of the President's Patent Planning Commission, which saved the U.S. patent system from being abolished.

Potter was president of the SPEE, from 1924 to 1925, of the American Society of Mechanical Engineers, and the American Engineering Council. Following his retirement he served as president of bituminous Coal Research, Inc. Potter was very dedicated to students and maintained office hours until he was 94 and did consulting for an additional year. He died on November 5, 1979, at the age of 97. ∎

contribution to the national defense by utilizing their facilities for specialized engineering training on the college level, without interrupting their regular programs leading to degrees.

The committee recommended that Congress authorize a college level program to train naval architects, draftsmen, marine engineering, aeronautical engineers, machine tool designers, and engineers, all of whom were in short supply and needed to supervise and increase production in industries essential to the national defense. Public Law 812 was quickly drafted, passed by the Congress, and on October 9 signed by the president. It created the Engineering Defense Training (EDT) program, with an appropriation of $9,000,000, for "the cost of short engineering courses of college grade, provided by engineering schools or universities of which the engineering school is a part . . . to meet the shortage of engineers with specialized training in fields essential to the national defense." [2]

As the program developed, it became necessary to expand the Washington staff. Roy A. Seaton, dean of engineering and architecture at Kansas State College of Agriculture and Applied Science and past president of the Society from 1932 to 1933, who was serving as a regional advisor to the program, was appointed director on November 25, 1940, and George W. Case, dean of technology at the University of New Hampshire, joined the staff to head the academic activities. They organized the EDT in Washington and established working relationships between the federal agencies and the participating institutions.

The Society publicized the program through a series of articles, which appeared in every issue of its *Proceedings* from December 1940 to December 1941, and frequently thereafter. The Office of Education stated that these articles "were of great value in stimulating interest in the program on the part of engineering colleges and their staffs." [3] At the Annual Meeting of June 1941, at the University of Michigan, a resolution was passed endorsing the "work of Deans Seaton, Potter, and Case and their associates under the supervision of the United States Commissioner of Education." [4]

The success of the program was immediate, and the following year the program was expanded to include chemists, physicists, and production supervisors. To reflect the program's more encompassing nature, its name was changed to the Engineering, Science, Management Defense Training (ESMDT) program. In 1942, it was again renamed as the Engineering, Science, Management War Training (ESMWT) program, which it remained until the program ended on June 30, 1945. The program was rather unique in that it was not a federal program conducted by the college and universities, but rather a collection of local programs created by the schools with support from the U.S. Office of Education on behalf of the federal government.

The program was highly successful in meeting the wartime needs for technically trained manpower. Over the five years of the program, 227 colleges and universi-

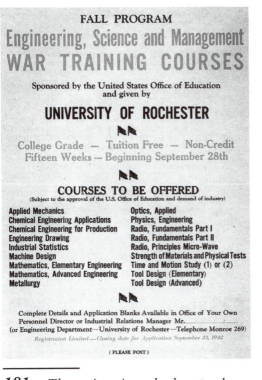

181. *The engineering schools not only trained the military, but offered an extensive number of courses for workers in defense-related industries. They were sponsored by the U.S. Office of Education and offered free to enrollees.*

ties offered 31,465 separate courses in engineering, some many times, to train 1.3 million people in areas including aircraft structures, explosives, plastics, surveying and mapping, communications, electronics, engineering drawing, production engineering, quality control, safety engineering, mechanical inspections and testing, and metallurgy. Another 450,000 people were trained in chemistry, physics, and production supervision. Of those who were involved, 94 percent were trained part-time while they were employed, making this the nation's first large-scale program in continuing education.

The five-year cost for the entire program was $60 million, of which about three-quarters was for engineering training. In contrast to the Student Army Training Corps program of World War I, the ESMWT program was conducted so that upon its conclusion it did not disrupt the regular engineering college programs.

Women, who were rare in engineering at the time, played a particularly important role in the program. In the preceding decade, less than 25 women each year received engineering degrees in the United States. In the ESMWT program, however, over 282,000 women, most of whom had not been previously employed and almost none of whom had been qualified to perform even simple engineering tasks, were trained and found employment in war industries in jobs customarily assigned to men. As a result, enough men were released from war industries to form nearly 19 infantry divisions. The significance of this may be realized by noting that the Italian campaign was successfully won with 11 divisions. Although the growth of women in engineering after the war would continue to be slow, their presence in the profession was no longer to be denied. By 1952, the number of women in the profession had increased to a level sufficient to found the Society of Women Engineers.

The contribution of the colleges was not limited to the ESMWT program. The Army Specialized Training Program (ASTP) and the Navy V-12 and V-5 programs utilized the engineering faculties and facilities. The army program was a failure from the point of view of the engineering colleges. It was designed by the military without the involvement of engineering educators. The courses were highly specialized and were 12 weeks in length, making it difficult to equate them with normal academic courses. Further, the Selective Service was unable to deliver the personnel as scheduled. Engineering colleges participated reluctantly as a national duty.[5]

The navy programs, in contrast, utilized a 16-week semester with practically standard college courses. The programs of both services ran year-round. The army trained 219,000 people, including 150,000 in the advanced courses for engineering, premedical, and language studies. From July 1943 to December 1945, the navy enrolled 179,000 people, with 71,000 of them in the V-12 program, which included 27,000 engineers.[6]

182. *At Iowa State, 100 women, sophomores or above with at least elementary college mathematics, spent 10 months, from February to December 1943, training for special assignments in engineering departments at Curtis-Wright Corporation. The "engineering cadettes" were taught a variety of skills, including how to weld airframes.*

Participation in World War II caused a shift away from economic concerns that characterized the 1930s to the very different set of problems associated with meeting the production needs of a war effort. There was a change between 1940 and 1950 in expectations about the role of higher education. No longer was higher education considered a by-product of prosperity, but rather, now it was viewed as integral to creating a growing economy and maintaining a strong national defense.

Expanded Research Activities

In both the United States and Canada, the war increased the awareness of the importance of academic research. The need for more knowledge and its application, coupled with increased amounts of money from the military, brought engineering colleges into research in a serious way. Engineering research with military

183. *In February 1948, midshipmen at the U.S. Naval Academy learned how a 60 kilowatt turbo-generator worked.*

ends was undertaken by faculty members and graduate students in many universities, often on projects that were highly secret and carried out without public knowledge. This altered the relationship between the federal government and the universities. The government specified the research to be performed, managed its conduct, and maintained the secrecy of the results. The performance of the academic researchers convinced the Congress and the executive branch that the federal government should be a dominant supporter of university research, and that universities had a special role in U.S. science and technology activities.

The Allied forces in World War II used as much petroleum in a single day as the entire Allied armies used throughout World War I,[7] which prompted major research and development in catalytic cracking and petroleum production. The loss of Malaya stimulated research in synthetic rubber, while efforts were expanded to produce asphalt for runways and roads, synthetic fibers such as nylon, plastics, and textiles, petroleum products and a wide variety of medicines. Developments occurred in electronics with radar, microwaves, communications, electronic computers, sophisticated control and navigation systems, and electronic instrumentation; in aeronautics and applied mechanics with high-speed aerodynamics, structures and fatigue of airframes, gas turbine engines, new fuels and lubricants, as well as new techniques in forging, pressing, milling, and testing high tensile light alloys; in metallurgy with duralumin, beryllium, titanium, and iridium, and high-temperature steel; and in high-speed production. The Manhattan Project, which possibly was the most scientifically advanced project of the war, led to breakthroughs in atomic energy. The implications of these technological changes went beyond immediate military applications. They laid the basis for significant commercial applications after the war.

During the years preceding the war and in the early years of the conflict, only two or three of Canada's then 11 engineering schools had significant graduate studies and research programs. Canadian military research activity was restricted, as Britain tended to guard jealously its research secrets. As the threat to the British Isles increased, however, more and more cooperative work was undertaken in Canada. The Canadian government recognized for the first time that the research competence and technological skills that existed in its universities were valuable assets to be used in the effort.

The Canadian universities operating through the National Research Council made significant contributions in the areas of radar, uranium fission, aviation medicine, defense against chemical warfare, the development of wooden aircraft, and explosives. Thanks to their successful response to the research challenge, by the end of the war, the universities enjoyed a new level of esteem.

There was a further stimulus with the launching of Sputnik I in 1957, and governments began to spend lavishly on education, particularly in science and engineering, in an effort to "catch up with the Russians." Universities responded with ambitious new and expanded programs of graduate study and research.

184. *After the war, engineering combined traditional and new disciplines. Students, as those at École Polytechnique de Montreal, studied engineering drawing in 1948.*

Before the war, a major fraction of all graduate enrollments in engineering in the United States was in part-time courses conducted in a few of the larger population centers. This, however, changed. While many part-time opportunities remained and even expanded, full-time enrollments grew. This growth was aided by the establishment, with federal government funds, of graduate scholarships, assistantships, and fellowships, and by expanded research activities. The undergraduate curriculum was redesigned to serve the double purpose of preparing some graduates for immediate employment and others for graduate study.

Changes in the Society

Discussion arose as to whether to hold an annual meeting in 1942 or to cancel it because of the war. The cooperation of all 12 of the engineering schools in the New York Metropolitan area was solicited, and an invitation extended. The agenda of the 1942 meeting of the Society was devoted largely to the work of the engineering colleges in the war effort. Having rationalized the holding of the fiftieth Annual Meeting in New York City in 1942, the Society decided to celebrate its "golden" anniversary the following year, which was the fiftieth calendar year since the founding of the Society in Chicago in 1893. As the committee stated:

> At a moment when all attention focuses on the winning of the war and the greatest possible utilization of the nation's resources for the earliest conceivable accomplishment of that all desirable end, it is particularly fitting that the SPEE should hold its Fiftieth Anniversary Meeting in Chicago, the city of its origin.[8]

The scope of engineering education was expanding, and the SPEE had to keep pace. At the fifty-fourth Annual Meeting held at Washington University in June 1946, under the presidency of Harry S. Rogers, it was voted to change the name of the Society to the American Society for Engineering Education. That year, the members of the Engineering College Research Association, an independent organization, voted to merge into ASEE effective January 1, 1947 and become the Society's Engineering College Research Council. One of the first outcomes of the merger was the appointment of a Joint Committee on Federal Relations between the new council and the Society's Administrative Council. This laid the ground work for more complete representation of the interests of engineering education in legislative matters.

Frederic Lendall Bishop, who became Secretary in 1914, retired in 1947 and was replaced by Arthur B. Bronwell of Northwestern University.

The influence of the Society was increasing. In 1947, a Research Foundation Bill (later known as the National Science Foundation Bill) was pending before Congress. Although, according to the record, engineering research had been expressly

185. *When the war ended, many veterans returned to campus under the GI Bill. They often came with new wives and young children, and their rooms at Duke University reflected the changed needs. The Wives Club flourished, while the Engineering Ball, for years one of the highlights of the fall season at Duke, was canceled in 1953 due to a lack of interest.*

omitted from the original bill submitted to hearings,[9] the new Engineering College Research Council was instrumental in having research included. In 1950, the Act was passed, and later that year, President Truman nominated three members of ASEE for the National Science Foundation's Board. They were Andrey A. Potter, Donald H. McLaughlin, president of Homestake Mining Co., and Edward L. Moreland, partner in Jackson and Moreland.

After the War

The United States and Canada emerged from the war in very healthy economic positions. Their industrial establishments had developed immensely during the years of conflict. With the industrial nations of Germany, France, Poland, Italy, Japan, and the USSR crippled by the war, the United States and Canada were able to sell abroad everything that could be produced.

The wartime training programs developed a large group of people who with the establishment of peace had a desire to obtain a more complete and systematic education in engineering, as well as in other fields. People were becoming aware that some form of college education was necessary for economic betterment. The U.S. Congress responded by passing the Serviceman's Readjustment Act of 1944, Public Law 346, as amended. Known as the "G.I. Bill of Rights," or more commonly as the "G.I. Bill," the Act provided education and training allowances for all World War II veterans for periods up to 48 months.

The response was immediate. As early as October 1946, 4.8 million veterans had applied for educational benefits, and applications were being processed at the rate of 10,000 per day. Of that group, 1.1 million enrolled in colleges and universities. It was projected that in the nine years subsequent to the end of the war, 2.5 million G.I.s would enroll in college, with 270,000 going into engineering.[10] Undergraduate enrollments in engineering jumped from 108,291 in 1940 to 230,180 in 1947.[11] Although enrollments declined to 180,646 in 1947, these great increases put tremendous pressure on the schools for classrooms, laboratories, housing, and faculty. The veterans saw things with a much more mature view than the younger college student and proved to be very capable students. Although their presence on the campus was transitory, the number of college students never decreased again to the prewar levels.

Like their U.S. counterparts, the Canadian universities had to cope with thousands of returning veterans eager to resume or undertake a college education. Similar to the United States, the federal government provided financial support for veterans to complete university programs, and many veterans opted for engineering. The number of engineering graduates increased from 746 in 1942 to 3591 in 1950, the peak year for graduating veterans.

186. *When they graduated, their children shared the proud moment, as shown here with a student who graduated in 1950 from the evening course at the Polytechnic Institute of Brooklyn.*

Canada's 11 engineering faculties performed well in accommodating the large influx of veterans. Professors carried extremely heavy teaching loads and taught classes of several hundred students, often in inadequate facilities. It was not until the veterans passed through the system, and student numbers dropped back almost to the immediate postwar levels, that the number of engineering faculties began to expand rapidly. Following an unprecedented postwar period of economic and industrial expansion in Ontario, the provincial government approved the establishment of engineering programs in the University of Western Ontario (1954), the University of Ottawa (1955), Carleton University (1957), the University of Waterloo (1957), McMaster University (1957), the University of Windsor (1958), and Laurentian University (1960).

In the United States, the West Coast schools and industries, particularly in the electronics field, grew dramatically as a result of the war. A small group of entrepreneurs, many of whom were graduate students or faculty members at Stanford, created a number of companies to develop and manufacture electronic equipment in the two decades before World War II. Litton Industries, Hewlett-Packard, and after the war, Varian Associates were begun in this way. These companies became important contributors to the defense effort and, in the process, grew significantly in assets and sales. Under the leadership of Stanford University's Dean of Engineering Frederick Terman, a major university–industrial relationship developed on the West Coast, primarily centered around Stanford. This was similar to the relationships that had developed a few decades earlier on the East Coast, with MIT and Harvard providing a stimulus and source of ideas for a large number of electronics firms that developed around Boston.

· · · · · · ·

An indication of the benefits and effect that this industrial relationship has had on Stanford is the increase in the government-sponsored research program in electrical engineering from about $20,000 per year before World War II to over $28 million in 1990 and 1991, and to over $79 million for all engineering research that year.[12] The California Institute of Technology and the University of California (Berkeley), which had become centers of activity in chemistry in the 1920s and 1930s and in nuclear physics in the 1930s, and had developed relationships with research laboratories established in California by several oil companies in the 1920s,[13] expanded their engineering departments after the war.

The transistor was developed in 1948 and found rapid application in computers and missile production. The miniaturization of transistors led to semiconductors of increasing density, which found application in a wide range of electronic devices. Computers grew in capability and speed, while their physical requirements and cost were reduced. Space vehicles were created, and they required new materials and increasingly complex instrumentation. Nuclear energy was being developed and installed for peacetime use. These developments caused a great increase in the

BIOGRAPHICAL SKETCH

FREDERICK E. TERMAN

Frederick Terman was an engineering teacher, administrator, researcher, author, and notable contributor to the development of electronics. He often is regarded as the principal person responsible for the establishment of a major electronics industry on the west coast of the United States.

He was born on June 7, 1900. Terman attended Stanford University, receiving a bachelor's degree in 1920 and the degree of electrical engineer in 1922. He was awarded a doctorate in electrical engineering by the Massachusetts Institute of Technology in 1924. He accepted a position as instructor of electrical engineering at Stanford in 1925, where he rose to professor and, in 1937, head of the electrical engineering department.

demand for electrical, mechanical, and industrial engineers, as well as physicists, chemists, and metallurgists. Increased affluence, which allowed more people to attend universities, and a rise in immigration after the war helped continue the expansion of university activities, including research and graduate studies, through the 1950s and 1960s.

The role of the university in research also began to change. Postwar legislation established the Office of Naval Research, the Atomic Energy Commission, and the National Science Foundation, and also expanded the activities of the National Institutes of Health (NIH). The AEC established the precedent of federally funded Research and Development centers, operating under contract to universities. The growth of the NIH extramural research program signaled government recognition of the importance of academic research in addressing national needs and agency missions. The establishment of the NSF broadened the government's support of research and training in all fields of science and engineering to increase scientific and technical knowledge for the general benefit of society. This complemented the research support in the service of specific agency missions.

International Activities

In 1945, Sidney S. Steinberg, dean of engineering at the University of Maryland, carried out a goodwill tour of Latin America, visiting 12 nations as a representative of SPEE.[14] His purpose was to promote closer cooperation among the faculty of the region and to foster the exchange of faculty and literature. In order to facilitate cooperation with groups in Central and South America, the newly named American Society for Engineering Education appointed a Committee on International Relations in June 1948.[15]

Steinberg made a second tour of Latin America in 1949. As a result of his efforts and contacts,[16] the first fully hemispheric Pan American Engineering Congress was held in July 1949 in Rio de Janeiro, Brazil. Immediately preceding the Congress, there was a meeting in Sao Paulo, Brazil to organize the Pan American Union of Engineering Societies (UPADI).[17] UPADI held its second convention at Tulane University, in August 1952.[18]

Cooperation with engineering schools in Western Europe was increased in the early 1950s, when ASEE cooperated with other organizations to start the United States and Europe Council of Engineering Societies, later known as the European–United States Engineering Education Conference (EUSEC). Conferences on engineering education among representatives from the United States, Canada, and a number of European countries were held in 1953 in London, in 1954 in Zurich, and in 1957 in Paris. The results of these meetings was a comprehensive comparative study of engineering education in various countries, pub-

In 1942, when the United States became involved in World War II, Terman moved to Harvard University to organize and direct the Radio Research Laboratory, which made improvements in electronic warfare including developments in radar countermeasures, surveillance equipment, jammers, and chaff used in the war. For this work he was awarded the Presidential Medal for Merit and decorated by the British Government. When he returned to Stanford in 1945, he was appointed dean of engineering, provost in 1955, and vice president in 1959.

Terman encouraged and supported Stanford students to commercialize the work of their studies. In this way, Terman and Stanford were instrumental in beginning Hewlett-Packard, Litton Industries, Varian Associates, and many other companies that formed a university-industrial complex on the west coast of the United States.

Terman served as vice president of the ASEE, president of the Institute of Radio Engineers, was a member of the National Academy of Sciences, and a member of the Committee of Twenty-Five chosen to establish the National Academy of Engineering. A prolific author, he completed eight books on electronics, radio engineering, measurements, and transmission line theory, as well as numerous articles.

Terman retired in 1965, and died on December 19, 1982.

lished in three volumes and distributed in the United States by the American Society of Civil Engineers.[19]

On a bilateral basis, ASEE sent missions to Japan, India, and the USSR. Jointly with the Unitarian Service Committee, the Society formed a Commission of Engineering Education, which was sent to Japan in 1951 at the request of the Supreme Commander of Allied Powers.[20] The ASEE coordinator for the mission was Harry P. Hammond, and the Committee on International Relations appointed 15 ASEE members to serve on the Japan Commission. Harold L. Hazen, dean of the graduate school at MIT, headed the mission to Japan.[21] The year after the mission, in line with its recommendations, the Japanese Society for Engineering Education was begun.

In November 1958, at the request of the International Cooperation Administration, ASEE sent a team of engineering educators to India for two months to help the country develop its engineering schools.[22] The team's report to the Indian government led to the establishment of the Indian Institute of Technology at Kanpur, which was created on the United States model of engineering education.

After Sputnik I went into orbit in late 1957, there was a national desire to catch up with the Russians quickly. To obtain the information about how the Russians were educating their engineers, ASEE organized a fact-finding group at the request of the Department of State and gave it the name, "ASEE Engineering Education Exchange Mission to the Soviet Union."[23]

International activities of the Society reached a high point in 1965 when the World Congress on Engineering Education was held in connection with ASEE's seventy-third Annual Meeting. Attended by 200 delegates from 33 foreign countries, this was only the second world congress on engineering education to have been held in 72 years, the first being the one at which SPEE was founded in 1893. Both meetings were held coincidentally in Chicago.

187. *Along with the traditional subjects, new disciplines were coming to the fore. Glenn Murphy was a pioneer in nuclear engineering education, and cotaught the nation's first nuclear engineering course at Iowa State College in 1952. A future ASEE president, Murphy headed three departments at Iowa State during his career.*

Atomic Energy Education

When the atomic bomb was dropped on Hiroshima in 1945 most of the engineering profession was just as startled by this development as was the general public throughout the world. Because of the unprecedented secrecy, both the theory and practice of the large-scale release of atomic energy were familiar only to the direct participants in the Manhattan Project, as the program to develop the bomb was called. But when World War II ended, scientists and engineers began looking for peacetime uses of this tremendous storehouse of energy. This was an entirely new field of technology, and the colleges of engineering prepared to introduce it into the curriculum as soon as possible.

In 1950, SPEE President Thorndike Saville appointed a Committee on Atomic

Energy Education. This committee set up five regional subcommittees, which arranged local meetings on atomic energy education. In 1955, a subcommittee chaired by Glenn Murphy of Iowa State College proposed a comprehensive study of present and future manpower requirements in the nuclear fields. This was approved by the executive board with a budget of $26,000. In addition, the Society, in cooperation with the Atomic Energy Commission and the National Science Foundation, organized and ran a number of summer schools on nuclear energy education, thereby providing many American engineering schools with qualified faculty members in this new field.

The United States Atomic Energy Commission built the first nuclear reactor for research purposes on a college campus at the Pennsylvania State University in 1958. Its purpose was to train nuclear engineers and reactor operators. By 1991, 33 higher education institutions in the United States had reactors, with their power varying from 1/10 watt at Manhattan College to 10 million watts at the University of Missouri at Columbia. These reactors operated at significantly lower power levels than the reactors at electric utilities, which typically generate from 300 million to 3 billion watts.

The Summer Institutes on Nuclear Energy Education were conducted through 1963. In 1964 and 1965, Nuclear Defense Institutes were run.

Improvement of Teaching

The need to improve the teaching abilities of engineering faculty members was a recurring theme in the Society throughout the early decades of the twentieth century. As the Committee on Engineering Education After the War, chaired by Harry Hammond, viewed the postwar needs of the engineering colleges, the concern came to the fore again. In its 1944 report, the Committee concluded that there is a:

> *need is for the systematic development of skill in teaching among younger faculty members and the creation of opportunities for broadening experience . . . it should be accepted as the responsibility of engineering college administrators to establish and direct programs of orientation and development of new and younger members of the faculty.*[24]

In 1949, the SPEE General Council decided that the recommendations of the Hammond report could be more effectively implemented if the Society developed a report which focused directly on the students and the teacher in the classroom.[25] At the Annual Meeting that year, a steering committee for the Committee on Improvement of Teaching was appointed, with B. Richard Teare as chairman. In June 1950, Teare asked to be replaced, and L.E. Grinter took charge. The com-

188. *At the University of Florida, Dean Joseph Weil, Professor Bill Fagan and a student examined the fuel supply for the school's first nuclear reactor, a subcritical device, in 1957.*

mittee consisted of 38 members, including many engineering college presidents and deans. Its work was supplemented by local institutional "committees on improvement of teaching." In this way, 1,000 to 1,500 people in over 100 colleges and universities became engaged in the work of the committee, and they generated over 150 reports and criticisms. The result was one of the most thorough analyses of the teaching-learning process undertaken by engineering educators. The committee's report, "Improvement of Engineering Teaching," [26] which was published in April 1952, recommended "that special schools or postgraduate training programs for the specific purpose of aiding teachers to improve their methods of instruction be established in strategically located institutions." [27] Grinter recommended that the Committee be dissolved and its activities be transferred to the Division of Educational Methods. [28]

In 1949, the General Council also appointed an Interim Committee for Young Engineering Teachers (CYET) for the purpose of interesting young engineering teachers in the Society to bring them into closer contact and collaboration with more mature members of the profession. [29] In 1955, the Committee proposed that:

a short term summer school be planned by the Educational Methods Division and CYET to precede the conference on a theme stressing pedagogical matters; . . . [and] a committee be appointed to study the feasibility of establishing an annual summer workshop for young engineering teachers . . . Educational theory and methods of teaching specific technical subject matter should be major factors of the curriculum. [30]

Both of these recommendations were acted upon. Immediately following the Society's 1958 Annual Meeting, a two-day summer school on "Principles of Learning in Engineering Education" was conducted. [31]

As a result of increasing sponsored research and growing demands for faculty members to serve as consultants, the prestige of these activities was being raised above that of teaching. In 1952, SPEE President Woolrich recommended to the Society's General Council that a committee be appointed to study the problem of how faculty efforts could be recognized and what kind of incentives were available "to encourage faculty members to give greater consideration to their primary function [commendable teaching]." [32] The Executive Board authorized the committee, which published three reports on how effective teaching could be recognized and rewarded. [33]

In 1956, SPEE President William L. Everitt believed that the problem for the next ten years would be the procurement and development of college faculties. At the time, only about 200 new PhD's a year were going into teaching. An advisory group under the chairmanship of Harold L. Hazen was appointed to formulate plans and a budget for a project. The project was funded, and the group was named the Committee for the Development of Engineering Faculties. Its report appeared in May 1960 as *Engineering Faculty Recruitment, Development, and Utilization.* [34]

• • • • • • •

■ BIOGRAPHICAL SKETCH

WILLIAM L. EVERETT

William Everett was a leader in electronics and communications engineering, whose textbook *Communications Engineering* profoundly influenced several generations of electrical engineers and laid the groundwork for many of the developments in telecommunications for half a century. The book was the first electrical engineering textbook to incorporate recent research results in a form suitable for classroom presentation.

Everett was born in Baltimore, Maryland, on April 14, 1900. His undergraduate studies at Cornell University were interrupted by service in the Marine Corps in World War I. He returned to the university where he became an instructor in electrical engineering while completing his baccalaureate degree in 1922. After two years working as an engineer at North Electric Manufacturing Company in charge of automatic PBX development, he enrolled at the University of Michigan, where he obtained a master's degree in 1926. He continued his studies at Ohio State University, publishing his book in 1932 and receiving a doctorate the following year.

Upon graduation, Everett accepted a faculty appointment at Ohio State. While there, he developed the principle of the radio altimeter, which became standard equipment on all larger aircraft, and in 1938 he organized the first broadcast engineering conference, which brought together engineers from the United States and Canada to discuss technical problems of radio stations.

In 1941, he was given a leave of absence from the university to serve during the war as director of the Operational Research Staff in the U.S. Army's Office of the Chief Signal Officer. In 1944, he accepted an offer to become head of the department of electrical engineering at the University of Illinois, with the condition that he remain in Washington for another year to complete his war work. For his accomplishments, he was awarded the War Department's Exceptionally Meritorious Civilian Award. When Everett moved to the University of Illinois in 1945, there were 29 undergraduates and no graduate students in electrical engineering. Four years later, there were 260 undergraduates and 156 graduate students. His goal was to not only expand the department, but to develop it from a teaching department to one whose faculty were engaged in both research and teaching. He was successful, and in 1949 was named dean of engineering. He continued to recruit outstanding faculty members and develop a strong research program. To keep himself abreast of technical advances, he accepted the editorship of a series of electrical engineering textbooks, and edited more than 100 books. He retired in 1967.

Bill Everett served as president of the ASEE from 1956 to 1957, of the Institute of Radio Engineers, and the Engineers Council for Professional Development. He was a founding member of the National Academy of Engineering, and after retirement from Illinois, chaired panels on telecommunications for the Academy and the Department of Commerce. Two years after his wife of 55 years died in 1978, he remarried and continued to enjoy outdoor activities. He died on September , 1986. ■

The Society had taken a very active role in the improvement of engineering teaching. From 1927 to 1959, it sponsored 57 summer schools for engineering teachers. Most of the programs dealt with specific disciplines.[35] In 1960, ASEE, in cooperation with The Pennsylvania State University and the Ford Foundation, initiated a two-week Summer Institute on Effective Teaching for Engineering Teachers. Conducted under direction of Otis E. Lancaster, the program continued each summer through 1963, and involved 247 participants from 130 colleges and universities. At its conclusion, the institute leaders recommended that a number of regional institutes of shorter duration be established so that a larger number of engineering teachers could participate.

A few regional institutes and workshops were held in 1966 and 1967, with ASEE encouragement. Then in 1967, the Society's Educational Research and Methods Division, chaired by Lawrence P. Grayson, took responsibility for the institutes. Under the overall coordination of Edward K. Kraybill of Duke University, a series of regional directors were appointed, brought together for training and orientation sessions, and charged to establish locally supported institutes that met the interests and circumstances in their locales. In 1967–68, ten regional institutes were held.[36] In the first five years, a total of 68 effective teaching institutes were conducted in every part of the United States and several in Canada, in both English and French. Over 3,200 teachers attended those institutes. The pattern was so successful that the Educational Research and Methods Division has continued the institutes every year since then, many of which have been held in conjunction with the ASEE Annual Conference.

Sputnik and Its Aftermath

The 1950s witnessed the early years of a nuclear arms race between the United States and the USSR, an American defense policy based on nuclear deterrents, increasing influence of the Communist party throughout the world, and the United States Congressional hearings on communism in America conducted by Senator Joseph McCarthy. There was a global tension and competition between the United States and the Soviet Union, the two most powerful nations in the world. It was referred to as a "Cold War."

When the United States brought World War II to a sudden halt by the use of atomic bombs, many people believed that atomic secrets were an American monopoly. They were rudely shocked by President Truman's announcement in September 1949 that "the Soviets had exploded an atomic bomb . . . approximately three years earlier than our experts had thought possible." Many felt that the Russian success was due to the stealing of secret formulas. In 1952, the United States exploded a still more powerful weapon, the hydrogen bomb, and this time

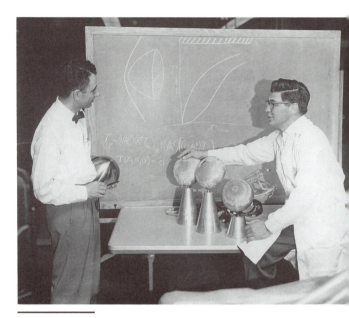

189. *As ambitions rose, aerospace engineering professors Sebastian Nardo (left) and Burton Erickson of the Polytechnic Institute of Brooklyn were using nose cone models in 1960 to study thermo stress and ablation as part of a research program in outer space flight.*

the Russians had a similar device only one year later. The feeling began to be prevalent in engineering and scientific circles that such achievements by the Russians must be based on something more substantial than the stealing of secret formulas.

When the Soviets launched a satellite into orbit in October 1957, before the United States space program could do the same, it became evident that America had a rival on the most advanced scientific and technological levels.

The resulting Soviet–American race for technological leadership and the national goal to land a man on the moon, gave rise to a scientific and technological

190. *At New Mexico State University, Captain Nelson explained the operation of a La Crosse missile to two students in 1960.*

boom. Funds for science and engineering education suddenly became available from private foundations and from federal and state governments appropriations. Faculty salaries rose, facilities and equipment improved, and research grants became plentiful. Academic standards were raised, and course requirements became more stringent. Scientists and engineers assumed new roles in government leadership, particularly during the Kennedy administration. This situation prevailed almost until the end of the period, assuring that research was fully integrated into the purposes of engineering colleges. Funds available to academic institutions increased significantly in the 1950s and 1960s, with the result that monies expended at universities for research and development increased from $334 million in 1953 to $2.6 billion in 1968.[37]

It was only after 1969, when America had landed a man on the moon and the nation's priorities began to change, that the amount of support for research declined. The number of graduate degrees awarded annually in engineering had a parallel rise, with the number of master's degrees increasing from about 1,300 in 1940 to 4,800 in 1950 to over 15,000 in 1968, while the number of doctor's degrees increased from about 100 to 500 to 2,900 over the same period.[38]

ASEE Studies

The evaluation of engineering education that had begun with the Mann and Wickenden reports continued. In 1940, the report, *Aims and Scope of Engineering Curricula,* conducted under the chairmanship of Harry Hammond, recommended that engineering education should stress fundamentals in the undergraduate years and organize the curriculum in parallel sequences of science–technology courses and humanistic–social subjects. The war, however, reversed these approaches.

Less than two years after the United States became an active participant in World War II, the ASEE began to make plans for restoring peacetime engineering education and, in 1944, appointed the Committee on Engineering Education After the War. This group, which had a membership largely similar to the committee that wrote the *Aims and Scope* report, was also chaired by Hammond. The technical demands of the war for new developments made clear the shortcomings of engineering education. Engineers required a deeper understanding of fundamentals that could be applied broadly and less emphasis on current technical practice.

In its report, *Engineering Education After the War,* the committee restated the earlier objectives and elaborated on the methods for their achievement.[39] It also made recommendations for extending engineering education at both ends of the spectrum: graduate work should be restored and broadened to include all areas of advanced specialization, and technical institutes should be strengthened by accreditation and by the acceptance of their graduates on a much wider scale than had

■ BIOGRAPHICAL SKETCH

LINTON ELIAS GRINTER

Linton Elias Grinter was born in Kansas City, Missouri, on August 28, 1902. He received a Bachelor of Science degree from the University of Kansas in 1923, a masters degree in 1924, and in 1926 became the first person to receive doctorate in civil engineering from the University of Illinois. In 1930, he was awarded a C.E. degree from the University of Kansas. After receiving his doctorate, he was employed as an engineer for Standard Oil Co. of Indiana, before joining the faculty at Texas A&M College in 1928, where he served as associate professor of civil engineering and then professor of structural engineering.

In 1937, Grinter moved to the Armour Institute of Technology, where he advanced from dean of the graduate division been done before. The report had a significant effect on shaping curricula after the war.

In 1951, the Engineers' Council for Professional Development asked ASEE to undertake a study of ways in which engineering education could keep pace with the rapid developments in science and technology, as well as how future engineers should be educated to provide the professional leadership needed over the next 25 years. This formal request represented a definite recognition that the development of standards and the enforcement of criteria should be separate functions.

In 1955, the committee, under the chairmanship of L.E. Grinter, issued a *Report on Evaluation of Engineering Education,*[40] which reemphasized the conclusions of the two Hammond Reports and set specific objectives for the profession in both the technical and social areas. It discussed in detail how the objectives could be implemented and suggested broad guidelines for dividing engineering curricula into stems that included humanities and social sciences, mathematics and basic sciences, engineering sciences, engineering specialty subjects and electives. The report also recognized that an undergraduate curriculum must serve a twofold purpose of preparing some students for graduate study and others for immediate employment.

· · · · · · ·

As an outgrowth of the Hammond and Grinter reports and their recommendations about the importance of the humanities and social sciences to engineering education, the Humanistic-Social Science Research Project was begun in 1954. It was designed to improve the study of liberal studies for engineers and to integrate these studies more thoroughly with the engineering curriculum. The final report, *General Education in Engineering,* which was distributed in 1956, provided detailed guidelines for humanistic studies in engineering curricula.[41]

To extend the findings of previous studies and formulate a set of educational criteria for engineering technology curricula, an evaluation of technical institute education was undertaken. The conclusions of the committee were presented in the report *Characteristics of Excellence in Engineering Technology Education.*[42]

Changing Curricula

These reports, coupled with the rapid growth of knowledge, the accelerated pace of technological advances, and the increasing complexities of social, technical, and economic relationships in modern society, had major effects on the development of engineering curricula during this period. The engineering programs of this period incorporated the natural sciences, social sciences, humanities, and communication arts into a strong core of mathematics, engineering science, and analysis, and tried

and director of civil engineering to vice president and dean of the graduate division. When the school merged with Lewis Institute to become the Illinois Institute of Technology in 1940, Grinter served as vice president, dean of the graduate school. In 1952, he became dean of the graduate school and director of research at the University of Florida. From 1969 to 1970, he was interim vice president of the university, and then for three years chaired the institute's ten-year self-study program before retiring in 1973.

He published over 200 papers and six books on structural engineering and theoretical mechanics during a professional career that spanned over 50 years. He served as president of the ASEE from 1953 to 1954, as well as president of the Engineers Council for Professional Development and of Sigma Xi. From 1953 to 1956, Grinter chaired a 40-man committee of the ASEE which prepared *Evaluation of Engineering Education,* otherwise known as the Grinter report. From 1969 to 1971, he chaired another ASEE committee that produced an evaluation of engineering technology education.

He was knighted in the Order of the North Star by the King of Sweden for his promotion of international relations between Sweden and the United States and was the first recipient of the Linton E. Grinter Distinguished Service Award presented by Engineers' Council for Professional Development. ∎

191. *In the 1960s, at the University of Michigan an electron microscope was used for research in materials science.*

192. *The blackboard was a handy way for Larry Baum (right), Washington State University's first Ph.D. recipient in engineering, to discuss a problem with mechanical engineering faculty member Robert Brun.*

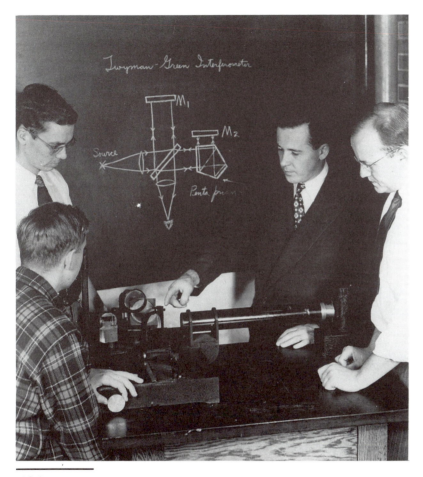

193. At the University of Rochester, Robert E. Hopkins, a leader in computer-designed lenses, instructed students in testing a Penta Prism commonly used in single-lens reflex cameras.

194. In Cornell University's high-voltage laboratory, a 750-kv a.c. transformer test set could create a discharge across a string of insulators (at center). Jets of water were used to simulate mist.

to bring these intellectual disciplines and fields of knowledge to bear on real and contemporary problems of society.

The general result is unique in American higher education. Engineering curricula attempt to provide within the confines of a four-year program both a broad general education and a specialized technical education of great and growing complexity. On one hand, there was an emphasis on fundamentals and an acceptance of a uniform first year to provide the engineer with the basic technical knowledge that would allow him to practice in a variety of occupations. On the other hand, there was a tendency to broaden the content of engineering programs in all branches, including some training in economics, management, social and humanistic studies, statistics, and computer programming.

In order to achieve both breadth and specialization, the general trend was to develop flexible, four-year undergraduate programs that could be followed by a year or more of graduate study. Indeed, the growth of graduate study was the most significant trend of the period. In the latter part of the period, graduate enrollment grew faster than undergraduate enrollment.

An Evolving **ASEE**

The ASEE continued to evolve with the changing demands of engineering education. Arthur Bronwell, who served as secretary since Bishop's resignation in 1947, resigned on February 1, 1955 to accept the position of President of Worcester Polytechnic Institute. W. Leighton Collins, professor of theoretical mechanics at the University of Illinois, was elected secretary by the executive board on December 13, 1954, and the headquarters moved to the University of Illinois on February 1, 1955.

The next ten years saw a significant growth in the Society and its staff. When Collins began, he spent half of his time teaching and half of his time running the small ASEE Headquarters office, staffed by three full-time secretaries, a bookkeeper, and a quarter-time editor. In 1962, a reorganization changed his title from Secretary to Executive Secretary. The reorganization also created the Technical Institute Council and elevated the Projects Management Group to the Projects Operating Unit headed by a vice president. To carry out the greatly expanding activity, the executive board decided to relocate the headquarters. Three committees debated whether it would be better situated in New York close to many of the other engineering societies or in Washington, DC, near the education societies. After much deliberation, it was concluded to move to Washington, and for the first time, the ASEE center was no longer located on a college campus. With the move in 1965, Leighton Collins became a full-time employee in charge of a staff of fourteen persons, and his title was changed to Executive Director. During this decade, the membership grew from about 7,500 in 1955 to 11,700 in 1965.

A number of consolidations among schools occurred in this period. In 1940, Armour Institute of Technology merged with Lewis Institute to become the Illinois Institute of Technology. In 1967, Carnegie Institute and Mellon Institute of Industrial Research became one institution, Carnegie-Mellon University, and Case School of Applied Science and Western Reserve University merged to become Case Western Reserve. In 1973, the engineering school at New York University merged into the Polytechnic Institute of Brooklyn to become the Polytechnic Institute of New York, which subsequently changed its name to Polytechnic University.

Rapid Growth in Canada

In 1950, there were 11 engineering colleges in Canada, stretching from Halifax to Vancouver. Even some of these had limited offerings. Although the École Polytechnique, for example, began offering a civil engineering program in 1873, diversification of its engineering curriculum did not occur until the university obtained a new charter in 1955. At that time, programs in chemical, electrical, geological, mechanical, metallurgical, and mining engineering, and in engineering physics were created.

This slow rate of growth changed following the launching of Sputnik I by the Soviet Union in 1957. As in other Western countries, the provincial governments in Canada undertook a decade-long program of expansion of postsecondary education facilities in order to catch up with Russian science and technology. Virtually every university engaged in an ambitious building program, and funds for new staff and equipment were readily available. Many engineering schools seized the opportunity to develop strong research programs to complement their traditional teaching functions. The doctorate became essential for those seeking an engineering academic career. By 1968, no fewer than 29 Canadian universities established faculties to teach engineering. Today, 31 universities offer engineering education under more than 40 program names.

The University of Waterloo established a school of engineering in 1957. Sir George Williams University in Montreal initiated engineering programs in 1963. The University of Guelph was incorporated in 1964 and five years later began offering degree programs in agricultural, biological, and water resources engineering. In 1969, the University of Quebec established engineering faculties on its campuses in Chicoutimi and Trois-Rivières. In 1974, the Quebec Legislative Assembly approved the merger of Sir George Williams University and Loyola College and the consequent formation of Concordia University.

For many years, the four western provinces each had one university. Then during the 1950s and 1960s, satellite campuses were established, some of which became independent institutions. The University of Calgary, created in 1966, evolved as a branch campus of the University of Alberta, while the University of Regina was a 1974 offshoot of the University of Saskatchewan. In 1972, Lakehead University in Thunder Bay, Ontario began offering engineering programs, becoming the only Canadian institution to offer both engineering and technology programs; the latter date from 1948.

The Royal Military College of Canada, which is one of the few institutions that offer instruction in both French and English, followed a pattern similar to the United States Military Academy at West Point. Although the institution had been awarding diplomas to its graduates since 1880, it was not until 1959 that the Ontario Legislature permitted the college to award degrees. The first degrees were granted in 1962 in chemical, civil, electrical, and mechanical engineering. Canada's other two military colleges, Royal Roads in British Columbia, which was created in 1942, and the Collège Militaire Royal de Saint-Jean in Quebec established in 1952, offer only the first two years of an engineering program. Students then transfer to the Royal Military College of Canada to complete their coursework.

By the midsixties, the effect of the postwar baby boom began to be felt at the postsecondary level. Engineering enrollments began an eight-year climb as the sons and daughters of servicemen reached college age. Given their growth, however, the engineering schools had little difficulty coping with the enrollment increases.

Goals Report

At the request of Engineers' Council for Professional Development, the Executive Board and General Council of ASEE voted in November 1961 to undertake a major new assessment of engineering education. Known as the "Goals of Engineering Education" study, Eric A. Walker, who had just completed a term as ASEE president and was president of the Pennsylvania State University, was appointed chairman. George A. Hawkins, dean of engineering at Purdue, and Joseph M. Pettit, dean of engineering at Stanford, became the chairmen of the undergraduate and graduate sections, respectively. On January 8, 1963, NSF funded the graduate part and the following month the undergraduate part.

· · · · · · ·

Like the Wickenden study, the Goals study was extremely comprehensive, with reviews being made of virtually every aspect of engineering education. Archie Higdon, who was chairman of the department of engineering at the U.S. Air Force

■ BIOGRAPHICAL SKETCH

ERIC A. WALKER

Eric Walker was chairman of the committee that developed the report *Goals of Engineering Education,* the most extensive assessment on the subject undertaken by the profession in the last half century.

Walker was born in Long Eaton, England, on April 29, 1910. At an early age, he moved with his parents to Canada, and then lived with an aunt in Wrightsville, Pennsylvania, during his high school years. He attended Harvard University on a scholarship, where he earned a B.S. in electrical engineering in 1932, an M.S. in business administration in 1933, and a ScD in electrical engineering in 1935. In 1933, he accepted a position as instructor

Academy, visited every engineering school campus to meet with the faculties and solicit their views. William K. LeBold of Purdue was the project coordinator, in charge of coordinating the research and gathering survey information about the state of engineering education. The study was scheduled to be completed in two-and-a-half years and included the issuance of a *Preliminary Report* as an intermediate step.

When the *Preliminary Report* was issued it contained two recommendations, among many others, that generated strong disagreement within the engineering community. The strongest reaction was to the recommendation that the master's degree be considered the first professional degree, with the bachelor's considered a general degree suitable for entry into employment in technical occupations and as preparation for graduate professional study. Many people believed it denegrated the bachelor's degree graduates, who they wanted to maintain as recognized engineers.

The second point of criticism was directed at the recommendation that ECPD accreditation, which had been granted since the council's inception by curricula, should be given to an engineering college as a whole. As a result, an *Interim Report* was written and circulated to engineering educators throughout the United States for comment. The two controversial recommendations were tempered. Among numerous observations and recommendations on virtually all aspects of engineering education, the report made the following points: society's needs in the decades ahead will call for engineering talent on a scale never before seen in the United States or elsewhere; the engineer of the future will be called upon to play an increasing role in the solution of complex social problems; and the future engineers will need greater technical competence to cope with the complexities of technological endeavors. The reactions were positive, and the final report was issued in January 1968.[43]

The Goals report was the basis for numerous discussions and meetings. Many of the recommendations were agreed to, but led to very little direct action. While it set the tone for engineering education over the next decade and more, unlike some previous studies, it did not result in definable new directions for the profession. The report, however, was more perceptive than directive, as many of its recommendations have come to fruition with the passage of time.

The 1960s

Although economic affluence would continue, America's self-confidence and self-assurance would be strained during the decade of the 1960s, as the nation endured the Cuban Missile Crisis, the assassination of President Kennedy, nuclear weapons protests, the unpopular war in Vietnam, university-based mass protests against the war, the antiestablishment "hippie" movement, the assassinations of Martin

of mathematics at Tufts College, where he was made head of electrical engineering in 1940. At the outbreak of World War II in 1942, Walker was appointed associate director of the Underwater Sound Laboratory at Harvard University, where the principal mission was the development of the homing torpedo.

After the war, the U.S. Navy wanted to retain the capability by moving the laboratory to a university site. Walker, who had just accepted a position as head of electrical engineering at Pennsylvania State University, was asked by the Navy to direct the new organization. It moved to Penn State as the Ordnance Research Laboratory. In 1951, Walker became dean of the College of Engineering and Architecture, vice president for research in 1956, and president later that year. Under his presidency, the student population of Penn State increased from 13,000 to 40,000, and the annual operating budget rose from $34 million to $165 million. When he retired in 1970, he became vice president for science and technology of the Aluminum Company of America until 1975.

Walker was president of the ASEE from 1960 to 1961, and of the Engineers Joint Council, as well as chairman of the Board of the National Science Foundation and the National Academy of Engineering. He has written more than 300 publications, and has served as a director of 10 industrial organizations. ∎

Luther King and Robert Kennedy, race riots in major cities, and severe environmental problems. All of these events had their effect on university life and on the education of the students of the era. By and large, the engineering schools did not participate in the counterculture movement and campus disruptions of the late 1960s. However, it did not follow that they were unaffected. The civil unrest and political turmoil were reflected in a desire to stop universities from performing military and classified research, in an occasional bombing of a research building, in the strong distaste for the ROTC, in which many engineering students participated.

In spite of the societal trends, the 1960s were the "Golden Age" for the research universities. Federal support for academic research more than quadrupled in constant dollars over a period of eight years. By 1968, 74 percent of sponsored academic research was supported by the federal government. The number of faculty involved in engineering research grew steadily, even as enrollments and

195. *The uses of light became more sophisticated in the early 1960s. Emmet N. Leith, of the electrical engineering and computer science department at the University of Michigan, is shown experimenting with techniques for holography.*

degrees were stable. The physical plant of universities expanded as new research facilities were built to house laboratories, equipment, professors, and graduate students. Universities took on a growing component of classified (secret) research for the Department of Defense. Teaching of graduate and undergraduate classes became a smaller proportion of the professors' responsibilities as they "bought" research time from their schedules with research grant funds.

Although engineering faculty and schools accepted research as a legitimate function of engineering education, and they readily increased their research activities in response to the availability of government funds, the deemphasis in teaching was in direct opposition to what the Society had been advocating for over half a century — that more, rather than less, attention should be directed toward improving engineering teaching. Continually increasing government funding through the present has continued to skew the emphasis between teaching and research toward research.

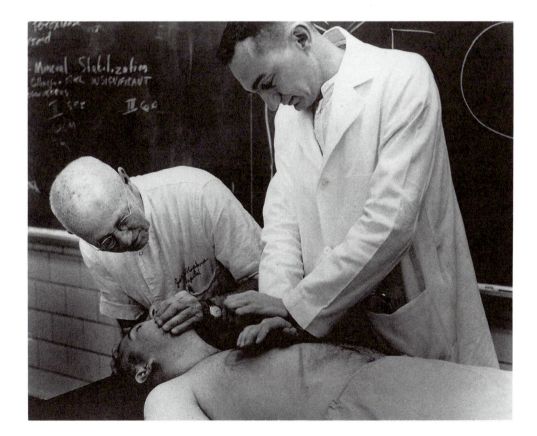

196. *William B. Kouwwenhoven, retired dean of engineering at The Johns Hopkins University, and a lecturer in surgery at the Hopkins Hospital in 1960, with surgeon Jim Jude developed the procedure now known as* cardiopulmonary resuscitation, *or* CPR.

197. *Students in the navy roomed dormitory style at Stevens Institute of Technology during the war.*

198. *In the summer of 1943, 800 officer candidates, including some from the active fleet, arrived at the University of Rochester as part of the U.S. Navy V-12 program. Chosen through testing procedures, all were required to take mechanical drawing.*

199. *The University of Illinois operated a diesel engine school for enlisted men during the war.*

200. *Cornell University conducted one for naval ensigns.*

201. *Virginia Polytechnic Institute trained army-enlisted men in electric motors and generators.*

202. *Dean A.A. Potter (center), who was instrumental in establishing the nation's wartime training programs, reviewed V-12 students in an electrical engineering laboratory at Purdue.*

203. *The float by the AIME chapter at Michigan Technological University showed its support of the war effort.*

204. *At Iowa State College of Agriculture and Mechanic Arts, the Student Defense Council broadcast weekly radio programs to inform students about various activities. Shown are Council members preparing for a Saturday program, "America Stands Firm."*

205. *Embry-Riddle Aeronautical University provided extensive training for pilots and mechanics. Shown are several students being instructed at the tail of a Stearman.*

206. *Embry-Riddle also provided training for British, as well as U.S., pilots. Many of those from Britain later flew Spitfires in the Battle of Britain.*

207. *At Cornell University, pilots were trained in flight maneuvers in a quonset hut built at an airstrip near the campus.*

209. *At the Ohio State University, men who were not in uniform learned about production supervision as part of a program in engineering defense training.*

208. *On June 6, 1944, D-Day, when the Allied Forces stormed the enemy-held beaches at Normandy, France, the men of the V-12 unit at the University of Rochester assembled to pray for the victory of their comrades overseas. The pastor of the Brick Presbyterian Church lead the prayer, while university president Alan Valentine stood at his left.*

210. *With most men in the service, courses were populated by women, such as these shown studying architectural engineering at Washington State University.*

211. *Employees of Consolidated Voltee learned about aircraft design at the Pennsylvania State College.*

212. *At the University of Cincinnati, women were trained to be airplane factory supervisors for the Goodyear Aircraft Corporation. They were known as the Goodyear Girls.*

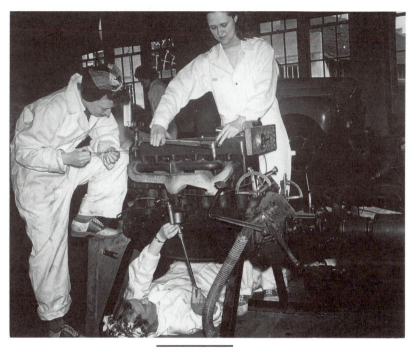

214. *The University of Idaho offered a course in automechanics for women during the war.*

213. *At Colorado State College of Agricultural and Mechanic Arts (now Colorado State University), women learned to adjust Curtis-Wright engines.*

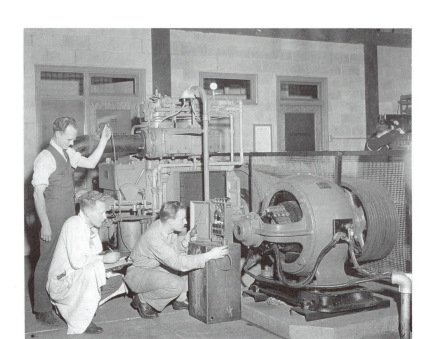

216. *At Marquette University, mechanical engineering students continued to learn to perform tests on diesel generators.*

215. *At the Michigan College of Mines and Technology, women studied the operation of a distillation tower in a unit operations lab.*

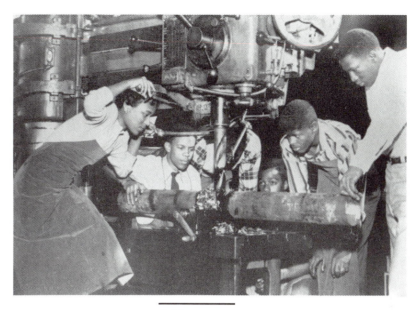

217. *At the Université Laval, students in 1945 worked with electrical power equipment.*

219. *In the 1950s, students at Tennessee State University learned to use a drill press.*

218. *Textiles were important in the South, and students at Southern College of Technology received instruction from John Alford, first head of the school's textile engineering technology department.*

220. *Electrical engineering students learned laboratory techniques at Notre Dame University in the 1950s.*

222. *In the 1940s, the CRL School of Electronics (now the Samuel I. Ward College of Technology at the University of Hartford) was training technicians to meet the demands of a growing electronics industry.*

221. *At Lehigh University, in 1953 students were studying a film transport mechanism as an example of an electro-mechanical servomechanism.*

223. *In 1954, at Iowa State College, work was progressing on a new process for recording color television signals on black-and-white film.*

224. *Students studying electronics technology at Ryerson Polytechnical Institute in the 1950s conducted tests on television transmitters and receivers.*

225. *With TV ownership becoming widespread in the mid-1950s, technology students at Southern College of Technology learned to repair them.*

226. *Electronics was advancing into new areas. At the Polytechnic Institute of Brooklyn's Microwave Research Institute, Anthony B. Giordano (a future ASEE President, third from right) and other researchers invented the gyrator for microwave networks.*

227. *The war brought electronic computers into being. At the University of Pennsylvania's Moore School of Electrical Engineering, the ENIAC (Electronic Numerical Integrator and Computer) was developed in 1946 for the U.S. Army Ordnance Department to calculate range tables for the artillery. The machine occupied a room 30 feet by 50 feet, weighed 30 tons, used 18,000 vacuum tubes, and had a mean time between failures of several hours. It had 16K bits of ROM and 1K bits of RAM.*

228. *In 1950, students and faculty at the University of California at Berkeley built the California Digital Computer for instruction and research. It had a magnetic memory capable of storing "10,000 ten-digit numbers with their signs."*

230. *Analog computers, which were well suited for real-time integration, were used at Michigan Technological University and many other engineering schools.*

229. *In 1963, a commercial IBM 1620 became the heart of the computer center at Ohio Northern University.*

232. *Sam Lazier, a professor at Queen's University, was conducting studies in the coastal engineering lab in 1950.*

231. *At the Davidson Laboratory of Stevens Institute of Technology, a contract with the Cunard Lines called for the study of the characteristics of the Queen Elizabeth 2.*

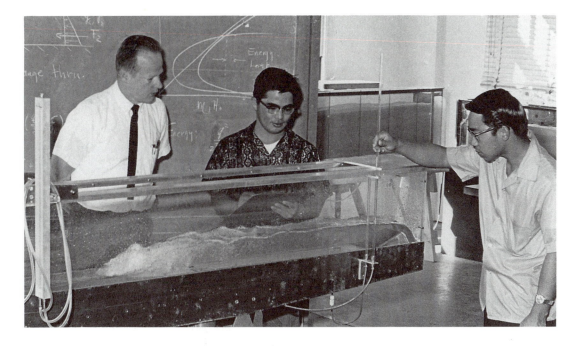

233. *At the University of Hawaii at Manoa, civil engineering students in the 1960s were studying a "hydraulic jump" in a wave tank.*

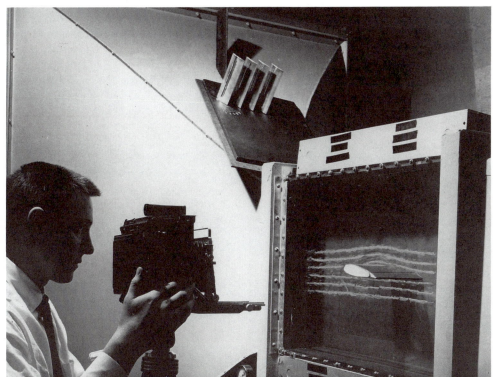

234. *At Purdue in 1957, smoke tests were performed to study air flow around a wing.*

235. *At Colorado State College of Agricultural and Mechanic Arts, agricultural engineers explained irrigation methods to Colorado farmers in 1952.*

236. *Cloud seeding to change the weather was a promising commercial technique. By 1968 the University of Wyoming's College of Engineering was using a twin-engine King Air Beech aircraft modified with extensive instrumentation and computer-directed data acquisition systems to study the atmosphere.*

237. *In the 1960s, University of Toronto faculty were studying air pollution with models of cities constructed in a low velocity wind tunnel.*

238. *Automobile safety was an important topic for research at Texas A&M University, when the state legislature designated the engineering college as the official research agency of the State Department of Highways and Public Transportation in 1948. The Texas Transportation Institute was created in 1950, and in 1966 the institute was conducting crash tests on roadway lighting fixtures.*

239. *At Purdue University, industrial engineering students learned how to lay out a plant in the early 1950s.*

240. *At Iowa State College, electrical engineering professor Warren Boast and some students in 1945 studied the illumination falling on the page of a book using an illuminometer.*

241. *At Cornell, a spherical photometer was used to measure total light flux in lumens by comparison with a standard source.*

243. *Engineering students could have fun, in addition to their intensive studies. After World War II, A. J. Paul La Prairie, who had served six years overseas with the Irish Regiment of Canada, and was the student "Direktor of Kultural Aktivities," began the regimental Lady Godiva Memorial Band in 1949. It has become a very popular group at the University of Toronto.*

242. *Beanied freshman at Worcester Polytechnic Institute were heckled by upperclassmen in 1965.*

244. In 1947, freshmen and sophomores vied for the most paddles at half-time of the first home football game at Worcester Polytechnic Institute. The Paddle-Rush is an old school tradition.

245. At Stevens Institute of Technology, freshmen and sophomores in 1953 played a game with a king-sized ball.

246. Otto Mattix, a student-created robot, was the hit of the Engineer's Fair at the University of Florida in 1955.

247. *In 1952, Spring Sports Day at Stevens Institute of Technology was a time for tossing books into a bonfire at calculus cremation ceremonies.*

248. *At the University of Rochester in 1950, a student found a creative way to use the orifice and weir tank.*

249. *Attendees at the 1967 ASEE Annual Conference held at Michigan State University were greeted with a nighttime window display.*

250. *The building at 1201 W. California, in Urbana, Illinois, served as the Headquarters for the American Society for Engineering Education from 1955 until 1965, when the Society moved to Washington, DC.*

251. *In addition to the technical session and comradery among the participants at the 1958 ASEE Annual Conference held at the University of Illinois, the members wives attended the annual tea.*

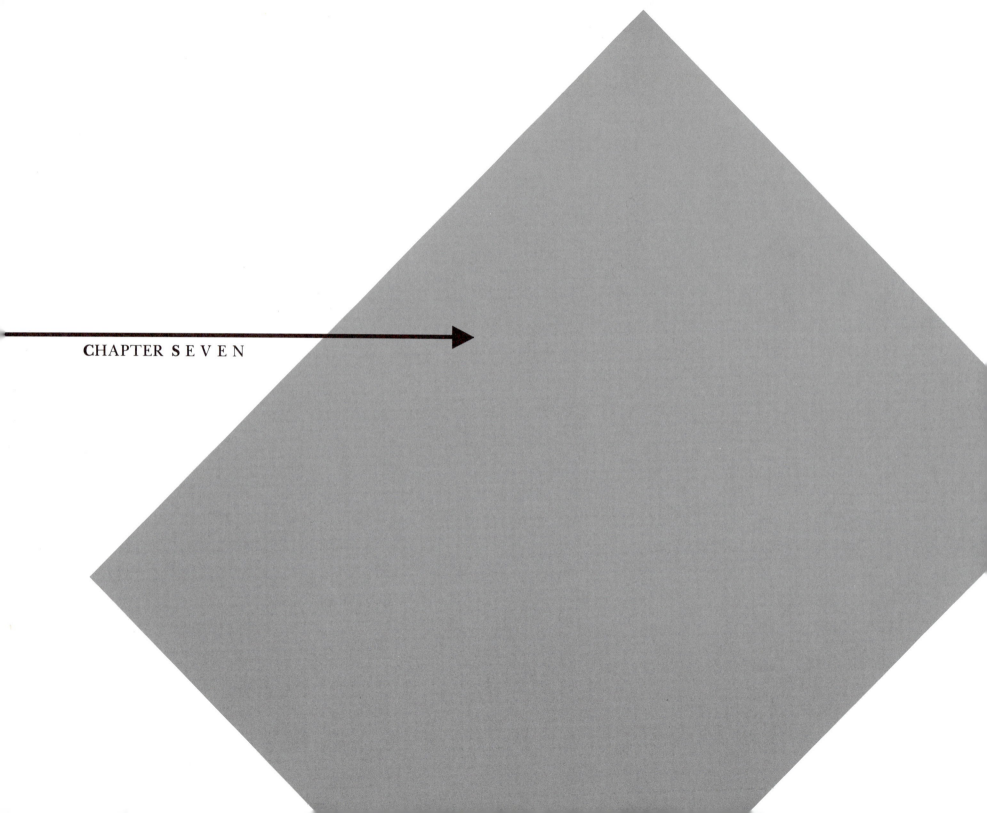

CHAPTER S E V E N

CHAPTER 7

DIVERSIFICATION: 1970–1990

. . . . . . .From the end of World War II to the OPEC oil crises of 1973, the United States and Canada enjoyed unprecedented economic growth. Rising employment and rising incomes brought living standards to heights undreamed of before the war. As the economic fabric of the two countries was transformed and they began to rely on leadership in technology for economic growth and national security, there were significant changes in engineering education.

In this period, the undergraduate curriculum was completely restructured and updated, with a turn away from the teaching of technological skills and techniques to a focus on engineering sciences, which were developed into a coherent body of knowledge. A large number of engineering disciplines and subdisciplines associated with advanced technologies were introduced, and a system of associate and baccalaureate degree programs in engineering technology were established to augment the engineering programs. A comprehensive system of graduate education was created, doctoral enrollments increased, and in many institutions extensive programs

219

of research were established. The curriculum changes were accompanied by the creation of a large number and array of modern textbooks at both the undergraduate and graduate levels, as well as a vast number of research publications.

Engineering enrollments traditionally have been very volatile, but never more so than in the 1970s and 1980s. A series of events and trends developed during these decades, which not only caused rapid changes in the numbers of students enrolled in engineering programs, but which continue to alter the composition of the student bodies and of the faculties in engineering schools in the United States and Canada.

The primary result has been to increase diversification in gender, racial composition, and national origin, but with student bodies and faculties shifting in different ways. At the undergraduate level, more women, blacks, and Hispanics enrolled in engineering programs, while foreign-born men, educated through the baccalaureate in their home countries, received large percentages of the doctorates awarded in engineering. Many of the foreign-born awardees have remained in the United States or Canada to join the faculty of engineering schools in increasing numbers.

The Vietnam War, which raged through the 1960s and into the early 1970s, was very unpopular, especially with young people. The consciousness of youth toward social concerns, personal relations, and affective matters was raised significantly. Many bright college-age students chose to study the social sciences, causing a drop in enrollments in engineering. Even though the number of 18 year olds in the United States and Canada increased rapidly as the baby boomers became of college age, freshmen enrollments in U.S. engineering schools declined from about 80,000 students in 1966 to 51,925 in 1973.

At the same time, in both countries, there were increased national commitments to social justice and affirmative action. Higher education came to be seen more as a right or opportunity, and less as a privilege. This change in attitude was accompanied by an unprecedented amount of student aid, particularly need-based aid, which focused admission policies on a "blind" basis. As a result, between 1970 and 1990, the United States moved toward universal access to higher education as more than 60 percent of the nation's 18- to 24-year olds enrolled in colleges and universities. As the number of white males pursuing engineering decreased, the numbers of women, blacks, and Hispanics in undergraduate programs increased.

All U.S. ground troops were removed from Vietnam in 1973, the same year that the OPEC countries forced a substantial increase in global oil prices. The OPEC action caused an economic upheaval throughout the developed countries of the world. An initial reaction to the price increases was a movement toward energy conservation and efficiency and a rapid upswing in oil and gas exploration. Several large projects were begun for the purpose of extracting and refining light oil from heavy oil and from the extensive deposits of tar sand in western Canada, while the search for conventional sources took place primarily in the arctic and offshore on the Atlantic coast and in the Gulf of Mexico and the Gulf of St. Lawrence. These developments provided a strong economic stimulus and increased the demand for engineering manpower not only in the petroleum industry, but also in the manufacturing and building industries.

The OPEC action also created regional disharmonies. Alaska and western Canada, for example, with large reserves of oil, suddenly found themselves wealthy. Life also improved in Nova Scotia and Newfoundland thanks to the discovery of offshore oil and gas. In contrast, the manufacturing industries of Quebec and Ontario, textiles, clothing, footware, and other consumer products, faced increasingly vigorous competition from imports. As a result, a conflict arose in Canada between the central provinces, which used most of the oil, and the Atlantic and western provinces that produced it. The producers wanted to obtain the higher world oil price for their oil, while the consumers wanted cheaper production from domestic sources.

With the Vietnam War over and a prospect of abundant engineering job opportunities, the popularity of engineering studies improved. In the United States, the number of undergraduates in engineering, which had decreased from 293,242 in 1968 to 186,705 in 1973,[1] began a rapid and steady rise. Students flocked to engineering schools and undergraduate enrollments of all population groups increased significantly for the next decade. Academic entrance requirements rose, class sizes increased, and facilities were used to capacity. The demand for places increased so greatly that by the early 1980s, most engineering faculties in the United States and Canada imposed limitations on their enrollments for the first time. By 1983, undergraduate engineering enrollments in the United States reached an all-time high of 406,144, more than double the number a decade earlier. Similar growth occurred in Canada.

In 1979, the Iranian revolution produced a reduction in world oil supplies and a new upsurge in prices by OPEC and its competitors, such as Mexico. This time, however, the higher prices were coupled with a global oil glut brought on by conservation measures. As a result, there was a precipitous drop in economic activity. The consequence was a worldwide economic recession that was particularly deep and prolonged. In the United States, there were double-digit inflation and high unemployment, while in Canada, the economic slowdown and disagreements between the Canadian and Alberta governments regarding oil pricing caused much of the work on the energy megaprojects to be curtailed. By 1983, more than 1 million Canadians, including more than 8,000 of Canada's 115,000 professional engineers were out of work.[2]

The softening job market in engineering was coupled with a change in demographics. The peak of the baby boom at 18 years of age, the age at which most people graduate from high school and undertake engineering studies, occurred in

1979, and then the pool of high school graduates declined. The result was another significant change in engineering enrollments. Following ten years of spectacular growth, enrollments reached a peak in Canada in 1982 and in the United States the following year. Four years later, a gradual decline in engineering graduates began.

In both the United States and Canada, the economic recession of the late 1970s and early 1980s was followed by the longest continuous period of economic expansion in recent history. From 1982 to 1988, 20 million new jobs were created in the United States. There was significant growth in the defense industries, as the United States began to strengthen its defenses against possible military confrontation with the Soviet Union. Thanks to their strong economies, unemployment in most parts of the two countries declined to traditional levels.

Engineering enrollments, however, did not increase in either nation, as the number of 18-year olds continued to decline. The sizes of the college-age population in the two countries will begin to increase in the mid-1990s, after a 25 percent decline from the early 1980s. Then enrollments are expected to increase once again. In the United States, a rising proportion of the 18–21-year-old population will be underrepresented minorities and women.

Women in Engineering

The last quarter of a century has witnessed a significant change in the people choosing to study and practice engineering. There has been a dramatic rise in the number of women and members of minority groups who have entered the profession. Although women and minorities have participated in engineering since the nineteenth century, their numbers remained small until the last 25 years or so.

As recently as 1970, only 358[3] women earned bachelor's degrees in engineering, accounting for a mere 0.8 percent of the degrees awarded. Then during the decades of the 1970s and 1980s, the number of women participating in the profession rose continually and rapidly. In 1987, 11,675 women in the United States received engineering bachelor's degrees, before a demographic decline in the number of 18-year-olds caused a drop in both male and female enrollments. By 1990, women comprised about eight percent of the engineering workforce in the United States, 16.5 percent of the full-time undergraduates, and 17.7 percent of the freshmen in engineering.

The increasing presence of women in the profession appears to be having an effect on the specialties chosen by students. Experience has shown that when women enter engineering programs, they select different disciplines than men. In 1990, for example, in the United States, women were awarded 15.4 percent of the engineering bachelor's degrees. However, they accounted for one-quarter to 40 percent of the degrees in materials, systems, industrial, chemical, biomedical, and

252. *The 1970s saw many more women enter engineering schools. In 1976, the first women were admitted to the U.S. Air Force Academy.*

253. *Women quickly became a regular sight in engineering schools, as in this chemistry laboratory at Cooper Union, where Professor Rebecca LaRue confers with students in 1988.*

254. *Women became more numerous at the École Polytechnique de Montreal and other Canadian engineering schools in the late 1980s.*

environmental engineering. In contrast, they accounted for only one-eighth to one-eighteenth of the degrees in electrical, mechanical, aerospace, petroleum, and marine engineering.[4]

Women's choices in engineering appear, so far, to be oriented toward disciplines that affect people more directly or are linked to the quality of life. Their engineering interests appear to be satisfied by subjects that are rooted in nature, as are the biological, physiological, and environmental sciences, rather than subjects that deal with invented or constructed technologies.

In the two decades of the 1970s and 1980s, women also made significant gains at the graduate level compared to white, non-Hispanic men. As late as 1973, 48 of the doctorates awarded by U.S. universities to U.S. citizens went to women and 2,800 went to white men. By 1990, women received 495 degrees, and white males about 2,200.

Since the entry of large numbers of women into engineering is a fairly recent trend, their impact on the field has not yet fully occurred. About 80 percent of the women who have earned baccalaureates in engineering received their degrees since 1980. As a result, the majority of women in the workforce are younger and less experienced than men. They occupy a smaller number of management positions in industry and are more likely to be assistant or associate professors in universities. As time progresses, and these ratios change, women will have an influence on the character as well on the numerical balance of engineering.

Enrollments of Minorities Increase

The decades of the 1970s and 1980s saw significant increases in the numbers of minority groups in U.S. engineering programs. The overall share of degrees awarded to African–Americans, Hispanic–Americans, Native–Americans, and Asian–Americans rose sharply at both the undergraduate and graduate levels. During the 20-year period, the minority share of bachelor's degrees in engineering more than doubled, and their share of doctorates awarded to U.S. citizens grew more than five times. The increase in the absolute numbers of individuals receiving degrees was even more dramatic.

In 1970, less than one percent of all new baccalaureate engineering degrees awarded in the United States went to African–American students. By 1990, 3.6 percent of these degrees went to this group. Similarly, in 1973, Hispanic–Americans accounted for 1.8 percent of all baccalaureate engineering awards. By 1990, degrees to Hispanics had risen to 3.2 percent.[5]

The rise of Asian–Americans in engineering was even greater. In 1973, 568 Asian–Americans received engineering baccalaureates and comprised 1.4 percent of the total number of engineering degrees awarded. In 1990, 5,989 Asian–Americans received degrees, accounting for 9.9 percent of the total.

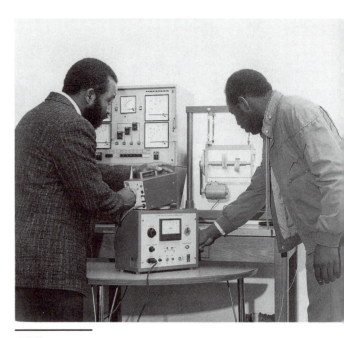

255. *In the 1980s, African–Americans began to increase in engineering, as seen in this view of the dynamics laboratory at the University of the District of Columbia.*

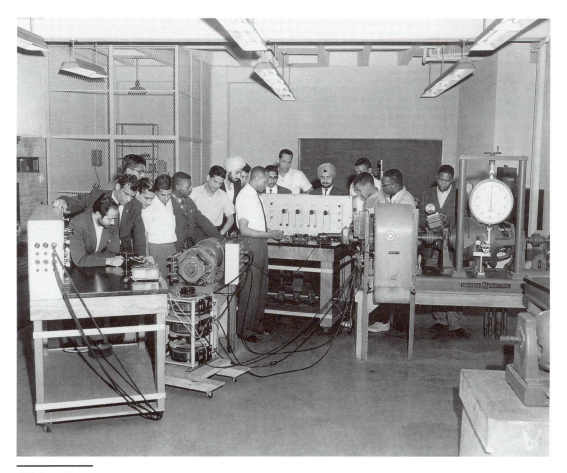

256. *There was great diversity in the backgrounds of students, as shown in this 1970 photo of Howard University's power systems laboratory.*

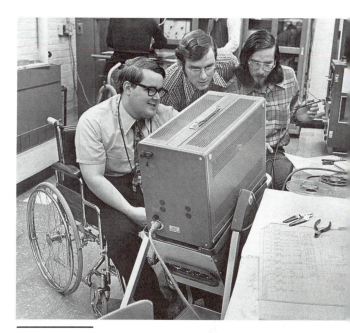

257. *In the late 1960s at Middlesex Community College, physically handicapped students, such as the one who with his laboratory partners is "trouble shooting" an audio tape machine, were given more opportunity for study.*

Minorities also made large gains at the graduate level. In 1973, of the 2,879 doctoral degrees in engineering awarded to United States citizens or permanent residents, 12 were awarded to African–Americans, 11 to Hispanic–Americans, and 54 to Asian–Americans. By 1980, the number of doctorates to nonforeign students awarded in the United States had declined to 1,769. But the minority share had increased, with African–Americans being awarded 19, Hispanic–Americans 25, and Asian–Americans 154. Over the next decade, doctoral degrees awarded to United States citizens and permanent residents increased once again, totaling 2,775 in 1990. While this was not quite as many degrees as received in 1973, the portion to minorities increased significantly. African–Americans received 36 doctoral degrees, Hispanic–Americans received 53, and Asian–Americans received 300.[6]

Enrollments of minority groups at both the undergraduate and graduate levels continued to rise through 1990, even as the total engineering enrollment of United States citizens declined in the period 1983–1990. In 1990, African–Americans and Hispanic–Americans constituted 12 percent of the full-time undergraduate students and 15 percent of the freshmen in engineering, and 6 percent of the graduate students. Asian–Americans accounted for 10 percent of the undergraduate enrollments and 12 percent of the graduate.

The choices minorities make differ from those of women. Hispanic–Americans are distributed among the engineering disciplines in approximately the same proportions as all students. African–Americans are distributed likewise, with perhaps a slight preference for electrical and industrial engineering. Asian–Americans, however, show a clear preference for electrical engineering, with almost half of all Asian–Americans choosing this as a major. It is clear that minorities, like women, will continue to gain a greater share of the degrees in engineering and become a more sizeable part of the engineering workforce. While their presence will make for a more diverse group, it is not expected to change the disciplinary balance in the field.

258. *Students learned about material testing equipment from Helen L. Plants, professor of theoretical and applied mechanics at West Virginia University.*

Changing Patterns of Study

Until about 40 years ago, engineering education was vocationally rather than scientifically oriented. Then a fundamental transformation occurred. Since the Second World War, the educational emphasis has shifted from engineering practice to fundamental principles and engineering science. In the 1970s and 1980s, there was another important program development with an increased emphasis given to communications and management skills, and to environmental and social issues. These changes occurred as a direct response to the needs of industry and the concerns of society.

The shifts in numbers was accompanied by changes in emphasis in enrollment among disciplines. In Canada, until about 1980, civil engineering was popular because the energy-related projects had significant civil engineering components. As the energy costs began to have a negative impact on the nation's balance of payments, governments began to emphasize industrial development in areas that had a high potential for export earnings, such as electronics, communications, advanced materials, and computer-aided design and manufacturing. As a result, enrollments in electrical and in mechanical engineering, and in several newly established computer engineering programs grew rapidly. On the other hand, as prices for minerals declined during the eighties, so did enrollments in mining, geological, and chemical engineering. These fluctuations in numbers and emphasis made it difficult for engineering faculties to cope with the demand.

Along with the shifts in enrollments, students took longer periods of time to complete their undergraduate engineering studies. Engineering programs, which were designed to be and traditionally had been completed in four years, now required from 4½ to 5 years to complete.[7] This lengthening of time was the result of a number of causes. Partially, it was due to the enrollment crunch and the difficulties students had in scheduling all of the required courses in a timely manner. More time was also needed because of the increasing difficulty of engineering courses, as more and more material was being covered in the same number of courses. And partially, it was due to the increased pressures on faculty members to seek federal grants, conduct research, and publish, leaving them little time to work with undergraduate students. The situation was similar in both the United States and Canada.

The increasing complexity of engineering caused some leaders in the profession to consider requiring five years for a baccalaureate degree in engineering. This had been tried in the past, but without success. After World War II, the University of Minnesota, Ohio State, Cornell, and Dartmouth all introduced five-year bachelor's programs, but each reverted to a four-year program because of its inability to attract students of high academic quality in sufficient numbers. As long as employers offered similar starting salaries to graduates of four- and five-year programs, there was little incentive for students to spend an additional year in school to receive the same level of credential.

Other leaders proposed retaining the baccalaureate program at four years, but making the master's degree the first recognized professional degree in engineering. This did not gain wide acceptance as many employers of engineers preferred hiring a person graduating in four years, and then providing additional company training as necessary. With the strong interest in retaining multiple purposes for engineering education—as a general education for people to enter other occupations, for immediate employment, and as preparation for graduate study—it is unlikely that the length of engineering programs will be increased.

259. *At Ryerson Polytechnical Institute co-op students in chemical engineering in 1990 received 20 months of paid, curriculum-related experience in industry as they pursued a bachelor's degree.*

Increased Emphasis on Research

Research has been a part of engineering education since the early part of the century. The dual tasks of investigation and imparting knowledge have been integral components of effective engineering teaching. However, since 1970, with a rise in support from all sources, there has been a tremendous increase in the involvement of universities in research.

In 1970, the ASEE reported that at its 201 member colleges and universities, 9,095 of the 16,247 full-time faculty members were engaged in separately budgeted research activities. They spent $288 million, of which $220 million was provided by the federal government.[8] In 1990, 226 U.S. colleges and universities reported that 13,826 of the 20,849 full-time faculty members were engaged in separately budgeted research and spent $2.4 billion.[9] Of this amount, $1.5 billion was provided by the federal government.

Today, colleges and universities perform directly about half of the basic research in science and engineering supported by the federal government. In addition, they administer the federally funded research and development centers, which are closely linked to the government's mission agencies that fund work in materials, defense, high-speed computing, environment, and many other areas. Clearly, academic institutions have become very significant research performers in the United States and, in many ways, have become the research arms of government agencies.

While federal support of engineering research in universities increased almost sevenfold between 1970 and 1990, funding from other sources increased even more rapidly. State and local government funding increased from $23 million in 1970 to $294 million in 1990, while business and industry increased from $21 million to $418 million over the same period. The role of the universities in research has become so great that the most heavily supported, about 170 universities, which perform about 90 percent of all academic research in science and engineering, have become known as research-intensive universities.

The close relationship that has evolved between the universities and the federal government has resulted in both benefits and problems. The external support has provided funding for upgrading facilities and purchasing modern equipment. Faculty who are engaged in frontier research bring up-to-date knowledge to their teaching, while students who participate in leading-edge investigations develop enhanced research skills that they later bring to the work force.

But as universities became more dependent upon governmental support of their research, with federal resources being more constrained and the rising costs for equipment, facilities, and personnel to do research, there were increasing pressures on the universities. As its support grew, the government increased its demand for accountability and efficiency, and imposed greater regulation, including restrictions on expenditures of federal funds, certificates of compliance with federal

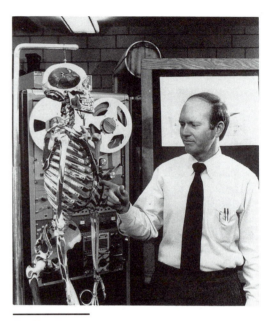

260. *In a continuing concern for people, engineers established programs in bioengineering. Charles Stanley, a mechanical engineering faculty member at West Virginia University, was explaining his research in 1983.*

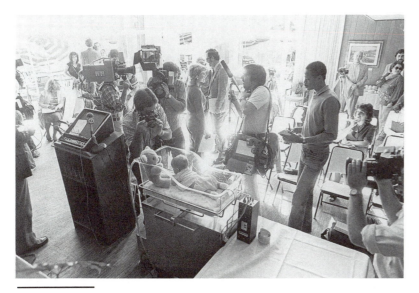

261. *In 1980, UCLA's Crump Institute for Medical Engineering displayed the isolette chamber for assisting premature babies in breathing, to reduce fatalities and disorders among newborns.*

263. *Cornell University established a submicron facility in 1978 for studying the properties of materials.*

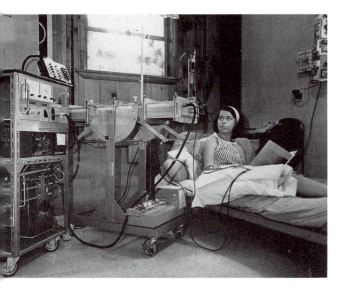

262. *At the University of Washington, mechanical engineers in 1971 helped develop an artificial kidney dialysis machine that could be used for treatment at home.*

264. *At UCLA, electrical engineering professor Frank Chen was studying lasers in 1979.*

265. *In a modern machine shop at the University of Vermont, students learned to use a numerically-controlled milling machine.*

statutes, and oversight to determine costs and monitor expenditures. The government also began to use criteria, such as economic payoffs, participation of underrepresented groups, and an expansion of the number of universities performing research, in addition to the overall excellence of the proposed research as a basis for making awards.

As the competition for funds became more intense, universities, in turn, began to use political influence to circumvent the competitive award procedures, possibly compromising their commitment to excellence. Further, in an effort to expand their research capabilities beyond what the federal government could provide, universities began to seek support from foreign sources, thus creating a concern that they were providing knowledge generated with U.S. government subsidies to foreign competitors of American firms.

Many people believe the delicate balance between education and research was being skewed by the strong emphasis on research. The reward system in many universities tilted in favor of research performance. The undergraduate teaching mission was deemphasized resulting in a drop in the individual attention that the students need from faculty members to develop. Some people admit that there was an imbalance, but that the huge benefits that have flowed from the emphasis on research far outweighed the distortions.

The situation has not developed to the same degree in Canada, to a large extent because the Canadian government provided much less support. In the United

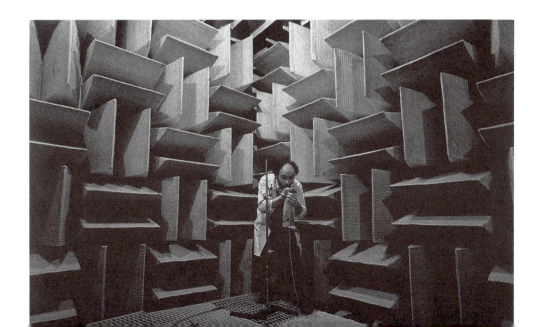

266. *An anechoic chamber, allowing absolutely no echos, was constructed at the École Polytechnique de Montreal in 1981 for acoustic research.*

States, defense spending, which supports a great deal of engineering research and development, is about three times the rate of Canada. In 1978, the Canadian government separated the National Research Council's "in house" research function from its program of postgraduate fellowships and university research grants. The latter was assigned to the newly formed Natural Sciences and Engineering Research Council. As a result of the separation and lower levels of funding, the government support for graduate education and university research was less influenced by the government's research priorities. In fact, in the 1980s, there was an outcry from scientists and engineers about the lack of government support, but the support increased somewhat when people realized that many of Canada's best students were pursuing the doctorate in the United States.

267. *Students use a modern chemistry lab at the Université Laval in 1985.*

Foreign Students in the United States and Canada

The number of foreign nationals receiving graduate degrees from U.S. and Canadian engineering schools rose dramatically between 1970 and 1990. The percentage of engineering master's degree students in Canada who were foreign students on temporary visas rose from 20 percent to 36 percent between 1972 and 1982. At the doctoral level, the change was even more dramatic, increasing from 23 percent to 55 percent.

In the United States in 1970, foreign nationals accounted for 505 or 14 percent of the 3,620 doctoral degrees awarded. By 1990, they received 2,649 or 49 percent of the 5,424 degrees granted. The large increase in degrees to foreign nationals compensated for the decline in degrees received by U.S. citizens and permanent residents, which dropped from 3,115 in 1970 to 1,768 in 1980. This trend caused significant concern in the United States, as it became increasingly difficult to meet the need for doctoral graduates in both the defense industries, where U.S. citizenship often is a condition of employment, and the engineering schools.

The United States and Canada reacted differently to the rising numbers of foreign nationals in their universities. United States engineering schools welcomed foreign students, who helped maintain graduate enrollments, provided assistance for research, and the approximately one-half of the doctoral graduates who remained in the United States after graduation contributed to the nation's economy. Asians, in particular, now account for some 70 percent of all foreign doctoral students and have been important for staffing the high-technology companies in Silicon Valley. Of the 10,000 Taiwanese who earned PhDs in the United States, four out of five have remained in America, including several eventual Nobel Prize winners.

While the U.S. did nothing to discourage foreign nationals from enrolling, it provided incentives in the form of government and corporate-sponsored fellowships to entice more Americans to study engineering at the graduate level. The result was that the number of doctorates awarded to U.S. citizens and permanent residents increased to 2,775 in 1990.

While there were benefits to U.S. universities and industry by the large enrollment of foreign students, their presence also caused problems. Since federally funded fellowships were not available to foreign nationals, many foreign graduate students were assigned to university-funded teaching assistantships. The use of teaching assistants with limited English skills or from cultures where expectations of women differ from those of the American culture drew a great deal of public criticism. Some foreign students did not communicate well with American-born undergraduate students, nor did they serve as adequate role models to induce these students to continue on to graduate school.

Further, as many of the foreign doctoral students could not work upon graduation in industries that were related to defense work, they sought positions in

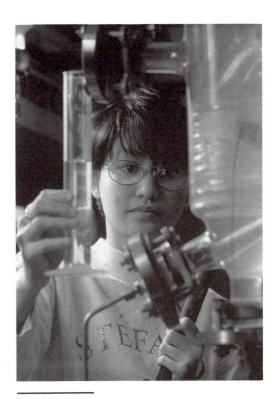

268. *At the University of New Haven, the laboratory was a place for experiential learning.*

university faculties. By the mid- to late 1980s, fully half of the new faculty appointments in engineering were to foreign nationals trained at the PhD level in American universities. As these individuals advance in seniority and take on more administrative authority the policies of the engineering schools may well be affected.

In contrast to the United States, most engineering faculties in Canada, in the late 1970s, began to impose severe limits on the number of foreign undergraduate students through either quotas or differential academic fees. These policies had a direct effect on enrollments at both the undergraduate and graduate levels. In 1988–89, foreign students made up 26 percent of the graduate enrollments in Canada, compared to 40 percent in 1982.

The issue of foreign influences in Canada was not limited to non-Canadians. Since the mid-1800s, the country has had a minority of French-speakers who were fiercely loyal to their heritage. From 1950 to 1970, the percentage of Quebec residents whose mother tongue was French decreased slightly from 83 percent to 81 percent. This alarmed many of them who could picture the French institutions being overwhelmed by English-speakers. The result was a movement to create *deux nations* in a single state. Quebec pressed for equality with the rest of Canada, with vastly increased powers inside and outside of the federal government. French became the official language and to a large extent the sole language of Quebec. New Brunswick officially became bilingual, and Ontario expanded French-language rights.

By 1987, the conflict for a distinct French society had become so intense that an accord was signed by the provincial premiers at Meech Lake. The accord restored the constitutional veto to all provinces, identified Quebec as a distinct society, increased provincial powers in immigration, restricted the federal government's spending powers, and provided a place for Quebec in nominating Supreme Court justices.[10] With Quebec separating the eastern from the western provinces, and the recent North American Free Trade Agreement, there is developing an increasing economic involvement between the United States and Canada that is weakening the necessity for East–West trade within Canada.

Industry–University Interaction

In the 1950s, most engineering faculty members were appointed for a nine-month period and would supplement their income by taking summer jobs in industry. These positions provided them with experience in the practice of engineering, with which they could make relevant their classroom presentations. As research and graduate work expanded during the 1960s and 1970s, the faculty member's summers were taken up by those activities. Although high-level consulting was encouraged, young faculty members faced strong pressure to secure research contracts and to publish. As a consequence, many of them rarely found time or incentive for industrial, "practical" engineering experience.

This began to change, although slowly, in the late 1970s and 1980s, as the United States and Canada became concerned about the Japanese "economic miracle." The prevailing notion today is that if the nations are to remain competitive in world markets, government, industry, and educational institutions must cooperate in developing and exploiting new technologies.

As Canada began to promote greater industrial development, new engineering schools were established. In northern New Brunswick, the Acadian population felt a need for French-language instruction in specialties that would accelerate the industrial development of the region. As a result, programs were established at the Université de Moncton in civil engineering in 1968 and in industrial engineering in 1972.

To meet the unique needs of Newfoundland as a cold-water, maritime region, the province's first and only engineering school was created in 1969 at the Memorial University of Newfoundland. In addition to programs in civil, electrical, and mechanical engineering, the university established the Centre for Cold Ocean Resources Engineering in 1975 and Canada's first program in shipbuilding engineering in 1979.

Engineering education continued to expand, as Simon Fraser University, which was established in 1965 to serve the lower part of British Columbia, added engineering in 1983. In 1984, the University of Victoria added engineering programs, first in electrical and computer engineering, and later in mechanical engineering.

Programs now are being developed in both the United States and Canada to promote a wide array of industry–university interactions. Engineering faculty members are being encouraged to spend leaves in industry engaging in research and development and to pursue industrial contracts for research. Well-qualified engineers in industry are encouraged to spend time working in the university environment. The universities also have begun to promote entrepreneurship and, in some cases, spin off high-technology companies. If anything, some concerns are being expressed that universities should be cautious and not serve as industrial laboratories, but rather should continue to focus on more fundamental research.

In the mid-1980s, the United States became concerned about its economic competitive position, particularly with regard to Japan. There was a consensus that while America was still leading in the development of new knowledge, that U.S. industry was too slow in turning research into marketable products. As a result, government agencies, lead by the National Science Foundation, began to emphasize closer working relationships between universities and industries and between universities and the national government laboratories. The National Science Foundation began to provide long-term, large-scale support for university-based engineering research centers. The centers were supported jointly by the government and corporate partners, with the aim to focus university research toward industrially relevant areas and improve the transfer time from laboratory to factory. While very successful in their approach, there was an outcry from the scientific community, which felt that with an increasing portion of the National Science Foundation's budget being devoted to industrial-driven ideas, there was less funding for cutting-edge research generated by individual researchers. There also was a concern that the universities might become so close to the industries that they would lose their independence and become too much like industrial research laboratories.

ASEE Expands Its Activities

As engineering education evolved during the 1970s and 1980s, the American Society for Engineering Education continued to provide leadership for the profession. It expanded its publication activities, carried on with the organizing of effective teaching institutes, and continued to conduct studies and issue reports on possible directions for the faculty and schools.

From its inception, the Society published a proceedings of the papers presented at its annual meeting. This continued for almost 20 years, until the early 1910s, when a monthly magazine was created, which, in 1916, was given the name *Engineering Education.* The *Proceedings* then were modified to focus almost exclusively on the business matters of the Society. In 1924, the two publications merged and the *Proceedings* became the bound set of monthly issues of the magazine. As a result, after that time, very few of the papers presented at the annual conference were published and made available to the general membership of the Society or to other engineering educators. Then in the 1970s, ASEE made significant strides toward establishing a more extensive literature of engineering education. Joseph M. Biedenbach, of the University of South Carolina, and Lawrence P. Grayson took charge of conference publications, and in the next 20 years they edited over 50 proceedings for the Society.

The first development occurred in 1971, when the Education Society of the Institute of Electrical and Electronics Engineers established the Frontiers in Education Conference (FIE). Its purpose was to provide a forum for people to discuss the latest developments in engineering instruction. It soon was evident that most of the presentors and attendees at the meeting were members of the ASEE. In 1973, the Education Society and ASEE's Educational Research and Methods Division entered into an agreement to cosponsor the FIE. Over the next two decades, the meeting was held successfully in all parts of the United States, as well as in Canada, England, and Austria, and the proceedings of the meeting grew from an 85-page document to over 850 pages a year.

In 1976, four ASEE divisions—Continuing Engineering Studies Division, Cooperative Education Division, Engineering Technology Division, and Relations With Industry Division—in cooperation with the Technical College Council, ini-

269. *The American Society for Engineering Education continued to meet the needs of its members in the 1970s and 1980s. In 1969, Leslie B. Williams (seated) who had become Executive Director chats with his predecessor W. Leighton Collins.*

270. *The banquet at the 1972 Annual Conference at Texas Tech University was a festive occasion.*

tiated the College Industry Education Conference (CIEC) to bring together people from universities and industry to discuss problems of mutual interest. This conference also has been successful in publishing a proceedings of its annual meeting.

After over a 60-year hiatus, the ASEE reinstituted the proceedings of its annual conference in 1978. This volume of papers presented at the meeting has been published annually since then. These three sets of proceedings have contributed substantially to the literature, making a huge number of papers on all aspects of engineering education widely and permanently available.

In addition to the proceedings, several ASEE divisions initiated journals, at various times during the second half of the twentieth century, to print papers and editorials of interest to their division members.

As enrollments increased significantly in the late 1970s, faculty shortages developed. In 1981, the ASEE and the American Association of Engineering Societies undertook a two-year study of the engineering faculty situation. Upon completion of this effort, the ASEE Board of Directors broadened the study to include all factors affecting the quality of engineering, with a concentration on the excellence of the faculty. It termed the new activity the Quality in Engineering Education Project.

271. *The Annual Conference was a chance to bring together leaders of industry, academia, and government. Participating in the Main Plenary Session at the 1990 meeting, from left to right were Nebraska Governor Kay A. Orr, GM President Robert Stempl, US West President Richard McCormick, ASEE President Lawrence P. Grayson, IBM Senior Vice President Patrick Toole, and University of Nebraska Chancellor Martin A. Massengale.*

The project's conclusions emphasized that teaching is a primary function of a university or college and that effective teaching should be an essential criterion for appointment or advancement. It was recommended that hiring institutions provide guidance and assistance to their faculty by offering preservice and inservice workshops for new faculty members.

The report noted that the then-current system for graduate engineering education was capable of significant expansion to meet the needs for more doctoral students. About one-sixth of the engineering schools produce about three-quarters of the doctorates granted in engineering, and almost half of the doctoral-granting schools produced fewer than 10 doctorates each in 1983. Part of the challenge was, and is, to make engineering faculty positions more attractive so that some of the best-qualified U.S. students wish to enter a system that leads to faculty appointment. One area that needed attention was teaching assistantships. In the mid-1980s, about 44 percent of all teaching assistantships were held by foreign nationals, many of whom had inadequate English-language skills.[11]

In response to the rapidly changing environment for engineering education and practice, the ASEE Board of Directors in 1986 appointed a task force and charged it to review the state of engineering education and identify ways of addressing the most important problem areas. Since the problems were well known, the task force concentrated on recommendations. The group considered the full spectrum of education, from precollege through graduate school. It called its report *A National Action Agenda for Engineering Education.*[12]

Recognizing that the four-year undergraduate curriculum cannot be expanded indefinitely to include an ever-increasing amount of technical and nontechnical subject matter deemed necessary for an engineering career, the task force recommended that the curriculum be designed to provide the knowledge base and capability for career-long learning. It suggested that the objectives and purposes of undergraduate laboratory instruction be rethought and more cost-effective approaches developed, and that engineering design, leading to the manufacturing and construction process, should be given a more central role in undergraduate curricula.

At the graduate level, it recommended that more degree programs should be directed toward engineering practice, rather than research, with more of a base provided for design, development, and manufacturing. Incentives should be developed to encourage more highly qualified U.S. students to seek the PhD and pursue careers as engineering faculty members. Since one's learning cannot stop with the awarding of a degree, an integrated system should be developed to provide high-quality, career-long educational opportunities for both faculty members and practicing engineers. Further, programs in mathematics and science, which prepare and motivate the nation's precollege youth to seek engineering careers, must be strengthened.

272. *At Washington State University, students and faculty tested a beam in a reaction frame at the Wood Materials and Engineering Laboratory in the 1980s.*

273. *At Dartmouth University's Thayer School, this student was learning about materials in 1979.*

274. *At the University of Alaska, students created runways with geotextiles.*

276. *By 1988, there was an increased emphasis on manufacturing processes, as seen in this photograph of the Manufacturing Systems Engineering Laboratory at the University of Wisconsin-Madison.*

275. *In the late 1960s students at the University of Hawaii at Manoa studied the strength of materials based on its microstructure.*

277. *In 1985, electrical engineering students at the State University of New York at Binghamton were learning microprocessor applications.*

278. *A midshipman investigated the characteristics of a ship's propeller operating at high speeds at the U.S. Naval Academy.*

279. *At the University of Kansas, graduate students in aerospace engineering ran wind tunnel tests to determine the influence of forebody shape on vortex flow.*

280. *In 1992, students and faculty at The College of Staten Island conducted experiments on the wake of an airfoil.*

281. *At the U.S. Air Force Academy, cadets conducted tests in wind tunnels that created air flows from subsonic to Mach 4.*

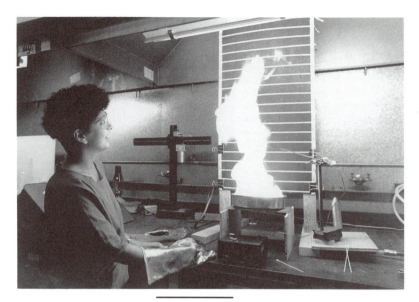

282. *A graduate student performs a combustion experiment in the fire sciences laboratory at Worcester Polytechnic Institute, which is the only school to offer both master's and doctoral degrees in fire protection engineering.*

283. *There is nothing like experience. In 1971, astronaut Neil Armstrong, first man to walk on the moon, accepted a position as university professor of aerospace engineering at the University of Cincinnati.*

284. *Civil engineering students at the University of California at Los Angeles participated in a 1988 building design competition.*

286. *At the University of California at Berkeley, faculty and students in 1972 gathered to watch the final load test on a one-third scale model of a curved box girder bridge.*

285. *At George Brown College, students were taught about refrigeration systems.*

287. *M. Dayne Aldridge, professor of electrical engineering at West Virginia University, tested a system he developed in the early 1970s to detect methane gas and air flow patterns in coal mines.*

288. *Cadets at Norwich University were learning about military bridge construction in 1970.*

289. *Students and faculty at the University of Hawaii at Manoa in 1982 were investigating a forced circulation solar water heating system.*

290. *Students at the University of Nevada, Reno conducted heat transfer experiments.*

291. *At Ryerson Polytechnical Institute, the electrical technology faculty erected a 35-foot vertical axis wind turbine to conduct research into wind as an energy source.*

292. *Since conventional oil recovery leaves much of the fuel in the ground, the Enhanced Oil Recovery Institute established in 1985 at the University of Wyoming has been investigating new approaches in petroleum engineering.*

295. *At the Institute of Northern Engineering at the University of Alaska Fairbanks, water samples were taken from a glacial kettle pond for study.*

293. *The environment has become an important concern in many engineering schools. In the late 1970s, civil engineering students at Texas A&M University were studying clean-up techniques in conjunction with an oil spill in the Gulf of Mexico.*

294. *Students collected soil samples at Michigan State University's Department of Civil and Environmental Engineering in 1991.*

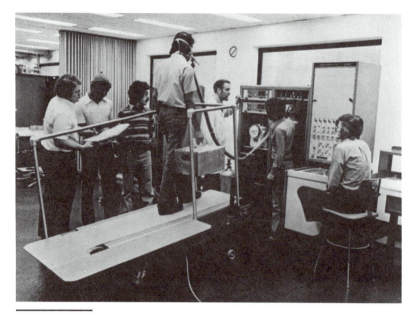

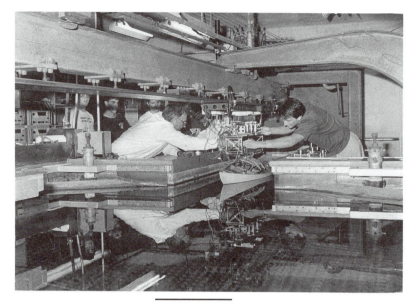

296. *Students in industrial engineering at the State University of New York at Buffalo worked in a human factors laboratory in the 1980s.*

297. *At Webb Institute, students tested models of boat or ship hulls in the 93-foot long tank, which allowed them to subject the models to various artificially created wave conditions.*

298. *Researchers in coastal and oceanographic engineering at the University of Florida in 1975 installed an instrument platform to record wave and erosion data in the field near Brevard County.*

299. *At the University of California at Los Angeles, researchers in 1978 used an ergometeric device to study the energy exerted by underwater work.*

300. *At the University of Hawaii at Manoa, a scuba diver in the early 1980s inspected an artificial reef constructed by ocean engineering students. Its purpose was to increase the local fish population.*

301. *In the early 1980s, the engineering school at the University of Michigan launched a balloon to study the ozone hole as part of its work in atmospheric, oceanic, and space sciences.*

302. *Where else but at the University of Alaska Fairbanks would someone be downloading data from a data logger buried in snow on the state's North Slope.*

303. *The Center for Advanced Training in Engineering and Computer Science at the University of Colorado at Boulder used microwave-delivered video with interactive audio to bring technical and engineering management courses to working professionals at their job sites.*

304. *At Iowa State University, engineering science and mechanics professor Anna Pate used acoustical methods to determine the quality of seeds in 1986.*

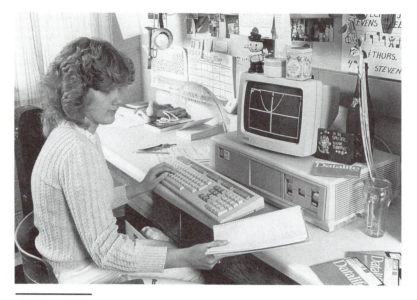

307. *By 1988, computers became a regular part of the dorm furnishings at Stevens Institute of Technology.*

305. *Computers are an integral part of engineering education. At Seattle University, students and faculty in the 1980s began using computer-aided tools to design electronic circuits.*

306. *In 1991, a computer classroom at Union College was used to teach a course in bridge design.*

308. *At the University of Puerto Rico-Mayagez, students raced their solar-powered car in the 1990 General Motors Sunrayce.*

310. *Students at Lakehead University teased 2007 miles per imperial gallon of gasoline out of their vehicle in the Shell Fuelathon Fuel Economy Competition.*

309. *Students have always been intrigued by using the devices they build. Competing with vehicles is very popular, as students at Texas Tech demonstrated with their participation in the 1992 Mini Baja.*

311. *At the University of California, Riverside, robot sumo wrestling was a popular event in 1990.*

312. *At Webb Institute, students tested their human-powered watercraft in the Long Island Sound.*

313. *A UCLA student launched a "Loony Lander" in the 1987 Egg Drop Competition. The lander survived the four-story fall without cracking the raw egg inside.*

314. *What began as Engineers' Day has become Engineers Week at UCLA. It is the occasion of an annual campus carnival, as shown in this 1985 photo.*

315. *At Michigan Technological University, students have fun in the snow.*

316. *Clemson University students expressed their thoughts by rearranging the letters on Earle Hall, the chemical engineering building on campus.*

317. *Newly graduated and commissioned midshipmen at the Naval Academy engage in an old tradition.*

CHAPTER **E** I G H T

. . . . . . .Engineering education is moving into a new era of development as a result of major changes occurring in economic, social, and political systems throughout the world, in addition to rapid advances in technology. The cold war is over. The Soviet Union has ceased to exist and has divided into a series of independent nations, each striving for economic development. Europe is evolving into a single, barrier-free economy. The nations of the Pacific Rim, led by Japan and closely followed by Korea, Taiwan, Hong Kong, and Singapore are experiencing rapid economic growth as a result of a commitment to technology and aggressive trade policies. And the United States, Canada, and Mexico have signed an agreement creating a North American Free Trade Zone. Military competition among nations is being replaced by economic competition; economic competition is being driven by technological competition.

In the past few years, there have been significant advances in robotics, high-performance computing, imaging technologies, semiconductors, superconductivity, space-based astronomy, and chemical separation technologies. Computers are revolutionizing ev-

261

erything, from communications, manufacturing, and molecular modeling to meteorology, agriculture, and medical diagnosis and treatment. Engineering is blending with computer science, chemistry, agricultural, and the medical and biomedical sciences to form new fields, such as urban engineering, geochemistry, environmental engineering, biotechnology, and space engineering. These new fields, along with advances in materials, instrumentation, conceptual and analytical techniques, and methods of processing and displaying information and data are forcing change in the content and scope of engineering education.

The effects of these advances may be as significant, and disruptive, as those that brought about the Industrial Revolution. Old industries are being reshaped and new ones are being created. Some jobs are disappearing, and others requiring different skills are evolving. There is a shift from a predominance on goods production to information, from manufacturing to service. Increasingly, engineers are being called upon to design and deliver products, systems, and services for global marketplaces.

New Roles for Engineering Education

Engineering schools, which always have been viewed as preparing the technical work force needed for industrial development, are becoming active participants in economic growth. Today, many universities in the United States and Canada are involved in securing and licensing patents, creating research parks, leasing incubator facilities, and even providing venture capital for companies. Students are learning concepts like *quality* and *reliability,* gaining more experience with design and being introduced to the principles and practices of manufacturing.

National priorities in the United States and Canada have begun to shift away from defense and more toward an unfolding array of human and social issues of enormous complexity and seriousness—how to control the proliferation of nuclear arms, how to cope with worldwide environmental concerns while still promoting economic growth, how to erase the problems of housing, hunger, and health. As a result, there has been a decrease in government funds available for military and space activities and an increase in funds for applying science and technology to domestic concerns, such as housing, transportation, health care, education, the environment, and energy. It is clear that engineering graduates of the future will be more concerned not only with technical developments, but also with the impact of those developments on society.

It has been usual for the engineer to focus primarily on the technical aspects of the job, leaving its moral and social implications to politicians, social scientists, and others. This attitude, however, is changing. While the design of a system to meet a set of requirements may be fairly straightforward technically, the human setting

318. *Jim Davis used audiographic tele-conferencing at the University of Wisconsin-Madison to interact with Japanese students in five states in 1991.*

into which the system will be placed can have profound implications for the design of the system. Engineers in the future must be sensitive to the societal and political forces that cause shifts in public policy and will have to deal with important non-technical constraints that arise out of legal, economic, aesthetic, and human considerations. They must be willing and have the ability to address questions of *what* should be done and *why* it should be done, in addition to how to do it.

Engineering has always been a form of public service, aimed at meeting the needs of people by conceiving, developing, and implementing solutions to technical problems of concern to society. It is the degree of interaction and the greater perceived impact that engineering solutions are having on people, however, that have increased dramatically in recent years. Technology today is affecting virtually every aspect of life in North America, and indeed in the world, from a country's gross national product (GNP), foreign trade and balance of payments, to the growth of cities and the production of goods and national defense, to the tallying of individual credit balances and tax returns. More than ever before, engineering is

319. *Ocean engineering students at Texas A&M University work with a submarine project at the Offshore Technology Research Center.*

being viewed as a service to society, taking into account the interaction of the technical with the social, physical, cultural, and political environments.

Programs are being developed at numerous universities, some at the senior level, others at the master's degree level, to acquaint the student with political and social processes and values, the structure of public systems, economics, social sciences, law, public health, rural, urban, and international development, civil welfare, business administration, environmental design, and public policy. These programs currently involve faculty from many parts of the university and often incorporate problem-oriented interdisciplinary courses. However, all of them are attempting to make students more conscious of the obligation the engineer has to society and to enlarge their outlook to include the human aspect of their future work. Although these programs involve a minority of students at present, they are an indication of a changing direction.

For engineers to fulfill their role in improving society, they must have the ability to identify needs and the knowledge to effect solutions. They must have the courage to take risks and the ability to inspire confidence in their efforts. They must be able to express themselves clearly in words, as well as in mathematics, and must understand theory as a basis for practice. They must be just as interested in cost and ability to manufacture as in product performance, because engineering achievement is measured not only by how well something is done, but by how soon and for how little. They must understand the societal environment in which they work and recognize that developing a supportive public opinion is often as important in completing a major engineering project as is the underlying science.

The present trend in engineering education is toward an emphasis on general, rather than technical, educational values in undergraduate college work, followed by one or more years of graduate work for specialized training, periodically supplemented by continuing education throughout one's professional life. This trend will continue.

As a result, an undergraduate engineering education of the future will be broadly conceived. It will provide a firm foundation in mathematics and science, a working knowledge of the technology in a field of specialization, and an understanding of the social, cultural, and political context of our society gained through study of the social sciences and humanities. It will not provide a complete professional preparation, for the majority of engineering graduates actually put their training to the uses of a general education. Rather, an undergraduate education will provide the basis for continued education and self-development throughout his or her career.

Master's programs will be strengthened and made an end in themselves, rather than being viewed as an intermediate step toward the doctorate. Their orientation will allow students to learn in-depth the technology of their speciality and the elements of professional practice, including an emphasis on design, development, production, and economics.

Doctoral programs will continue to provide a firm understanding of the science and engineering fundamentals underlying a broad field of study and give opportunities for significant research to expand the frontiers of knowledge.

Postscript

The hallmarks of engineering education in America have been adaptability and stability. These seemingly incongruous qualities have blended very well to allow engineering schools to develop in response to national as well as local and regional needs.

Engineering education in America evolved from a combination of borrowed and indigenous elements, which in many ways reflected the character of the continent. The collegiate plan of organization and most of the traditions of the professoriate can be traced back to the older universities of England, which formed the models for the early arts colleges of the United States and Canada. Engineering curricula, which began in the United States almost a century before it started in Canada, were derived originally from French models, as was the concept of a professional school of engineering. Early approaches to the teaching of shop and manual arts were based on schooling in Russia, while the emphasis and methods of research and the model for graduate education came from Germany.

Although early developments in the United States were more adaptive than creative, in several respects, American schools have exercised conspicuous leadership. They pioneered in the introduction of laboratory instruction for the individual student as an integral part of the curriculum, in the provision of distinctive training in the economic and management phases of engineering, and in the development of cooperative education.

Engineering education was promoted initially to satisfy the needs of the military, but quickly developed as an effort to satisfy the civil needs of a rapidly growing country. Americans created land-grant colleges and engineering experiment stations to stress "the application of science to the common purposes of life"[1] and evolved the modern research university, blending advanced research with student instruction. Faculty and schools have been linked to industry and the community, through consulting, joint relationships, and the establishment of incubator facilities, among other activities.

As individual engineering schools were created to meet the needs of their respective regions, a variety of forms and settings evolved. There are free-standing independent institutions of technology, major colleges within broad-based state universities, developing colleges that are part of branch campuses, and departments or divisions within small, mostly independent liberal arts colleges. To cope with this diversity, American schools have assumed responsibility for setting minimum standards for engineering programs and assuring that they are met through voluntary, peer-controlled accreditation. This has created a system of engineering schools that are national in scope, but local in character.

Engineering schools have continued to display their adaptability to serve national and regional needs. They have demonstrated a willingness to change to meet military requirements in times of war and the needs of industry and the economy in times of peace. Engineering education, as a whole, has adopted a broad view toward national trends, with schools throughout the nation establishing curricula with similar goals and objectives, while simultaneously being highly responsive to local and regional differences. Strong programs in electronics have developed in California, coal mining in West Virginia, automotive engineering in Michigan, ocean engineering in Newfoundland, petroleum engineering in Texas, communications in Hawaii, and agricultural engineering in Iowa, among many other examples.

In contrast to the variety of changes that have occurred in content and approach during the last century, engineering curricula have maintained a remarkable stability. In their more essential qualities, engineering curricula today are what they were one hundred years ago. In form, they retain the structure of the typical undergraduate course, with a "major" or field of concentration, a requirement of "breadth," and a system of electives. Engineering education has evolved as a distinctive type of college program based primarily on the principles and applications of physical sciences and mathematics — with associated studies in humanities and social sciences — intended to precede and supplement, but not supplant, an extended period of on-the-job learning. The undergraduate education is assumed to provide the more general while the initial on-the-job development will provide the more specific, preparation for an engineering career. The numerous changes in curriculum content that have taken place in the course of a century do not invalidate these observations.

The stability and fundamental soundness of the core features of engineering curricula may be ascribed to the external review and vetting that the programs receive. In many disciplines, the university is accepted as the gatekeeper for the professions, but in engineering, the national associations and professional societies have taken the lead in analyzing the undergraduate degree programs, and they continually press to raise academic standards and modify course work to meet the changing needs of the country.

Impetus for curriculum reform comes from outside the university before it takes place within the institution. As a result, there are few, if any, branches of higher education that are more severely tested by objective realities, nor are there any in which the content of curricula is scrutinized more constantly and critically by the members of its profession for its relevance, in consequence of the rapid advance of knowledge and technical practice and the enforced limitations of time.

The interests in maintaining national standards while responding to the needs of a wide variety of industries for engineers create divergent demands for curriculum reform. The diversity among schools allows individual institutions to respond to the pressures in different ways in an attempt to meet the needs in their locales and enhance the desirability of their graduates on the job market. The vetting of engineering programs by the profession assures that all schools meet minimum standards of quality. The resulting forces create a progressive tension in which the schools, as a whole, respond well to the most pressing needs of industry and the nation's economy.

The twin characteristics of adaptability and stability will continue to serve engineering education well. In the twentieth century, engineering schools in the United States and Canada have met the needs created by four major wars, a worldwide depression, a post-World War II baby boom, and an explosion in scientific and technical developments. The recent vigorous economic competition among nations and growing concerns for the world's energy and environment create new reasons for change.

In recent decades, American and Canadian universities, through their programs of education, research, and scholarship, have become increasingly vibrant and important contributors to the process of economic development. In the coming decades, the universities' contributions to economic growth will require a great deal of both advanced education and knowledge-generating research. The pivotal issue for engineering education as it approaches the twenty-first century is to educate, initially and throughout their lives engineers from a diverse population pool, while maintaining the research emphasis to increase knowledge. Through its strength and adaptability, engineering education will succeed.

320. *American universities are beginning to expand to Europe. Georgia Institute of Technology was the first American university to offer a graduate engineering program in Europe leading to Master of Science and Ph.D. degrees, when Georgia Tech Lorraine opened in Metz, France in 1990.*

321. *At Rensselaer Polytechnic Institute, graduate students can design and test a microchip on a computer-aided design system at the Center for Integrated Electronics.*

322. *Students at East Tennesee State University use design software to study computer aided manufacturing in the school's Department of Technology.*

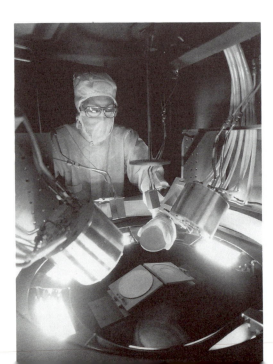

323. *At Texas A&M's Texas Engineering Experiment Station, industrial sponsors can join the Program for Automation in Manufacturing to help improve manufacturing processes such as automation, robotics, and quality assurance.*

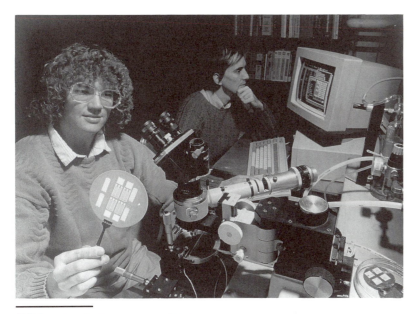

324. *At the University of Wisconsin-Madison, assistant professor Denice Denton examines a silicon wafer with test devices used to characterize polymer films.*

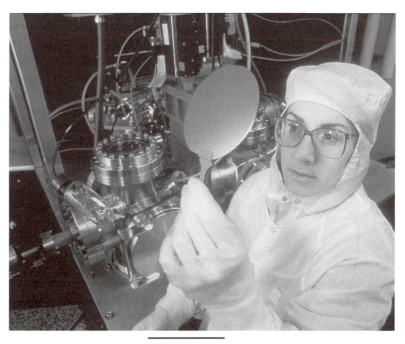

325. *Silicon wafers containing integrated electronic circuits are developed at the Center for Advanced Electronic Materials Processing at North Carolina State University.*

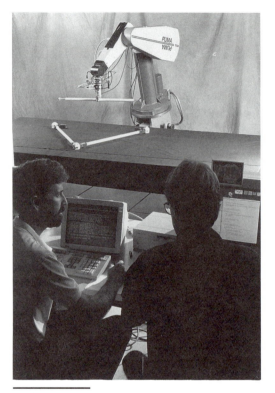

326. *At the University of California at Los Angeles, electrical engineering professor Kang Wang works in his laboratory with an ultra-high vacuum chamber that is used for the deposition of thin films by molecular beam epitaxy.*

327. *At the Rensselaer Polytechnic Institute/NASA Center for Intelligent Robotic Systems for Space Exploration, a robot arm is controlled by a special computer to assemble a structural truss for a space station.*

328. *In order to meet modern seismic safety standards and avoid the damage and loss of life sustained in the 1988 earthquake in the San Francisco Bay area, the University of California at San Diego successfully completed a large scale test that will be used to retrofit existing double-decked freeways in California.*

329. *Electrical engineering student Susan Casseday reviews data collected by the Doppler radar system at Colorado State University.*

330. *Students at the University of Kentucky examine electric current harmonics drawn from an utility grid by an adjustable speed drive.*

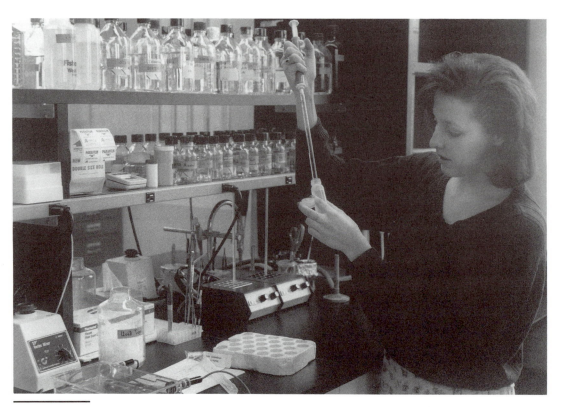

331. *At Worcester Polytechnic Institute, a senior conducts an experiment in recombinant DNA in the fast-growing department of biology and biotechnology.*

332. *At the University of Wisconsin-Madison, materials science and engineering professor Frank Worzala and graduate student Ann Redsten examine a prosthetic knee made of ion-implanted titanium.*

333. *Herman Weed, biomedical engineering professor at The Ohio State University, watches graduate student Alan Mortensen adjust a prototype chair designed to help wheelchair-bound passengers get around in an airplane.*

334. *The Colorado State University Solar Car crossing the finish line at the Indianapolis 500 during the General Motors Sunrayce USA contest in 1991.*

335. *Civil engineering students at the University of Hawaii at Manoa hold up their concrete canoe, which won the 1992 Pacific Southwest Regional Conference's competition.*

Name	Affiliation at Time of Assuming Office
DeVolson Wood, 1893–94	*Stevens Institute of Technology*
George F. Swain, 1894–95	*Massachusetts Institute of Technology*
Mansfield Merriman, 1895–96	*Lehigh University*
Henry T. Eddy, 1896–97	*University of Minnesota*
John B. Johnson, 1897–98	*Washington University*
Thomas C. Mendenhall, 1898–99	*Worcester Polytechnic Institute*
Ira O. Baker, 1899–1900	*University of Illinois*
Frank O. Marvin, 1900–01	*University of Kansas*
Robert Fletcher, 1901–02	*Dartmouth College*
Calvin M. Woodward, 1902–03	*Washington University*
C. Frank Allen, 1903–04	*Massachusetts Institute of Technology*
Fred W. McNair, 1904–05	*Michigan College of Mines*
Charles L. Crandall, 1905–06	*Cornell University*
Dugald C. Jackson, 1906–07	*Massachusetts Institute of Technology*
Charles S. Howe, 1907–08	*Case School of Applied Science*
Frederick E. Turneaure, 1908–09	*University of Wisconsin*
Henry S. Munroe, 1909–10	*Columbia University*
Arthur N. Talbot, 1910–11	*University of Illinois*
William G. Raymond, 1911–12	*State University of Iowa*
William T. Magruder, 1912–13	*The Ohio State University*
Gardner C. Anthony, 1913–14	*Tufts College*
Anson Marston, 1914–15	*Iowa State College of Agriculture and Mechanics Arts*
Henry S. Jacoby, 1915–16	*Cornell University*
George R. Chatburn, 1916–17	*University of Nebraska*
Milo S. Ketchum, 1917–18	*University of Colorado*
John F. Hayford, 1918–19	*Northwestern University*
Arthur M. Greene, Jr., 1919–20	*Rensselaer Polytechnic Institute*
Mortimer E. Cooley, 1920–21	*University of Michigan*
Charles F. Scott, 1921–22, 1922–23	*Yale University*
Perley F. Walker, 1923–24	*University of Kansas*
Andrey A. Potter, 1924–25	*Purdue University*
George B. Pegram, 1925–26	*Columbia University*
Ora M. Leland, 1926–27	*University of Minnesota*
Robert L. Sackett, 1927–28	*The Pennsylvania State College*
Dexter S. Kimball, 1928–29	*Cornell University*
Robert I. Rees, 1929–30	*American Telephone and Telegraph Company*

Name	Affiliation at Time of Assuming Office
Harold S. Boardman, 1930–31	*University of Maine*
Herbert S. Evans, 1931–32	*University of Colorado*
Roy A. Seaton, 1932–33	*Kansas State College*
William E. Wickenden, 1933–34	*Case School of Applied Science*
Clement C. Williams, 1934–35	*University of Iowa*
Douglas S. Anderson, 1935–36	*Tulane University*
Harry P. Hammond, 1936–37	*Polytechnic Institute of Brooklyn*
Samuel B. Earle, 1937–38	*Clemson Agricultural and Mechanical College*
Karl T. Compton, 1938–39	*Massachusetts Institute of Technology*
Olin J. Ferguson, 1939–40	*University of Nebraska*
Donald B. Prentice, 1940–41	*Rose Polytechnic Institute*
Alfred H. White, 1941–42	*University of Michigan*
Henry T. Heald, 1942–43	*Illinois Institute of Technology*
Robert E. Doherty, 1943–44	*Carnegie Institute of Technology*
Harry S. Rogers, 1944–45, 1945–46	*Polytechnic Institute of Brooklyn*
Huber O. Croft, 1946–47	*University of Iowa*
Charles E. MacQuigg, 1947–48	*The Ohio State University*
Clement J. Freund, 1948–49	*University of Detroit*
Thorndike Saville, 1949–50	*New York University*
Francis M. Dawson, 1950–51	*State University of Iowa*
Solomon C. Hollister, 1951–52	*Cornell University*
Willis R. Woolrich, 1952–53	*University of Texas*
Linton E. Grinter, 1953–54	*University of Florida*
Nathan M. Dougherty, 1954–55	*University of Tennessee*
Maynard M. Boring, 1955–56	*General Electric Company*
William L. Everitt, 1956–57	*University of Illinois*
Frederick C. Linvall, 1957–58	*California Institute of Technology*
William T. Alexander, 1958–59	*Northeastern University*
B. Richard Teare, Jr., 1959–60	*Carnegie Institute of Technology*
Eric A. Walker, 1960–61	*The Pennsylvania State University*
Robert W. Van Houten, 1961–62	*Newark College of Engineering*
Glenn Murphy, 1962–63	*The Iowa State University of Science and Technology*
Kurt F. Wendt, 1963–64	*University of Wisconsin*
Elmer C. Easton, 1964–65	*Rutgers, The State University*
George D. Lobinger, 1965–66	*Westinghouse Electric Corporation*
Robert H. Roy, 1966–67	*The Johns Hopkins University*

Name	Affiliation at Time of Assuming Office
Melvin R. Lohmann, 1967–68	*Oklahoma State University*
Carl C. Chambers, 1968–69	*University of Pennsylvania*
Merritt A. Williamson, 1969–70	*Vanderbilt University*
George A. Hawkins, 1970–71	*Purdue University*
Harold A. Bolz, 1971–72	*The Ohio State University*
Joseph M. Pettit, 1972–73	*Georgia Institute of Technology*
John C. Calhoun, Jr., 1973–74	*Texas A&M University*
Cornelius Wandmacher, 1974–75	*University of Cincinnati*
Lee Harrisberger, 1975–76	*University of Texas of the Permian Basin*
George Burnet, 1976–77	*The Iowa State University of Science and Technology*
Otis E. Lancaster, 1977–78	*The Pennsylvania State University*
Joseph J. Martin, 1978–79	*University of Michigan*
Charles E. Schaffner, 1979–80	*Syska & Hennessy, Inc.*

Name	Affiliation at Time of Assuming Office
Vincent S. Haneman, Jr., 1980–81	*University of Alaska*
Daniel C. Drucker, 1981–82	*University of Illinois*
Joseph C. Hogan, 1982–83	*Notre Dame University*
John C. Hancock, 1983–84	*Purdue University*
Richard J. Ungrodt, 1984–85	*Milwaukee School of Engineering*
Robert N. Mills, 1985–86	*General Electric Company*
Edmund T. Cranch, 1986–87	*Wang Institute of Graduate Studies*
Robert H. Page, 1987–88	*Texas A&M University*
Lawrence P. Grayson, 1988–89	*U.S. Department of Education*
Anthony B. Giordano, 1989–90	*Polytechnic University*
Curtis J. Tompkins, 1990–91	*West Virginia University*
Leighton E. Sissom, 1991–92	*Sissom & Associates, Inc.*
J. Ray Bowen, 1992–93	*University of Washington*
George E. Dieter, 1993–94	*University of Maryland-College Park*

SECRETARIES/EXECUTIVE SECRETARY/ EXECUTIVE DIRECTORS

Name	Affiliation at Time of Assuming Office
Secretaries (volunteer)	
John B. Johnson, 1893–95	*Washington University*
C. Frank Allen, 1895–97	*Massachusetts Institute of Technology*
Albert Kingsbury, 1897–99	*New Hampshire College*
Edgar Marburg, 1899–1900	*University of Pennsylvania*
Henry S. Jacoby, 1900–02	*Cornell University*
Clarence A. Waldo, 1902–04	*Purdue University*
Milo S. Ketchum, 1904–06	*University of Colorado*
William T. Magruder, 1906–07	*Ohio State University*
Arthur L. Williston, 1907–09	*Pratt Institute*
Henry H. Norris, 1909–1914	*Cornell University*
Frederic L. Bishop, 1914–1947	*University of Pittsburgh*
Arthur B. Bronwell, 1947–55	*Northwestern University*

Name	Affiliation at Time of Assuming Office
Secretary/Executive Secretary/Executive Director (part-time to full-time)	
W. Leighton Collins, 1955–69	*University of Illinois*
Executive Directors (full-time)	
Leslie B. Williams, 1969–74	*University of Delaware*
Francis X. Bradley, Jr. (Acting), 1974–75	*American Society for Engineering Education*
Donald E. Marlowe, 1975–81	*The Catholic University of America*
W. Edward Lear, 1981–86	*University of Alabama*
F. Karl Willenbrock, 1986–89	*Southern Methodist University*
Thomas J. Perry (Interim), 1989–90	*American Society for Engineering Education*
Frank L. Huband, 1990–	*National Science Foundation*

Chapter 2

1. Artz, F.B., *The Development of Technical Education in France 1500–1850*, The M.I.T. Press, Cambridge, MA, 1966, pp. 99–100; and Emerson, George S., *Engineering Education: A Social History*, Crane Russak, NY, 1973, pp. 29–33.

2. LeBold, William K., "Engineering Education," in *Encyclopedia of Educational Research*, 4th ed., Robert L. Ebel, ed., The Macmillan Co., London, 1969, pp. 435–443.

3. McGivern, James G., *First Hundred Years of Engineering Education in the United States (1807–1907)*, Gonzaga University Press, Spokane, 1960, pp. 107–108.

4. Guggisberg, F.G., "The Shop," *The Story of the Royal Military Academy*, Cassell and Co., London, 1900.

5. Fitzpatrick, J.C., ed., *The Writings of George Washington from the Original Manuscript Sources, 1745–1799*, U.S. Government Printing Office, Washington, DC, 1931–1944 (39 volumes), Vol. 3, pp. 323–325.

6. Heath papers, Massachusetts Historical Society, Boston (roll 1, frame 62) John Adams to William Heath, February 18, 1776.

7. Fitzpatrick, J.C., *op. cit.* 5, Vol. 12, p. 40.

8. *Ibid*, Vol. 16, p. 48.

9. Ford, W.C., et al, eds., *The Journals of the Continental Congress, 1774–1789*, U.S. Government Printing Office, Washington, DC, 1904–1937 (34 volumes), Vol. 25, p. 725.

10. *Ibid*, Vol. 25, p. 738.

11. *The Centennial of the United States Military Academy at West Point, New York 1802–1902*, U.S. Government Printing Office, Washington, DC, 1904, Vol. 1, pp. 213–214; Vol. 2, pp. 49–50.

12. Committee on History and Heritage of American Civil Engineering, *The Civil Engineer — His Origins*, American Society of Civil Engineers, New York, 1970, p. 37.

13. *Ibid*, p. 37.

14. *The Centennial of the United States Military Academy at West Point, New York, 1802–1902*, U.S. Government Printing Office, Washington, DC, 1904, p. 263.

15. Mc Givern, J.G., *op. cit.* 3, pp. 37–38.

16. The degrees were made retroactive to 1802 for all graduates of the Military Academy, under a law drafted by General Douglas MacArthur.

17. Cullum, George W., *Biographical Register of Officers and Graduates of the United States Military Academy*, Houghton Mifflin Co., Boston, 1891, Vol. 3, p. 2300; and Wellington, A.M., "The Engineering Schools of the United States III," *Engineering News*, Vol. 27, April 2, 1892, p. 318.

18. Graham, Gerald S., *A Concise History of Canada*, The Viking Press, New York, 1968, p. 74.

19. Curti, Merle, *The Growth of American Thought*, 3rd ed., Harper & Row, Publishers, New York, 1964, p. 351.

20. "The State of Undergraduate Science and Engineering Education," draft of unpublished report, National Science Foundation, Washington, DC, June 1992, pp. 2–7.

21. Benton, J.R., "Do the National Engineering Societies Discredit Engineering Education?," *Bulletin of the SPEE*, Vol. 8, September 1917, p. 35.

22. This is brought out clearly in articles dealing with the founding of the American Medical Association, American Society of Dental Surgeons, and American Bar Association; see McGivern, J.G., *op. cit.* 3, pp. 107–108.

23. *Ibid*, p. 57.

24. Doty, Paul, and Dorothy Zinberg, "Science and the Undergraduate," Chapter 4 in *Content and Context*, Carl Kaysen, ed., McGraw-Hill, New York, 1937, p. 155.

25. Webb, Lester A., *Captain Alden Partridge and the United States Military Academy 1806–1833*, American Southern, Northport, AL, 1965, p. 23; and Johnson, Allen, and Dumas Malone, eds., *Dictionary of American Biography*, Charles Scribner's Sons, New York, 1959, Vol. 7, Part 2, p. 281.

26. Ellis, William A. ED., *Norwich University, 1819–1911, Her History, Her Graduates, Her Roll of Honor*, The Capital City Press, Montpelier, VT, 1911, Vol. 1, p. 2.

27. Emerson, G.S., *Engineering Education: A Social History*, *op. cit.* 1, p. 142.

28. McGivern, J.G., *op. cit.* 3, pp. 46–48.

29. From letter of Stephen Van Rensselaer of November 25, 1824, to Samuel Blatchford, and included in the act incorporating the Rensselaer School, passed by the

New York State Legislature, March 21, 1826; see Rezneck, Samuel, *Education for a Technological Society,* Rensselaer Polytechnic Institute, Troy, New York, 1968, p. 3.

30. Calhoun, Daniel H., *The American Civil Engineer, Origins and Conflict,* The Technology Press, distributed by Harvard University Press, Cambridge, 1960, p. 45.

31. Wickenden, William E., "A Comparative Study of Engineering Education in the United States and Europe," in *Report of the Investigation of Engineering Education 1923–1929,* Society for the Promotion of Engineering Education, Lancaster, PA, 1930, Vol. 1, pp. 811–812.

32. Emerson, G.S., *op. cit.* 1, p. 146.

33. Rezneck, S., *op. cit.* 29, p. 44.

34. Gianniny, O. Allan, Jr., "The Overlooked Southern Approach to Engineering Education: One and a Half Centuries at the University of Virginia, 1836–1986," in *Proceedings of the 150th Anniversary Symposium on Technology and Society, "Southern Technology: Past, Present, and Future,"* Howard L. Hartman, ed., College of Engineering, University of Alabama, Tuscaloosa, March 3–4, 1988, p. 151.

35. Gianninny, O.A., Jr., *op. cit.* 34, p. 152.

36. Norrell, Robert J., *A Promising Field, Engineering at Alabama, 1837–1987,* The University of Alabama Press, Tuscaloosa, 1990, pp. 4–14, 26, 31.

37. Norrell, Robert J., "A Promising Field: Engineering Education at The University of Alabama," in *Proceedings of the 150th Anniversary Symposium on Technology and Society, "Southern Technology: Past, Present, and Future,"* Howard L. Hartman, ed., College of Engineering, University of Alabama, Tuscaloosa, March 3–4, 1988, pp. 20.

38. Dineen, J.O., "A Short History of Engineering at The University of New Brunswick," unpublished article, The University of New Brunswick, April 1962.

39. *The Education and Status of Civil Engineer, in the United Kingdom and in Foreign Countries,* Institution of Civil Engineers, London, 1870, p. 173.

40. Greene, Benjamin Franklin, *The True Idea of a Polytechnic Institute,* originally published in 1849, reprinted by Rensselaer Polytechnic Institute, 1949, p. 56.

41. Rezneck, S., *op. cit.* 29, pp. 83–84.

42. Wickenden, W.E., *op. cit.* 31, Vol. 1, p. 542.

Chapter 3

1. Bruce, Robert V., *The Launching of Modern American Science, 1846–1876,* Alfred A. Knopf, New York, 1987, p. 279.

2. Wickerham, James P., *A History of Education in Pennsylvania,* originally published in 1866, reprinted by Arno Press, New York, 1969, pp. 431–432; McGivern, James G., *First Hundred Years of Engineering Education in the United States (1807–1907),* Gonzaga University Press, Spokane, 1960, p. 87.

3. *World Book Encyclopedia,* Vol. 19, 1975, p. 75.

4. *Historical Statistics of the United States, Colonial Times to 1970,* Part 2, U.S. Government Printing Office, Washington, DC, 1975, series Q 321, p. 731, and series Q 47, p. 788.

5. Armytage, W.H.G., *A Social History of Engineering,* Pitman Publishing Corporation, New York, 1961, p. 178. Also, McGovern, James G., *First Hundred Years of Engineering Education in the United States (1807–1907),* Gonzaga University Press, Spokane, 1960, p. 92.

6. Fletcher, Robert, "A Quarter Century of Progress in Engineering Education," *Proceedings of the SPEE,* Vol. 4, 1896, pp. 31–50 at 37. Wickenden, William E., "A Comparison of Engineering Education in the United States and Europe," in *Report of the Investigation of Engineering Education 1923–1929,* Society for the Promotion of Engineering Education, Lancaster, PA, 1930, Vol. 1, pp. 750–1015 at 816.

7. Norrell, Robert J., *A Promising Field, Engineering at Alabama, 1837–1987,* The University of Alabama Press, Tuscaloosa, 1990, pp. 37–38.

8. *Historical Statistics of the United States,* Part 2, *op. cit.* 4, series W 99, p. 959; series P 110, p. 683; series P 228, p. 689; series P 232, p. 691; and series P 265, p. 694.

9. *The Education and Status of Civil Engineer, in the United Kingdom and in Foreign Countries,* Institution of Civil Engineers, London, 1870, pp. 169–171.

10. *Atlantic Monthly,* July 1876, quoted in John W. Oliver, *History of American Technology,* The Ronald Press Company, New York, 1956, p. 301.

11. Re-quoted in Emerson, George S., *Engineering Education: A Social History,* Crane, Russak, New York, 1973, p. 276.

12. Zaret, Matthew Elias, *An Historical Study of the Development of the American Society for Engineering Education,* doctoral dissertation, School of Education, New York University, available from University Microfilms, Inc., Ann Arbor, 1967, p. 28.

13. *Ibid,* pp. 29–30.

14. Calvert viewed this as "a deeper struggle between two cultures—school and shop—for control of the whole process of socialization, education, and professionalism of mechanical engineers in America." See Calvert, Monte A., *The Mechanical Engineer in America 1830–1910,* The Johns Hopkins Press, Baltimore, 1967, p. 62.

15. *Ibid,* pp. 56–57. See also Brittain, James E. and Robert C. McMath, Jr., "Engineers and the New South Creed: The Formation and Early Development of Georgia Tech," *Technology and Culture,* Vol. 18, No. 2, 1977, pp. 175–201 at 176 and 189.

16. Calvert, M.A., *op. cit.* 14, p. 281.

17. Zaret, M.E., *op. cit.* 12, p. 31.

18. Fletcher, R., *op. cit.* 6, p. 37.

19. Bennett, Frank M., *The Steam Navy of the United States,* Warren and Co., Pittsburgh, 1896, pp. 733–736.

20. Norrell, Robert J., "A Promising Field: Engineering Education at the University of Alabama," in *Proceedings of the 150th Anniversary Symposium on Technology and Society, "Southern Technology: Past, Present, and Future,"* Howard L. Hartman, ed., College of Engineering, University of Alabama, Tuscaloosa, March 3–4, 1988, p. 123.

21. Terman, Frederick E., "A Brief History of Engineering Education," *Proceedings of the IEEE,* September 1976, pp. 1399–1407.

22. Quoted in Oliver, John W., *History of American Technology*, Ronald Press, New York, 1956, p. 361.

23. Gianniny, O. Allan, Jr., "The Overlooked Southern Approach to Engineering Education: One and a Half Centuries at the University of Virginia, 1836–1986," in *Proceedings of the 150th Anniversary Symposium on Technology and Society, "Southern Technology: Past, Present, and Future,"* Howard L. Hartman, ed., College of Engineering, University of Alabama, Tuscaloosa, March 3–4, 1988, p. 161.

24. Armytage, W.H.G., *op. cit.* 5, p. 175.

25. "Address of Professor DeVolson Wood," *Proceedings of the SPEE*, Vol. 2, 1894, p. 23.

26. Porter, H.F.J., "How Can the Present Status of the Engineering Profession be Improved?," *Transactions of the American Society of Mechanical Engineers*, Vol. 14, November 1892, p. 487.

27. *Stillman Williams Robinson, A Memorial*, The Ohio State University, Columbus, 1912, p. 65.

28. *Index to Volumes I–XX of the Proceedings, 1893–1912*, SPEE, 1914, p. 4.

Chapter 4

1. Hammond, H.P., "Promotion of Engineering Education in the Past Forty Years," *The Journal of Engineering Education*, Vol. 24, No. 1, September 1933, pp. 44–66 at 46.

2. *Stillman Williams Robinson, A Memorial*, The Ohio State University, Columbus, 1912, p. 65.

3. Davis, Joseph Baker, "In Behalf of the University of Michigan," *Ibid*, p. 15.

4. Baker, Ira Osborn, "In Behalf of the University of Illinois," *Ibid*, p. 33.

5. "Origin of the Society," *SPEE Index to Volumes I–XX 1893–1912 of the Proceedings, Society for the Promotion of Engineering Education*, 1914, p. 4.

6. "Proceedings," *Proceedings of the SPEE*, Vol. 1, 1894, pp. 8–9.

7. Allen, C. Frank, "Historical Sketches of the Society," *The Journal of Engineering Education*, Vol. 22, No. 2, October 1931, p. 80; Talbot, Arthur N., "Origin of the Society for the Promotion of Engineering Education," *The Journal of Engineering Education*, Vol. 24, September 1933, pp. 41–42; Hammond, H.P., *op. cit.* 1, p. 44.

8. Moriarty, Catherine, *John Galbraith, Engineer and Educator*, University of Toronto, Canada, 1989.

9. "Origin of the Society," *op. cit.* 5, p. 4.

10. "Address of Professor DeVolson Wood," *Proceedings of the SPEE*, Vol. 2, 1894, p. 21.

11. *Proceedings of the SPEE*, Vol. 1, 1893, p. 7.

12. "Address of Professor DeVolson Wood," *op. cit.* 10, pp. 22–23.

13. "Proceedings," *Proceedings of the SPEE*, Vol. 2, 1894, p. 2.

14. *Historical Statistics of the United States, Colonial Times to 1970*, Part 2, U.S. Government Printing Office, Washington, DC, 1975, Series S 32, p. 820.

15. Hammond, H.P., "Promotion of Engineering Education in the Past Forty Years," *op. cit.* 1, p. 57.

16. Zaret, Matthew Elias, *An Historical Study of the Development of the American Society for Engineering Education*, PhD dissertation, School of Education New York University, 1967, available from University Microfilms, Inc., Ann Arbor, MI.

17. *Report of the Investigation of Engineering Education, 1923–1929* (also known by the name of the study director William E. Wickenden as the Wickenden Report), Society for the Promotion of Engineering Education, Lancaster, PA, 1930, Vol. 1, p. 548.

18. "Entrance Requirements for Engineering Colleges," Report of the Special Committee, *Proceedings of the SPEE*, Vol. 4, 1896, pp. 101–173 at 103–104.

19. McGivern, James G., *First Hundred Years of Engineering Education in the United States (1807–1907)*, Gonzaga University Press, Spokane, 1960, p. 147.

20. Turneaure, F.E., "Recent Developments and Past Tendencies in Technical Education," *Proceedings of the SPEE*, Vol. 17, 1909, p. 20.

21. *The Evolution of Engineering Education in Canada*, Canadian Council of Professional Engineers, Ottawa, 1990, p. 1.

22. Magruder, William T., "Report of the Committee on Statistics of Engineering Education," *Proceedings of the SPEE*, Vol. 14, 1906, pp. 94–96.

23. Hammond, H.P., "Promotion of Engineering Education in the Past Forty Years," *op. cit.* 1, p. 45.

24. Aldrich, William A., "The Hale Engineering Experiment Station Bill," *Proceedings of the SPEE*, Vol. IV, 1896, pp. 187–215.

25. Seaton, R.A., "How Industry can Cooperate with Engineering Colleges in Furthering Research," *Proceedings of the SPEE*, Vol. 33, 1925, pp. 205–214 at 206–207.

26. Plants, H.L., and C.A. Arents, "History of Engineering Education in the Land-Grant Movement," *Proceedings of the American Association of Land-Grant Colleges and State Universities*, Vol. 2 of the Centennial Convocation, 1961, p. 93.

27. Roe, J.W., "Cooperative Plan of Engineering Education," *Management Engineering*, May 1922, p. 269.

28. Zaret, M.E., *op. cit.* 16, p. 150.

29. Timbie, W.H., "Cooperative Courses at the Massachusetts Institute of Technology," *Proceedings of the SPEE*, Vol. 35, 1927, p. 280.

30. Timbie, W.H., "A Cooperative Course in Electrical Engineering Conducted by M.I.T. and the General Electric Company," *Bulletin of the SPEE*, Vol. 10, June 1920, p. 459.

31. Schneider, Herman, "Cooperative Course in Engineering at the University of Cincinnati, *Proceedings of the SPEE*, Vol. 15, 1907, pp. 391–398; also "Two Years of the Cooperative Course at the University of Cincinnati, Vol. 16, 1908, pp. 279–294.

32. *1993 Directory of Engineering and Engineering Technology Cooperative Education Programs*, Cooperative Education Division, American Society for Engineering Education, Washington, DC, January 1993.

33. "Greetings from A.L. Rohrer," *P.T.M.*, published by the General Electric Com-

pany, Vol. 1, No. 2, April 1926; and Evans, F.L., "When Test Men Used Rubber Gloves," *P.T.M.*, Vol. 1, No. 3, July 1926.

34. McGivern, J.G., *op. cit.* 19, pp. 107–108.

35. *1992 Annual Proceedings,* National Council of Examiners for Engineering and Surveying, Clemson, SC, 1992.

36. Canadian Council of Professional Engineers, personal correspondence, July 20, 1992.

37. Zaret, M.E., *op. cit.* 16, p. 81.

38. Adams, Henry, *The Education of Henry Adams,* The Modern Library, Inc., New York, 1931, p. 466.

39. Historical Statistics of the United States, *op. cit.* 14, Part 1, Series H 600, p. 379; Series H 753, p. 386.

Chapter 5

1. Armytage, W.H.G., *A Social History of Engineering,* Pitman Publishing Corporation, New York, 1961, p. 268.

2. *Historical Statistics of the United States, Colonial Times to 1970,* Part 2, U.S. Government Printing Office, Washington, DC, 1975, Series Q 152, p. 716.

3. *Ibid,* Series Q 153, p. 716; Series Q 566 and Q 567, p. 768.

4. Armytage, W.H.G., *op. cit.* 1, p. 206.

5. Burlingame, Roger, *Engines of Democracy,* C. Scribner's Sons, New York, 1940, pp. 450–451.

6. *Proceedings of the SPEE,* Vol. XV, 1907, pp. 17–18; and Jackson, D.C., "Present Status and Trends in Engineering Schools," Engineers' Council for Professional Development, 1939.

7. Mann, Charles R., *A Study of Engineering Education,* Bulletin 11, Carnegie Foundation for the Advancement of Teaching, 1918.

8. "Report of the Special Committee on the Report of the Joint Committee on Engineering Education," *Proceedings of the SPEE,* Vol. XXVII, 1919, pp. 103–112 at 105–106.

9. "Preliminary Report of a Committee Appointed by the Advisory Commission of the Council of National Defense to Study the Relation of the Engineering Schools to the National Government During the Present Emergency," *Bulletin,* Society for the Promotion of Engineering Education, Vol. VIII, No. 1, Sept. 1917, pp. 2–4.

10. Mann, C.R., "The Effect of the War on Engineering Education," *Bulletin,* Society for the Promotion of Engineering Education, Vol. IX, No. 4, December 1918, pp. 109–110; and Manley, Louis K., "Army Education in War Issues," *Bulletin,* Vol. IX, No. 3, Nov. 1918, p. 90.

11. McKibben, Frank P., "The Colleges and The War," *Bulletin,* Society for the Promotion of Engineering Education, Vol. IX, No. 9, May 1919, pp. 379–381.

12. Committee on Education and Special Training, War Department, "Student Army Training Corps," *Bulletin,* Society for the Promotion of Engineering Education, Vol. IX, No. 2, October 1918, pp. 56–59.

13. Daggett, Parker H., "Present Status of Engineering Registration," *The Journal of Engineering Education,* Vol. XXII, No. 10, June 1932, pp. 869–872.

14. *Report of the Investigation of Engineering Education 1923–1929,* Society for the Promotion of Engineering Education, Lancaster, PA, 1930, Vols. 1 and 2.

15. Hammond, H.P., "Engineers' Council for Professional Development Begins Inspection of Engineering Colleges," *Proceedings of the SPEE,* Vol. XLIII, 1935, pp. 310–311.

16. *59th Annual Report,* Accreditation Board for Engineering and Technology, New York, September 30, 1991, p. 57.

17. Johnson, J.B., "Some Present Tendencies in Higher Technical Education," *Proceedings of the SPEE,* Vol. IX, 1901, pp. 180–208.

18. Talbot, A.N., "The Engineering Teacher and His Preparation," *Proceedings of the SPEE,* Vol. XIX, 1911, pp. 22–32.

19. Magruder, W.T., "The Good Engineering Teacher, His Personality and Training," *Proceedings of the SPEE,* Vol. XXI, 1913, pp. 27–38.

20. Thomas, G.B., "Summer Course for College Teachers," *Bulletin of the SPEE,* Vol. IV, March 1914, pp. 49–51.

21. Hammond, H.P., "The Summer School for Engineering Teachers," *Proceedings of the SPEE,* Vol. XXXIV, 1926, p. 835; and Wickenden, W.E., "Summer Schools for Engineering Teachers, Their Aims and Methods," *Proceedings of the SPEE,* Vol. XXXIV, 1926, p. 778.

22. Hammond, H.P., "The 1933 Session of the Summer School for Engineering Teachers," *Proceedings of the SPEE,* Vol. XL, 1932, pp. 515–516.

23. Hammond, H.P., "Sessions of the Summer School for Engineering Teachers for 1932," *Proceedings of the SPEE,* Vol. XXII, No. 6, Feb. 1932, pp. 443–444; and *Year Book,* Supplement to Vol. XXII, No. 4, December 1931.

24. *Proceedings of the SPEE,* Vol. XLIV, 1936, p. 285.

25. *Ibid,* Vol. XLIV, 1936, p. 285.

26. Whitehead, T. North, "The Engineer as a Servant of Society," *Proceedings of the SPEE,* Vol. XLV, 1937, pp. 101–109 at 109.

27. Earle, S.B., *Proceedings of the SPEE,* Vol. XLVI, 1938, pp. 20–21.

28. Potter, A.A., *Proceedings of the SPEE,* Vol. XLVI, 1938, p. 146.

29. "Report and Progress on Special Committee on Aims and Scope of Engineering Curricula," *Proceedings of the SPEE,* Vol. XLVII, 1939, p. 475; and *The Journal of Engineering Education,* Vol. XXX, No. 5, January 1940, p. 475.

30. *Report of the Committee on Aims and Scope of Engineering Curricula, The Journal of Engineering Education,* Vol. XXX, No. 7, March 1940, pp. 555–556 (Proceedings, Vol. 47, 1939).

31. "Report of the Committee on Statistics of Engineering Education," *Proceedings of the SPEE,* Vol. X, 1902, pp. 231–257, at 239.

32. Dupree, A. Hunter, *Science in the Federal Government: A History of Policies and Activities to 1940,* Harvard University Press, Cambridge, 1957, p. 324.

33. Wickenden, W.E., "Research Relations Between Engineering Colleges and Industry," *Journal of the American Institute of Electrical Engineers,* Vol. 45, 1926, p. 987.

34. Potter, A.A., and G.A. Young, "Tendencies in Research at Engineering Colleges," *Journal of the Society of Automotive Engineers*, Vol. 20, July 1927, p. 623.

35. Wickenden, W.E., *op. cit.* 33, p. 987.

36. Potter, A.A., "Research Relations Between Colleges and Industry," *Journal of the American Institute of Electrical Engineers*, Vol. 45, 1926, p. 1272.

37. "Graduate Study, Report of Progress," *Proceedings of the SPEE*, Vol. XLIII, 1935, p. 315.

38. "Report: Progress in Engineering Education," *Proceedings of the SPEE*, Vol. XLVI, 1938, p. 674.

39. Hammond, H.P., "Graduate Study," *Proceedings of the SPEE*, Vol. XLIII, 1935, p. 315.

Chapter 6

1. Seaton, Roy A., "Engineering Defense Training," *Proceedings of the SPEE*, Vol. XLIX, 1941, pp. 47–48; and "Report of the Committee on Acceleration of the Regular Engineering Program," *Proceedings of the SPEE*, Vol. L, 1942, p. 155.

2. Armsby, Henry, H., *Engineering, Science, and Management War Training, Final Report*, U.S. Office of Education, Bulletin no. 9, U.S. Government Printing Office, Washington, DC, 1946, p. 71.

3. *Ibid*, p. 19.

4. "Minutes of the Business Sessions," *Proceedings of the SPEE*, Vol. XLIV, 1941, p. 135.

5. Saville, Thorndike, "Achievements in Engineering Education," *Proceedings of the SPEE*, Vol. LX, 1953, pp. 222–235 at 229; and Dougherty, Robert E., "The ASTP Situation," *Proceedings of the SPEE*, Vol. 51, 1943, pp. 448–449 at 448.

6. Herge, Henry C., "Wartime College Training Programs in the Armed Services," American Council on Education, Washington, DC, 1945, p. 70.

7. Armytage, W.H.G., *A Social History of Engineering*, Pitman Publishing Corporation, New York, 1961, p. 270.

8. "50th Anniversary Meeting, Chicago, June 18, 19, 20, 1943," *Proceedings of the SPEE*, Vol. L, 1942, p. 571.

9. "Minutes of the Council Meeting, June 18, 1947," *The Journal of Engineering Education*, Vol. 38, No. 2, 1947, p. 106.

10. Armsby, Henry H., "A Reexamination of the Compton Report in the Light of Enrollment in Engineering Curricula, Fall of 1946," *The Journal of Engineering Education*, May 1947, p. 683.

11. Story, Robert C., and Henry H. Armsby, "1949 Enrollment in Engineering Colleges," *The Journal of Engineering Education*, February 1950, p. 4.

12. "1992–1993 Directory of Engineering Graduate Studies & Research," American Society for Engineering Education, Washington, DC, 1992, p. 61.

13. Norberg, Arthur L., "The Origins of the Electronics Industry on the Pacific Coast," *Proceedings of the IEEE*, September 1976, pp. 1314–1322.

14. "College Notes," *The Journal of Engineering Education*, Vol. 36, 1946, p. 386.

15. "Meeting of the Executive Board," *The Journal of Engineering Education*, Vol. 38, 1948, p. 773.

16. Steinberg, S.S., "Engineering Mission to Latin America," *The Journal of Engineering Education*, Vol. 40, 1950, p. 91.

17. Steinberg, S.S., "Organization of the Pan American Union of Engineering Societies (UPADI) and the First Pan American Engineering Congress," *The Journal of Engineering Education*, Vol. 40, 1950, pp. 266–267.

18. "In the News," *Journal of Engineering Education*, Vol. 43, 1953, p. 89.

19. Saville, Thorndike, "The EUSEC Report on Engineering Education and Training in Western Europe and the United States," *Journal of Engineering Education*, Vol. 69, 1961–1962, pp. 73–78.

20. "Commission on Engineering Education," *Journal of Engineering Education*, Vol. 41, No. 9, June 1951, p. 593.

21. Shimizu, Kinji, "How the Report of the American Advisory Mission to Japan for Engineering Education, 11951, Influenced Japanese Engineering Education," *Journal of Engineering Education*, Vol. 46, No. 3, November 1955, p. 260.

22. Dougherty, N.W., "Engineering Education in India," *Journal of Engineering Education*, Vol. 49, No. 9, May 1959, p. 755.

23. "ASEE Engineering Education Exchange Mission to the Soviet Union, November, 1958, Final Report," *Journal of Engineering Education*, Vol. 49, 1958–1959, pp. 839–911.

24. "Report of Committee on Engineering Education After the War," *Proceedings of the SPEE*, Vol. 51, pp. 589–614.

25. "Report of Committee on Improvement of Teaching," *Journal of Engineering Education*, Vol. 43, 1953, p. 34.

26. "Improvement of Engineering Teaching," *Journal of Engineering Education*, Vol. 43, 1953, p. 33.

27. "Improvement of Engineering Teaching—Report of the Committee on Improvement of Teaching," *Journal of Engineering Education*, Vol. 43, September 1952, p. 46.

28. "Minutes of the General Council Meeting," *Journal of Engineering Education*, Vol. 43, 1953, p. 59.

29. "Report of the Secretary," *Journal of Engineering Education*, Vol. 39, 1949, p. 25.

30. Weinberg, Philip, "Report of the ASEE Committee for Young Engineering Teachers," *Journal of Engineering Education*, Vol. 46, November 1955, pp. 284–285.

31. *Journal of Engineering Education*, Vol. 49, February 1959, p. 533.

32. "Minutes of the Executive Board," *Journal of Engineering Education*, Vol. 43, 1953.

33. Schmelzer, R.W., "Recognizing and Rewarding Good Teaching," *Journal of Engineering Education*, Vol. 45, 1955; Case, H.W., "Report on Survey Conducted by Committee on Recognition and Incentives for Good Teaching," *Journal of Engineering Education*, Vol. 46, 1956, p. 81; and Johnson, Lee H., "Ways to Increase the Prestige and Improve the Status of a Good Teacher," *Journal of Engineering Education*, Vol. 46, 1956, p. 132.

34. Hazen, Harold, "Engineering Faculty Recruitment, Development, and Utilization," *Journal of Engineering Education,* Vol. 50, No. 9, May 1960, pp. 757–828.

35. "Engineering Summer Schools, 1927–1959," *Journal of Engineering Education,* Vol. 49, February 1959, p. 533.

36. Kraybill, Edward K., "Effective Teaching: Institutes for Engineering Teachers," *IEEE Transactions on Education,* Vol. E-12, No. 2, June 1969, pp. 85–88.

37. *Historical Statistics of the United States, Colonial Times to 1970,* Part 2, U.S. Government Printing Office, Washington, DC, 1975, Table 24, p. 52, and Table 25, p. 55.

38. Bronwell, A.B., "Enrollment in Engineering Colleges," *Journal of Engineering Education,* Vol. 39, No. 6, February 1949, p. 7; Armore, Sidney J., and Henry H. Armsby, "Engineering Enrollments and Degrees in ECPD-Accredited Institutions: 1957," *Journal of Engineering Education,* Vol. 48, No. 6, February 1958, p. 420; and data from Engineering Manpower Commission, American Association of Engineering Societies.

39. *Report of Committee on Engineering Education After the War,* written by a committee of the SPEE chaired by H.P. Hammond, *The Journal of Engineering Education,* Vol. 34, No. 9, May 1944.

40. *Report on Evaluation of Engineering Education (1952–1955),* also known by the name of the study director as the (L.E.) Grinter Report, American Society for Engineering Education, June 1955.

41. *General Education in Engineering, Report of the Committee for the Humanistic-Social Science Research Project, Journal of Engineering Education,* April 1956, Vol. 46, No. 8, pp. 619–750.

42. *Characteristics of Excellence in Engineering Technology Education, Journal of Engineering Education,* Vol. 53, 1963, pp. 631–648.

43. *Final Report: Goals of Engineering Education,* committee chaired by Eric A. Walker, American Society for Engineering Education, January 1968.

Chapter 7

1. Enrollment data from the Engineering Manpower Commission, American Association of Engineering Societies, Washington, DC.

2. *The Evolution of Engineering Education in Canada,* Canadian Council of Professional Engineers, Ottawa, 1990, p. 14.

3. "Women in Engineering," *Engineering Manpower Bulletin,* No. 109, May 1991.

4. *Ibid.*

5. "Minorities in Engineering," *Engineering Manpower Bulletin,* No. 110, June 1991.

6. "Engineering Degree Statistics and Trends—1990," *Engineering Manpower Bulletin,* No. 106, December 1990.

7. Cranch, Edmund T., and Gene M. Nordby, "Engineering Education: At the Crossroads Without a Compass?," *Engineering Education,* Vol. 76, May 1986, pp. 742–747.

8. "Engineering College Research and Graduate Study," *Engineering Education,* Vol. 61, No. 6, part 2, March 1971, p. 570.

9. "Engineering College Research and Graduate Study," *Engineering Education,* Vol. 81, No. 2, March 1991, p. 58.

10. Bothwell, Robert, Ian Drummond, and John English, *Canada Since 1945: Power, Politics, and Provincialism,* revised edition, University of Toronto Press, Toronto, 1989, p. 396.

11. "Quality in Engineering Education," *Engineering Education,* Vol. 77, No. 1, October 1986, pp. 16–24, 49–50.

12. *A National Action Agenda for Engineering Education,* American Society for Engineering Education, Washington, DC, 1987.

Chapter 8

1. This phrase originally was used by Count Rumford in 1799 in a prospectus for The Royal Institution of Great Britain; see Ricketts, P.C., *History of Rensselaer Polytechnic Institute,* John Wiley, New York, 1934, p. 4. Steven Van Rensselaer used it in a letter of November 5, 1824, to Samuel Blatchford defining the purpose of the Rensselaer School; see Rezneck, Samuel, *Education for a Technological Society,* published by the Rensselaer Polytechnic Institute, Troy, 1968, p. 3.

PHOTOGRAPHIC CREDITS

Note: Italic numbers denote photograph numbers, non-italic numbers preceded by a B denote a page number for a biographical photo.

Alabama, University of, W.S. Hoole Special Collections Library, *42, 153*
Alaska-Fairbanks, University of, *274, 295, 302*
Brach, Philip L., *271*
California at Berkeley, University of, College of Engineering, *286*
California at Berkeley, University of, The Bancroft Library, *34, 39, 53, 156, 170, 228*
California, Los Angeles, University of, *261, 264, 284, 299, 313, 314, 326*
California, Riverside, University of, *311*
California, San Diego, University of, *328*
California Institute of Technology, *86, 115*
Case Western Reserve University, *71, 94, 120*, B134
Chase Ltd., *269*
Cincinnati, University of, Archives, *135, 162, 212, 283*, B84
Clemson University, *47, 164, 316*
Colorado at Boulder, University of (Andy Katz, photographer), *303*
Colorado State University, *83, 90, 154, 213, 235, 329*
Columbia University, Avery (from the C.D. Arnold Collection) Library, Architectural and Fine Arts, *1, 2, 3, 10*
Columbia University, College of Engineering, *35, 167*
Cooper Union for the Advancement of Science and Art, The, *111, 253*
Cornell University, *30, 50, 60, 64, 72, 75, 82, 194, 200, 207, 241, 263*, B44
Dartmouth College, *66, 273*
District of Columbia, University of, *255*
Duke University Archives, *176, 185*
East Tennessee State University, *322*
École Polytechnique, *139, 184, 254, 266*
Embry-Riddle Aeronautical University, *205, 206*
Florida, University of, *174, 188, 246, 298*, B186
Fritz, Bruce , *276, 318, 324, 332*
George Brown University, *285*
Georgia Institute of Technology, *95, 96, 143, 320*
Hartford, University of, *222*
Hawaii at Manoa, University of, *233, 275, 289, 300, 335*
Howard University, *256*
Idaho, University of, Library, *161, 214*
Illinois, University of, *97, 103, 104, 129, 134, 168, 169, 180, 199, 250*, B68, B182
Iowa State University of Science and Technology, *57, 87, 91, 165, 182, 187, 204, 240, 304*, B82
John Wiley & Sons, *104, 122*
Johns Hopkins University, The Ferdinand Hamburger, Jr. Archives of The, *144, 196*
Kansas, University of, *279*
Kentucky, University of, *113, 177, 330*
Lakehead University, *310*
Laval, Université, *217, 267*
Lehigh University Libraries, Special Collections, *109, 221*
Library of Congress, *11*
Maine, University of, *121*
Marquette University, *216*
Massachusetts Institute of Technology, *54, 69, 73, 80, 85, 133*, B122
McNamara, Patrick E., *334*
Michigan, University of, *26, 37, 38, 78, 112, 132, 150, 191, 195, 301*
Michigan State University, *31, 249, 294*
Michigan Technological University Archives and Copper Country Historical Collections, *93, 105, 107, 116, 178, 203, 215, 230, 315*
Middlesex County College, *257*
Milwaukee School of Engineering, *102, 117, 126, 127, 159*
Mississippi State University, *108*
Missouri-Rolla, University of, *32, 41, 43, 92, 171*
National Archives, *13*
Nevada, Reno, University of, *290*
New Brunswick, University of, *22, 33, 89*
New Haven, University of, *268*
New Mexico State University Library, Hobson-Huntsinger University Archives, *123, 190*
New Mexico State University Library, Rio Grande Historical Collections, *48, 118, 172*
New York at Binghamton, State University of, *277*
New York at Buffalo, State University of, *296*
Notre Dame University, *45, 220*
North Carolina State University Archives, *128, 325*
Norwich University, *17a-b, 20, 28, 141, 288*, B26
Ohio Northern University, *229*
Ohio State University, *44, 65, 67, 98, 106, 125, 131, 209, 233*, B54
Pennsylvania, University of, *227*
Pennsylvania State Historical Society, The, *25*
Pennsylvania State University Archives, The, *63, 76, 88, 100, 101, 149, 163, 211*, B140, B192
Pittsburgh, University of, *68, 145, 146*, B126
Polytechnic University, *61, 62, 155, 175, 179, 186, 189, 226*
Puerto Rico at Mayaguez, University of, *308*
Purdue University (J.C. Allen & Son, Inc, contributors), *130, 136, 158, 166, 202, 223, 234, 239*, B170
Queen's University, *140, 232*
Rensselaer Polytechnic Institute, *27, 29a-b, 46, 51, 52, 152, 321, 327*, B32
Rochester, University of, *74, 157, 181, 193, 198, 208, 248*

INDEX